DOCUMENTS
....

DOCUMENTS

Artifacts of Modern Knowledge

Annelise Riles, Editor

THE UNIVERSITY OF MICHIGAN PRESS............ ANN ARBOR

Copyright © by the University of Michigan 2006
All rights reserved
Published in the United States of America by
The University of Michigan Press
Manufactured in the United States of America
⊗ Printed on acid-free paper

2009   2008   2007   2006   4   3   2   1

A CIP catalog record for this book is available from the British Library.

Library of Congress Cataloging-in-Publication Data

Documents : artifacts of modern knowledge / Annelise Riles, editor.
    p.   cm.
    Includes bibliographical references.
    ISBN-13: 978-0-472-09945-0 (cloth : alk. paper)
    ISBN-10: 0-472-09945-0 (cloth : alk. paper)
    ISBN-13: 978-0-472-06945-3 (pbk. : alk. paper)
    ISBN-10: 0-472-06945-4 (pbk. : alk. paper)
    1. Ethnohistory—Methodology.   2. Ethnohistory—Research.
I. Riles, Annelise.
GN345.2.DF63   2006
302.2'244—dc22   2006008020

Contents

Illustrations

Acknowledgments

I AM GRATEFUL TO Professor Bonnie Honig, Director of the Center for Law, Culture, and Social Thought at Northwestern University, for sponsoring the conference at which these papers were first presented, to Leticia Barrera, Jane Campion, Marie-Andrée Jacob, Amy Levine, Sergio Muñoz-Sarmiento, and Simon Stern for their research assistance, and to Donna Hastings for her assistance in preparing the final version of the manuscript. Raphael Allen at the University of Michigan Press has done more for this manuscript than any author could ever hope for, and we thank him for his vision, his confidence, and his care. Most of all, I thank Debbora Battaglia, Mario Biagioli, Don Brenneis, Tony Crook, Bryant Garth, Iris Jean-Klein, George Marcus, Bill Maurer, Hirokazu Miyazaki, Kunal Parker, Adam Reed, and Marilyn Strathern for helping me to appreciate once more, and perhaps articulate a little better, what is at issue in this collective project.

Introduction

In Response

Annelise Riles

FROM CINEMA TO ADVERTISING, management studies, and even military and police science, ethnography is enjoying something of a renaissance. Across the social and human sciences, the arts, and the professions, ethnography excites, provokes, and intrigues. In the academy in particular, in disciplines from law, sociology, and economics to literary criticism, scholars are turning to ethnographic work as a way out of overdetermined paradigms, as a theoretically sophisticated antidote to the excesses of theory.

This volume foregrounds a particular aspect of the ethnographic enterprise. Our specific focus is not the new *subjects* of ethnographic work, per se, but the *nature* of ethnographic knowledge itself. And within that knowledge, we draw attention to a particular aspect or dimension of ethnographic work: the act of *ethnographic conceptualization and response*. We are interested in how ethnographers conceive, grasp, appreciate, see patterns—or rather, in a telling colloquialism, how certain insights or patterns "come to them." We explore, through experiment as much as analysis, how ethnographers become caught in others' conceptualizations (Wagner 2001) and stopped in their analytical tracks, how they appreciate and empathize. And most of all, we draw attention to, and experiment with, anthropologists' *response* to their subjects, and to one another, as a form of ethical and epistemological engagement.

The volume is organized around one particular ethnographic artifact, *the document*. Why a focus on an artifact rather than a shared theoretical or methodological perspective? And why documents, of all things, a subject that Bruno Latour has termed "the most despised of all ethnographic subjects" (1988, 54)? Documents provide a useful point of entry into contemporary problems of ethnographic method for a number of reasons. First, there is a long and rich tradition of studies of documents in the humanities and social sciences. Second, documents are paradigmatic artifacts of modern knowledge practices. Indeed, ethnographers working in any corner of the world almost invariably must contend with documents of some kind or another. Documents thus provide a ready-made ground for experimentation with how to apprehend modernity ethnographically.

At the moment when scholars in other fields are, in increasing numbers, embracing ethnography, anthropologists, whose discipline gave birth to the method, pose questions. Anthropologists are now profoundly aware of their own complicity in local articulations of global political forces, and they are concerned about the ethical implications of their relationship to their subjects (Turner 1997). Experiences with translocal forces of decolonization, economic turmoil, and militarization have sewn fears that ethnographic accounts of particular places may actually obscure, rather than illuminate, the impact of wider political and economic forces. In a world in which the people anthropologists formally referred to as "informants" now often attend academic conferences and speak in the language of anthropological theory, moreover, uncanny connections and ironic alliances abound in anthropological discussions of the way globalization has altered the nature of the "field" and the task of fieldwork (Marcus 1999b, 4; Tsing 2005). At the same time, anthropologists' ethnographic encounters with new agents and artifacts—subjects such as financial instruments, biotechnologies, social movements, robots, scientific and legal theories, even academic bureaucracies—have raised new questions about the limits of traditional ethnographic description and analysis.

Moreover, if anthropologists ever truly believed that facts were "collected" in the "field" rather than produced collaboratively in the intersubjective experience of the ethnographic encounter, they have abandoned any such pretense. Gupta and Ferguson, for example, critique conventions of "spatial separation" and temporal sequence that separate "the field" from "home" and with these, the moment of data gathering from the moment of writing and analysis (1997a, 12). Marilyn Strathern (1991) likewise analyzes conventions of scale at work in understandings of ethnographic data, and also the "aesthetic of relationality" animating both ethnographic research and anthropological analysis (Strathern 1995). Anthropologists have definitively critiqued such conceptual categories as culture, society, or statehood, which once were the workhorses of ethnographic research. And the enduring legacy of the critiques of ethnographic writing practices of the 1980s (Clifford and Marcus 1986) has been doubts about the conventions of ethnographic narrative. One way to rephrase many of these concerns is to say that a once productive distance ethnographers maintained, implicitly or explicitly, purposefully or not, between ourselves and our objects of our study, between the things studied (the data) and the frames we used to study them (the analysis), between theorizing and describing, has now definitively collapsed.

Anthropologists' current questioning of fieldwork method marks out, in a practical and engaged way, large and important political, philosophical, and epistemological questions that are the province of no particular discipline. Already, enthusiasts of ethnography in other disciplines have begun to confront these questions as well. The early embrace of ethnography in science and technology studies and in film studies (e.g., Ruby 1992), for example, has given way to reflexive concerns much like the anthropological crises of representation of the 1980s (Lynch 1993). But for anthropology in particular, the future direction of the discipline now depends on finding answers to some very old and deceptively simple questions: What exactly differentiates ethnography from, or joins it to, journalism, fiction writing, cultural theory, historiography, or political activism? What notions of truth, and what ethical, political, or aesthetic commitments, does it embrace and demand? Who and what is ethnography for? How does description incorporate, supplement, or counterbalance ideas and ways of thinking in social theory? In recent decades anthropologists have pinpointed and dissected the methodological, political, and epistemological problems ethnographers confront in the field, and at their desks, with great acumen and skill. But the question of what ethnography should *become*, what should count as ethnography, in light of this internal critique, of what is the skill or the art of ethnographic work in the aftermath of the debates about politics and epistemology, still remains out of focus.

Articulations of the limits of conventional fieldwork have generated a number of proposals for how ethnography should be done. Many current proposals focus on new *subjects* of anthropological research—on identifying new institutions, new conditions for ethnographic work, or new objects of study, from laboratories to war zones (Franklin and McKinnon 2001; Greenhouse, Mertz, and Warren 2002; Ong and Collier 2005). George

Marcus's notion of "multi-sited" research (1998, 117) addresses the perceived limits of locality, for example. Another strand of proposals has focused on the character of relations between anthropologist and the people they encounter in the field—on moving away from a model of "informant relations" toward a focus on political, ethical, and conceptual collaboration with the people the ethnographer encounters in the field (Gupta and Ferguson 1997b; Marcus 1999b; Tsing 2005). Gupta and Ferguson propose a more actively engaged ethnographic practice focused on the concept of "political location" rather than fieldwork locale, for example (1997a, 39). A third strand of proposals has focused on the stylistic conventions of ethnographic writing and representation (Clifford and Marcus 1986; Marcus 1995, 1996; Raffles 2002).

This volume offers, by experiment and example as much as by argument, another view of the path forward, one that is surely related to both problems of rapport between field-worker and informant, and stylistic conventions of ethnographic writing, but is also not reducible to these. The focus here is on *ethnographic response*. The book proceeds through a series of ethnographic studies of one class of salient artifacts that ethnographers are now bound to encounter in modern fieldwork contexts from law to science, to the arts, religion, activism, and market institutions: documents. The chapters concern documentary practices in diverse ethnographic contexts. Adam Reed's essay juxtaposes the prison intake records of a maximum security prison in Papua New Guinea with prisoners' own "autographs" modeled on these intake records. Don Brenneis analyzes the aesthetic features of a recommendation form produced by an American funding organization. Marilyn Strathern writes about the production of a university mission statement. Mario Biagioli asks what the names affixed to large-scale multiauthored scientific papers document. My chapter considers the negotiation of a document at a United Nations international conference. Carol A. Heimer compares the medical documents produced in neonatal intensive care units to the "family" documents produced by the parents of the patients. Hirokazu Miyazaki's chapter addresses the uses of documentation in mortuary rituals he witnessed in a peri-urban Fijian community.

What I term ethnographic response may or may not require long-term fieldwork; it can involve subjects that are familiar or strange; it certainly does not depend on sociological constructs and conventions such as notions of society, locality, state, and culture that have come under such heavy critique in anthropological theory in recent years (Clifford 1988;

Gupta and Ferguson 1997a, 1997c; Moore 1993; Strathern 1992; Taussig 1997). Ethnographic response is part art and part technique, part invention and part convention, part the ethnographer's own work and part the effect of allowing others to work upon the ethnographer. It is theoretically informed but not theoretically determined. Hence the volume brings together ethnographers working from the standpoint of very different problems and paradigms, and it makes no effort to reconcile these differences. The volume includes a chapter by an organizational sociologist (Heimer); a philosopher of science (Biagioli); and five chapters by anthropologists working in various subdisciplines from linguistic anthropology to legal anthropology.

In this introduction, I retrace the trajectory of this project, from the initial reasons for the focus on documents to the response it ultimately offers to the challenges of doing ethnography in conditions in which the distance between anthropologist and informant, theory and data are no longer self-evident or even ethically defensible. I conclude with the surprise of our project: the emergence of questions of reception and appreciation, as integral aspects of the ethnographic enterprise, to be valued and worked on alongside questions of production and representation.

Artifacts of Modern Knowledge

Practices of documentation are without a doubt ubiquitous features of late modern life. From bus tickets to courtroom transcripts, employment applications to temple donation records, election ballots to archived letters, documents appear at every turn in the constitution of modern bodies (Scarry 1987), institutions (Ferguson 1990), states (Lass 1988), and cultures (Foster 1995). The ability to create and maintain files is the emblem of modern bureaucracy (Dery 1998), part of what Thomas Osborne has called the establishment of "the ethical competence to rule" (1994, 290). In modern criminal law, for example, efforts to limit the power of the state often take the form of demands that the state document its case against defendants in records accessible to the public (Sarat and Scheingold 2001).

Historians tell us that the word *documentation* was coined by the American Documentation Institute at its founding in 1937 to connote the joinder of new information technologies with a universalist rationalist philosophical outlook (Otlet 1934; cf. Farkas-Conn 1990, 4–36).[1] At about the same time, documentation also became the target of critique of both phenomenologists and Marxists (Day 2001, 729). Walter Benjamin, for example, condemned the fetishization of capitalist technology at the heart of the documentation project, and Martin Heidegger attacked the universalist pretensions of documentation in an argument that now finds a new audience in latter-day critiques of technological utopianism (e.g., Brown and Duguid 2000). The document therefore references *both* a utopian modernist vision of world peace through transparency and information exchange (Day 2001, 727) that had its roots in an earlier Victorian celebration of the public archive (Joyce 1999, 41; cf. Thomas 1992, 104), and also an ongoing critique of that vision.

Most recently, the changing character of the document has been at the heart of the seemingly endless excitement surrounding new information technologies. Kenneth Megill, for example, writes, "In the electronic age, 'document' is becoming a verb" (1996, 25). No longer a physical object, the document becomes "a response to a query," pure "function" (27), he argues. Corporate how-to books and intellectual property scholars describe a new world order built around new forms of Internet-based documents. Much of the debate about the consequences of the information revolution for the law revolves around the question of whether, and under what circumstances, an electronic communication is "like" a paper document (for the purposes of forming a contract or recording a deed, for example (e.g., Whitman 1999; Ealy and Schutt 2002).

As Giddens (1990) and others have suggested, modern knowledge is characterized by a persistent endeavor reflexively to seek further knowledge about itself. One of the principal instruments of this self-knowledge has no doubt been the document. Many of the buzzwords of the moment—from transparency to accountability—are in practical terms calls to documentation (Rosga 2005).

But if documents are so ubiquitous, why are documents also so "despised," as ethnographic subjects, in Latour's terms? Documents are special ethnographic subjects in one sense: they are also paradigmatic artifacts of ethnographic research. Field-workers document empirical phenomena in the world—and they do so concretely by producing documents (field notes, field reports, ethnographic archives)[2] or by consulting others' documents in archives (Comaroff and Comaroff 1991).[3] In other words, the document has a special status in the humanistic sciences as an artifact of what Carlo Ginzburg describes as "an epistemological model," a paradigm of interpretation, prevalent in fields as diverse as art criticism, detective novels, and psychoanalysis as well as ethnography: "a method of interpretation based on discarded information, on marginal data, considered in some way significant" (1989, 101).

In this respect, the subject of documents demands that ethnographers treat their own knowledge as one instantiation of a wider epistemological condition: As George Marcus writes, there is "an affinity between bureaucrats, officials, professionals, and left-liberal scholars that may be disturbing to the latter but which progressive scholars would have to take self-consciously into account in pursuing future projects" (1999a, 9). Holmes and Marcus have coined the term *para-ethnography* to describe the knowledge practices of actors in the world such as central bankers that are, in many respects, analogous to the anthropologist's own (Holmes and Marcus 2005). As a result, Marcus writes, "many of the spaces in which anthropologists work call into question the use and value of anthropological representation" (1998, 241).

Two chapters in this volume present this problem in particularly poignant form. In Marilyn Strathern's and Don Brenneis's chapters the bureaucrats they observe producing documents are literally themselves, or rather versions of themselves cast in the temporary role of bureaucrats, whether seconded to the bureaucratic state as evaluators of national research grant proposals (Brenneis) or serving in the capacity of university administrators (Strathern).

We have here one important reason for taking up the subject of documents, then. Documents are artifacts of modern knowledge practices, and, in particular, knowledge practices that define ethnography itself. Therefore, the ethnography of documentary practices—whether at a step removed from the academy, as in the case of the chapters by Heimer, Riles, Miyazaki, or Reed, or closer to home, as in the case of the chapters by Biagioli, Brenneis, and Strathern, affords an opportunity to reflect and work upon ethnographic practice in a particular way—not straight on, in the guise of critique or self-reflexivity, but laterally, that is, ethnographically. To study documents, then, is by definition also to study how ethnographers themselves know. The document becomes at once an ethnographic object, an analytical category, and a methodological orientation.

....

On Ethnographic Interest: "As If" Naïveté

But it is important, from the standpoint of our theme of ethnographic conceptualization, to acknowledge that this explanation of the project is not actually where this project began. The idea for this project originated rather in the course of fieldwork a decade ago among international organizations and NGOs (Riles 2000). I had become drawn, entirely by accident, into NGO workers' and government employees' preoccupations with conference reports, funding proposals, and nongovernmental organization newsletters. Slowly, by force of involvement in the mundane activities of daily bureaucratic life, I backgrounded the theoretical concerns that had initially framed my project and succumbed to the pull of these documents, as my interlocutors in the field experienced it.

Back from the field, I discovered that other ethnographers had similarly experienced the pull of documents. Early conversations with Reed and Miyazaki about practices of document production, collection, and dissemination they had observed caught us off guard. It certainly was an unanticipated point of collegial engagement, and at first glance, these conversations seemed to have nothing to do with anything of theoretical importance. But it was clear that the interest our research subjects had shown in documents had become contagious. Our subjects' interest had the effect of producing interest *in us*, the researchers. As we puzzled over how to "make something of documents," we turned to Brenneis's work (1994) on funding proposal documents as a model. In the months that followed, we learned of Biagioli's and Heimer's own encounters with similar phenomena in the field. What struck us was the energy that animated these conversations about the details of others' documentary practices, and the way that energy put other possible points of theoretical and methodological difference in the background as we pretended naively to indulge in the "ethnographic material."

This realization in turn prompted more fundamental questions about how interest is generated in humanistic research—where did this interest in documents come from? And what might it tell us about how theoretical questions emerge from the ethnographic encounter and are maintained through the retrospective experience of analyzing ethnographic data? Might there be lessons here about what to do at moments at which dominant theoretical paradigms no longer seem to generate the interest they once did? With a kind of leap of faith, the contributors to this volume decided to take their shared interest in documents as ethnographic artifacts as a basis for rethinking these fundamental questions surrounding the practice of ethnography and its relationship to theory, even though it was not clear at the outset what to make of documents analytically or where the subject might lead us theoretically. An initial meeting at Northwestern

University in 2000 provided the first impetus for a dialogue that since has become considerably richer and more nuanced as the years have passed.

Disparate Contexts

Our initial commitment to documents as ethnographic objects had a kind of purposeful naïveté to it, therefore (Marcus 1998, 124). But the fascination was always also, if implicitly, theoretically strategic. Becoming ethnographically engrossed in documents provided a kind of hiatus from theoretical debates that had blocked each of us, in different ways. By way of introducing the essays that follow, let me sketch out some of the different theoretical contexts we brought to our newfound ethnographic object.

Carol A. Heimer: Responding to the Weberian Tradition

As Carol A. Heimer explains in her chapter, organizational sociologists since Max Weber have looked to documents as crucial technological elements of bureaucratic organization (Weber 1968). Starting from a view of the organization as a more or less rational instrument, sociologists have considered how documentary practices shape behavior within organizations (Ouchi and Wilkins 1985). For example, Raffel (1979) describes how hospital medical records create alliances, and Smith (1990, 216) shows how social relations are "mediated" through items such as passports, birth certificates, application forms, and bills. Henderson considers how changes in the instruments of design technology in turn lead to other changes in organizational structure (1999).[4] Wheeler analyzes record keeping as a tool of social control made potent by a number of special characteristics of the file—its legitimacy or authority, its permanence, its transferability, its facelessness, and the fact that files can be combined and organized in a number of different ways (1969, 5). This approach is prevalent in the sociological literature, but it also has advocates among anthropologists interested in the effects of documentary practices on social organization and development (Goody 2000).

In her chapter, Heimer points out that the debate for sociologists has concerned the impact of documents on the degree of formality within the organization (Stinchcombe 2001). The assumption here is that documents strip away context, she explains, and hence enable the routinization of innovation (Hargadon and Sutton 1997), what Smith terms documents' "co-ordinating function" through the production of multiple copies of a document (Smith 1990, 213), and the more general "planned and organised character of formal organisation" (1990, 217; cf. Henderson 1999). This emphasis on the instrumental uses of documentary technologies within institutions dovetails with a number of sociological studies of the social and cognitive effects of writing technologies (Ong 2002) and, more recently, of new digital documentary forms.[5]

Although Heimer does not dispute the more general Weberian claim, she turns to ethnography to describe the range of uses of documents that characterize hospital employees' and family members' experiences of neonatal care. Specifically, she contrasts the "case analysis" of medical experts with the "biographical analysis" of the family members among whom she conducted ethnographic research and demonstrates that both forms of knowledge are structured by documentary forms. Heimer's careful attention to the uses of family members' documents and the kinds of "objects" (children) they produce nicely parallels the contrast Adam Reed draws in his chapter between the uses of "warrant cover" documents by prison wardens and prisoners themselves in the maximum security Papua New Guinea prison in which he conducted fieldwork. Documents, Heimer demonstrates, can also enable forms of cognition that are quite the opposite of formal bureaucratic reasoning.

Adam Reed: Responding to the Foucauldian Tradition

As Adam Reed explains in his chapter, it has become commonplace in the humanities and social sciences to analyze the constitutive effects of documents—the ways documents produce the very persons and societies that ostensibly use them (e.g., Foucault 1991). Historical anthropologists working on colonial documents have focused attention on "the role of inscriptions of various kinds in the making of ideology and argument" (Comaroff and Comaroff 1992, 34), and hence on what these documents suggest about colonists' relationships to their subjects (Dirks 2001; Stoler 2002). Bernard Cohn (1987), for example, discussed how the documentation of population in colonial India served to objectify, and hence reify, particular sociological categories. Thomas (1990), likewise, emphasized the panopticon-like devices of control at play in colonial report-making in Fiji. Voss and Werner have described the technologies of classification at work in the production of documents (1999, i). Nicholas Dirks and others have borrowed from Foucault to describe the colonial archive, and the documents it contains, as a technology that "encodes a great many levels, genres, and expressions of governmentality" (2002, 59; Joyce 1999, 53).

For Foucault, the critique of the constitutive power of the modern bureaucratic document necessarily extended to practices of documentation in the social sciences also. It was with this social scientific usage of the document as evidence in mind that Michel Foucault summed up his life project as "the questioning of the document":

> Of course, it is obvious enough that ever since a discipline such as history has existed, documents have been used, questioned, and have given rise to questions; scholars have asked not only what these documents meant, but also whether they were telling the truth, and by what right they could claim to be doing so. . . . But each of these questions, and all this critical concern, pointed to one and the same end: the reconstitution, on the basis of what the documents say, and sometimes merely hint at, of the past from which they emanate and which has now disappeared far behind them; the document was always treated as the language of a voice since reduced to silence, its fragile, but possibly decipherable trace. (1972, 6)[6]

In his work on forgery as a preoccupation of historians, likewise, Carlo Ginzburg describes the ways in which the evaluation of documents' authenticity has historically involved evaluations of the text's rhetorical dimensions (1999, 55) and he argues for an appreciation for the ways in which proof and rhetoric are inexorably intertwined (1999, 57). Historical anthropologists in particular have purposely treated historical documents "not as repositories of facts of the past but as complexly constituted instances of discourse that produce their objects as real, that is, as existing prior to and outside of discourse" (Axel 2002, 14).

This tradition, then, foregrounds a series of questions about how social science, policy science, and related documentary traditions render the world real for themselves (Sprenger 2001, 27).[7] Some writers have chosen to treat realism as a rhetorical stance, a matter of presentation rather than simple fact. Clarke (1999), for example, discusses what he terms "fantasy documents"—documents produced by organizations outlining contingency plans in the event of mass disasters such as a nuclear war or a massive environmental disaster—as "rationality badges" (1999, 16), that is, statements to the public that things are under control. Scholars and artists working in documentary film, likewise, have queried how the realism that is the hallmark of the documentary genre is produced.[8]

This work, along with several traditions of work on documents in literary criticism, treats documents as cultural texts—as receptacles of (politically or culturally) meaningful knowledge to be "read" by the theorist/observer (Bloomfield and Vurdubakis 1994; Inoue 1991).[9] The new historicist tradition of literary criticism, for example, has read documents such as bills of mortality, accounting tables, maps, and bookkeeping ledgers as evidence of a wider "cultural logic" that motivates the form of the documentary text (Miller 1984, 125).[10] In the same way, many ethnographers have understood themselves to be "reading" narratives of modernity. Key themes in these readings have included notions of trauma, loss, nostalgia, excess, ambiguity, plurality, and phantasm (Ivy 1998; Morris 2000; Siegel 1997).

Yet as Reed discusses in his chapter, there are a number of limitations to these discursive and textual paradigms. These limitations, moreover, have by now been well articulated and understood within the discipline of anthropology. Rappaport (1994) challenges the focus on textual meaning with the observation that for the Peruvian activists with whom she worked, the textual meaning of documents was rarely accessible and hence largely irrelevant. Carol Greenhouse has drawn attention to "the extent to which text fails to cover the surface of social life, that is, the ways in which interpretivists might be predisposed to assume that accessible articulatory practices in the public sphere comprise the full range of articulatory *needs*" (Greenhouse 2002, 18) and she has argued that "to limit discussion of ethnography to its representational aspects is to restrict ethnography to the symbolic dimensions of experience" (2002, 17). Ian Hodder (1994) argues that unlike human informants, the document does not so readily "talk back" to the ethnographer. The problem with a purely textual or discursive approach, he argues, is that sometimes documents may be intended to be representational, and sometimes not. Where they do "represent," they often do so differently than through the representational system of symbols found in oral or written language: precisely because they endure over time, they can also "work through the evocation of sets of practices within individual experience" (1994, 396). The temporality of the object also has implications for its meaning: an image that is at first metaphorical over time becomes a cliché, for example: "An artifact may start as a focus but become simply a frame, part of an appropriate background" (1994, 398).

Reed also has a larger concern about the Foucauldian treatment of documents: its emphasis on the "hegemony of document technology" tends itself to become fairly hegemonic, he argues. Scholars working in this tradition tend to focus on one "highly specific" aspect of documentary practices, their strategic or instrumental character. This analytical frame makes it difficult for scholars to grasp what else actors may do with documents, or indeed how else documents may be "good to think with" for scholars as much as for their subjects. This question then becomes the context of Reed's analysis of prisoners' emulation of prison documents.

Mario Biagioli: Responding to Science and Technology Studies

One tradition of scholarship that has engaged the subject of documents with particular élan is science and technology studies. Actor-network theorists Bruno Latour and Steve Woolgar have described scientific documents as "inscriptions" (1986; cf. Hevier 1998), and scientific work as the practice of producing, circulating, and evaluating these inscriptions. Latour and Woolgar describe scientists as "compulsive and almost manic writers" who spend their days making lists, filling in forms, writing numbers on samples, and drafting and redrafting articles (1986, 48). They draw attention to "transcription devices," such as the centrifuge machine, that "transform pieces of matter into written documents" such as graphs or diagrams that in turn are manipulated into documents of yet other kinds (Latour and Woolgar 1986, 51). Documents in this understanding are "immutable, presentable, readable and combinable" artifacts used to mobilize networks of ideas, persons, and technologies (Latour 1988, 26).[11]

From the standpoint of this volume, one important contribution of the actor-network approach is its methodological and epistemological stance. Latour and Woolgar refuse to treat labels on petri dishes as of a fundamentally different order than academic articles. Both are "inscriptions" for them. In this understanding, the distance between documentary practices in the world and critical analysis of those practices that some social scientists take for granted is replaced with a series of chains of artifacts—our documents, their documents, each capable of being manipulated into ever further forms of one another.

This focus draws on the insights of ethnomethodology (Lynch 1993), and Heimer and Reed pick up on Garfinkel's ethnomethodological analysis of clinical records in their own chapters.[12] Brenneis likewise draws on Richard Harper (1998)'s usage of the ethnomethodologists' notion of the document's career (Meehan 1997) to describe how, as a result of the division of labor within the International Monetary Fund bureaucracy he studied, the document changes social and material form as it moves from one setting (the study mission for example) to another (the archive) (cf. Laurier and Whyte 2001).

But Biagioli asks why this approach, which has broadened our understanding of what counts as an actor, ignores the issue of authorship—the subject's and one's own. In a turn of phrase that says much about his own approach to ethnographic artifacts, Biagioli writes that science studies scholars treat names "as units to be counted, not as documents *to be opened up*" (emphasis added). His wider concern, as with Reed's view of Foucauldian modes of analysis, in other words, is that science studies approaches tend to become overdetermined, and even at times mechanical in their theoretical claims. This concern becomes the context for Biagioli's investigation of scientists' practices of naming in academic articles.

Annelise Riles: Responding to Politics and Gender as Analytical Categories

One tradition of social scientific work on documents and other technocratic artifacts engages the document in a modality or critique. This tradition is exemplified by the work of Geoffrey Bowker and Susan Leigh Star (1999). Bowker and Star seek to "demystify" technology (1999, 9) by presenting an exhaustive survey of documentary processes across disparate cultures and institutional domains. They are interested in how information technologies such as data entry procedures constrain or enable by the way they "categorize" (1999, 36). They emphasize, for example, the political effects of bureaucratic classifications based on race, class, gender, or sexual orientation (1999, 26), and they seek to recover the "practical politics" of categories (1999, 45) by digging up the "conflict and multiplicity" that is "buried beneath layers of obscure representation" (1999, 47).

Bowker and Star call for a high-tech, politically engaged sociological analysis that would use new computer technologies, for example, "to describe this territory" (1999, 31). They write, "We need a topography of things such as the distribution of ambiguity; the fluid dynamics of how classification systems meet up—a plate tectonics rather than a static geology" (31). This new objectivism—which Michael Lynch (1993, 66) has termed "Left Mertonianism"—differentiates Bowker and Star from the more reflexive tradition of Foucauldian work on documentary categorizations. They critique what they view as the outdated and reactionary character of the ethnographic perspective: "By the very nature of the method . . . we also shared the actors' blindness. The actors being followed did not themselves see what was excluded: they constructed a world in which that exclusion could occur" (1999, 48).

Bowker and Star's critique of ethnography captures the particular ethical gloss of much contemporary work in the humanities and social sciences and the challenge it poses for ethnography. From law to science and technology studies, from anthropology to philosophy, the epistemological and political conflicts that characterized the academy in the 1980s have given way to a desire to *instrumentalize* academic knowledge. We now want to share with our subjects a set of tools and thus become potential allies, critics, or adversaries—in sum, we see ourselves as actors engaged in a singular plane by virtue of our shared objects, rather than observers. We seek a renewed connection with our publics; we want anthropology to be connected and relevant to the world we have too often kept at a remove (e.g., Nader 2001; Di Leonardo 1998).[13] As a result, ethnographers are now taking the artifacts of others' instrumentality as transparent things in the world, with straightforward uses *for us*.

But in my chapter, I seek to come to terms with the limits of analytical categories such as "politics" and "gender" to understand events seemingly laden with political and gendered implications. Like Reed, Heimer, and Biagioli, I am attentive to the consequences of this overdetermined analytical frame. Specifically, I am concerned that it obscures those aspects of "gender" that are most salient and those aspects of "politics" that are most powerful, from technocrats' own point of view. I worry that a failure to appreciate the efficacy of technocratic knowledge, in the rush to critique it, ironically renders ethnography itself nonefficacious in the face of politics and gender (as is explicitly suggested by Bowker and Star's critique of the ethnographic method) (cf. Jean-Klein and Riles 2005). This then becomes the context for my investigation of an explicitly political and gendered meeting—a meeting of states at the United Nations to draft a document on gender.

Don Brenneis and Marilyn Strathern: Responding to Technocracy

Finally, for Brenneis and Strathern, documents invoke a different kind of context—the context of their own enrollment in projects of producing and evaluating bureaucratic documents. They are both concerned with finding ways of coming to terms with the exhaustions surrounding the bureaucratization of the academy and its accompanying effects on both the production of knowledge and the agency of the scholar-turned-bureaucrat (Brenneis 1999; Strathern 2000).

For the authors in this collection, then, the theoretical contexts are disparate and diverse. But what the authors share is *a technique of response.* That is, they seek out a way of engaging with existing paradigms in the social sciences and humanities, from Weberian sociology to identity politics-driven activism, to Foucauldian history to science studies, that does not reject or critique these outright, and indeed that acknowledges their productive contributions. In fact, the authors are engaged, animated by the problems they identify at the limits of these paradigms, by what these paradigms make it impossible to observe, enact, or describe. Collectively, the authors seek a way to respond to rather than critique these problems.

The contributions of Heimer and Reed together provide a kind of response to the Weberian tradition of studies of the role of files within modern organizations: although neither author displaces Weberian arguments, each rephrases those claims with ethnographic understandings of other kinds of uses of the same artifacts. Likewise, for Reed, but also for Brenneis and Riles, documents provide an ethnographic alternative to the Foucauldian tradition—a way to respond in practice to the critiques of that tradition Greenhouse, Hodder, and others have articulated. Strathern and Brenneis both return to ethnography as a response to their own interpellation into bureaucratic practices. They respond by treating the artifacts of bureaucratic work—recommendation forms in Brenneis's case, and the university mission statement, in Strathern's—as ethnographic artifacts. Hence in a practical and concrete way, the volume demonstrates a collective hope in ethnography: ethnography emerges as a technique of response, at a moment at which one acknowledges the limits of existing theoretical paradigms, but also the limits of the critique of such paradigms.

Artifacts

We are not by any means alone in searching for places of respite from overdetermined theoretical paradigms or outworn descriptive tropes. But what differentiates this project is that many of the chapters engage this widespread concern from a particular ethnographic direction, that is, through the redeployment of Marilyn Strathern's notion of the "artifact" (1988, 1990). For Strathern, the artifact is something one treats *as if* (Leach

1986; Vaihinger 1924; Wagner 1986) it were simply a found object in the world. And yet, it is by definition always the artifact of ethnographic work as much as a found object. Specifically, it is the fruit of the ethnographic effort of working through one's theoretical concerns not by deductive analysis but laterally, through the ethnographic apprehension of, or empathy for, others' analytical concerns. An artifact-centered anthropological practice neither fetishizes objectivity (Gupta and Ferguson 1997a, 38) (the artifact is an *as if* found object) nor indulges in self-reflexivity (the subject is the artifact, not the anthropologist). In Roy Wagner's terms, it "obviates" existing theoretical oppositions (Wagner 1986) rather than resolving them or turning to a third hybrid category. As Strathern has shown in other ethnographic contexts, to take other people's knowledge practices as an ethnographic subject is also necessarily to think "laterally" about the epistemological and aesthetic commitments of one's own knowledge. Concretely, the artifact is what the ethnographer looks for in the field.

But the artifacts on display in this collection are special artifacts. They include the bracket, in Riles's chapter; the bullet point in Strathern's; the grid-shaped tabular chart in Miyazaki's; the warrant cover in Reed's; the name in Biagioli's; and the case and the child in Heimer's. The difference here is that the ethnographic subject (bureaucratic practice) and the ethnographic method are both the ethnographers own, albeit at different moments in time (at one moment, Strathern and Brenneis are thinking as committee members; at another moment they are thinking as ethnographers).

In their chapters, Strathern and Brenneis deal with the conflation of subject and object in ethnographic studies of modernity, in other words, by daring to take that conflation one step further, by bringing the moment of ethnographic observation into the moment of bureaucratic participation. Ironically, by collapsing these moments, they are able to continue to think about themselves and their own practices *as if* they were thinking laterally about them, as ethnographic objects. The discovery and articulation of new ethnographic themes in these mundane practices becomes a kind of bureaucratic instrument of its own, a weapon for conditions in which, as they explain, critique on the one hand, and bureaucratic engagement on the other, are always already assimilated into the very practices the academic anthropologist would wish to critique or engage.

From this standpoint, a number of provisional themes—ways of talking across individual chapters in the "meantime" (Weston 2002) of the project—emerged.

Temporality

Questions of temporality appear and reappear across all the chapters in the volume. As Brenneis puts it, working with documents necessarily entails moments of document making and moments of evaluating. Biagioli analyzes scientists' names as the "hinge between two distinct moments" in scientific production—the development of scientific claims and scientific publication. My chapter considers a moment of UN conference document drafting, bracketing, at which units of time and of analysis, two entities one normally would think of as of entirely different orders, collapse into one. I describe the formal techniques intrinsic to the negotiation process that negotiators deploy to unwind the two, and hence to bring both temporal and analytical closure to the negotiations.

Our attention to the way moments of document creation anticipate future moments in which documents will be received, circulated, instrumentalized, and taken apart again implicitly engages a wide range of work in the humanities and social theory. Temporal analysis is now widely taken as an alternative to what is interpreted as the overly static nature of social theory. In many parts of the humanistic social sciences, alternative understandings of temporality indexed, for example, by Heideggerian notions of "becoming" as opposed to "being" serve as a ground for the critique of the hegemony of modern and technocratic temporal practices. Likewise, for many scholars, a focus on pragmatist concepts of "emergence" enables a more dynamic, nondeterministic, complex understanding of social life.

Our focus on the temporality of technocratic artifacts such as documents responds to these projects by demonstrating that expert knowledge itself is far less hegemonic and far more interesting than the caricatures of technocratic knowledge often make it out to be. Moreover, we are interested not just in drawing a contrast between technocratic and "everyday" temporalities but in tracing the engagement between these (e.g., Heimer). At the same time, treating documents as artifacts also draws explicit attention to the temporal nature of social and cultural theory itself. Some of the authors find in the temporalities of documents, for example, counterpoints to the urge to produce an aesthetic of complexity in one's own analysis simply by setting one's analytical categories in motion (Miyazaki).

Form Filling

As a response to the instrumentalization of documents, and also to their treatment as mere texts to be read, several of the contributions to this volume focus on questions of form—the uses of the formal and aesthetic properties of documents, the relationship of form to information technology, and the question of how attention to document form might engender a rethinking of the document's instrumental or informational purposes (cf. Danet 1997). Reed considers how the form of the prison intake document, as experienced and then emulated by prisoners, prefigures the past and future agency of those who complete it and are subjected to it, while Brenneis analyzes the kind of interaction anticipated by the NSF recommendation letter form. Brenneis' chapter builds upon earlier work in which he has shown how documents serve not only as instruments for collecting and conserving information about individuals but also as the means by which individuals inform about themselves through the pleasures of self-objectification and mimesis (Brenneis 1994). Here, Brenneis echoes James Aho (1985), who argues that the invention of double-entry bookkeeping is explained not by its instrumental uses but by its rhetorical ones: double-entry bookkeeping created an aura of transparency. This rhetoric has gone largely unnoticed by scholars, Aho argues, because it is a rhetoric of instrumentalism—a rhetoric that convinces and appeals by adopting the language of antirhetoric—of uses, functions, and effects.

Documents are by definition artifacts of a particular genre, or form. As scholars in informational design theory have pointed out, documentation implies a particular set of aesthetic commitments (Henderson 1999; Kinross 1989): "the belief in simple forms, in reduction of elements, apparently not for reasons of style but for the most compelling reason of need—the need to save labor, time, and money and to improve communication" (Kinross 1989, 138). All of the chapters in this volume address questions of documentary form, from the aesthetic rules that govern the production and completion of documents to the evaluation and appreciation of documentary genre.

In particular, most of the chapters concern, in one way or another, a set of aesthetic practices associated with the production, use, and circulation of documents that distinguish documents from other genres of texts, that is, practices of form filling. Miyazaki's chapter, for example, describes a tabular record prepared in advance of a mortuary gift-giving ritual by Fijian clan members, to be filled in during the ritual itself in order to produce a record of the gifts received. In Miyazaki's analysis, at the moment of its making, the table anticipates certain kind of future form-filling practices. At the moment of its completion, likewise, the spatial arrangement of columns and rows to be filled in effectuates a particular experience of the exchange taking place at that moment.

Recently, ethnographers of modernity have taken an interest in subjects that overflow and subvert workhorses of sociological interpretation such "culture" and "society." Form filling turns out to be a highly interesting terrain for a postsocial, postcultural, even postrelational humanistic scholarship of this kind. As I have suggested in another context, the form is a self-contextualizing entity (Riles 2000): the gaps in the form to be filled in contain within themselves all the terms of analysis one would need to understand or complete them. The question then becomes methodological as well as theoretical: what might an ethnography of such a self-analyzing, self-contextualizing object look like? What might it contribute?

The authors in this collection are by no means the first to pay attention to documentary form. Sociological studies of organizations have long treated the form and material qualities of documents as influential on the character of communicative practice. For example, in an historical study of the evolution of the memo form in the late nineteenth century and early twentieth century, Orlikowski and Yates consider how different "genres" of bureaucratic communication (memos, letters, meetings) (1994, 301) are both produced by and influential upon ideologies of managerial behavior and actors' communicative practices (310–11), and how new documentary technologies both trigger, and are influenced by, new ideologies of managerial behavior (311).[14]

But in some of the chapters, the ethnographic treatment of documentary forms and of associated practices of filling them out pushes the boundaries of social analysis by refusing to contextualize documentary form in arguments about its social contexts and institutional purposes. Instead, the authors produce empathetic accounts of the aesthetic qualities of the form and its effects. Brenneis, for example, deploys insights from linguistic anthropology to not so much to analyze fellowship reference forms as to make it possible for readers, most of whom routinely process such forms in large quantities as part of the mundane aspect of their institutional lives, to see these objects a second time, as if new. Reed's description of the documents produced by prisoners draws at times on prisoners' exegesis, but also reflects his own appreciation of these documents. This ability to appreciate, what Bateson (1987) termed empathy toward pattern, is an effect of ethnographic work: only through ethnographic engagement did the authors come to appreciate the document's form. And yet this is a differently empirical enterprise: Rather than simply describing a documentary form as an instantiation of existing analytical categories and problems, the authors respond to that form with further replications and extensions.

....

Authorship and Agency

In her chapter, Carol A. Heimer observes that "the bureaucratic uses of documents often assume that someone outside the organization will have a rather different relation to the subjects of their documents." In other words, documents anticipate and enable certain actions by others—extensions, amplifications, and modifications of both content and form. All of the contributors are concerned with these practices of extending, completing, or recycling, as modalities of authorship and of agency. We are interested in how diverse types of agency are produced, stretched, or abbreviated through the medium of the document; in short, in the responses, human and nonhuman, that documents demand or offer up. Brenneis's analysis of recommendation forms, for example, shows how they anticipate and call forth certain disciplined responses from evaluators that nevertheless sometimes leave room for surprises. Reed shows how prisoners respond to the forms prison officials use to describe and categorize them by producing other exemplaries of the form as self-descriptions.

Drawing on Strathern's earlier work (1988) on agency, Miyazaki argues that the ritual form of Fijian gift presentations, and the documents participants use to capture its effect, are both open and closed at once: on the one hand, only certain responses to the speeches, or notes in the boxes on the document's form, will do. But at the same time, these documents cannot complete themselves. Each must await completion, in a successive temporal moment, by another agent. In Miyazaki's analysis, what is crucial is that the gift-giver momentarily places his agency "in abeyance"—he submits to the evaluation of the gift-receiver—and this act of abeyance also ultimately compels the gift-receiver's response. One insight of our ethnography likewise concerns the capacity of documents to place their own agency in abeyance, such that what is made visible in the document, rather, is the creativity of another agent (the point of the completed reference form, for example, is what is said about the candidate, not the nature of the form or the questions it poses). This is not to deny that documents allow only for certain kinds of responses and self-descriptions. But it does suggest that to critique bureaucratic processes for the way they assert agency over us, and for the limitations they place on our own creativity and agency, would miss the very means by which bureaucratic processes compel others' creativity in the first place (see Riles, this volume; Strathern, this volume).

In particular, in his discussion of scientific names as documents, Biagioli draws attention to authorship as a corrective to current conceptions of agency in critical theory. Against current work that reduces authorship to a kind of agency, Biagioli asks how names at the top of scientific publications come to be documents of scientific agency. Commenting on the way authorship is presumed to be multiple and fragmented in scientific circles in ways that mirror claims in critical studies of authorship, Biagioli nevertheless insists on a crucial difference between scientific notions of authorship and those of critical theory. Scientists deploy authorship in a "documentary" sense, he argues: authorship is precisely the physical presence of the name on a byline and all the privileges and liabilities this brings with it. This documentary practice of authorship is what allows scientists to criticize authorship in policy debates while still holding onto it as a mundane practice.

Biagioli's attention to the character of documentary authorship necessarily invokes questions about the status of authorship within the humanistic social sciences. What can be learned about ethnographic authorship from scientists' mundane understandings of authorship? How is it that the same critiques of authorship that have been so destabilizing in the human sciences have so little practical force in the lives of scientific authors? Against Foucault, Biagioli points out that responsibility for one's artifacts is as important to the constitution of scientific truths as epistemological authority. Responsibility, in other words, does not end with challenges to authority. His description raises the question of responsibility, as a corrective to questions of epistemological authority, in ethnographic authorship.

Ethnography as a Modality of Response

I mentioned earlier that the contributions in this volume are unique in their manner of seeking to respond to, rather than merely critique, the limits they find in humanistic theory. The same could be said of the authors' engagement with their ethnographic artifacts. One way of thinking about agency, temporality, and form collectively is to say that we are interested in how documents themselves elicit particular kinds of *responses*. Recommendation forms anticipate their own completion, for example; or UN documents that call for action on particular social problems anticipate that state bureaucracies will review these calls and respond with further policies and documents. In focusing on the responses that documents effectuate or command, we are responding also, as ethnographers, to our documentary subject. To return to the larger theme of ethnographic practice, we are necessarily thinking about questions of ethnographic epistemology, ethics, and aesthetics "through the grain" (Shaw 1999) of the documentary practices we describe: the ultimate question is what kind of response ethnographic objects such as documents might demand, enable, or compel *of us*.

The authors take different approaches, here. For example, when Heimer describes her subject as "comparison itself," she subtly but crucially asks her reader to consider the parallels between bureaucratic and sociological knowledge. Brenneis focuses not so much on parallels between academic and institutional knowledge as on actual social, material, and conceptual relations between them. Brenneis builds specifically on projects in linguistic anthropology that focus on the artifactual quality of texts and on "entextualization practices" (Silverstein and Urban 1996) to treat documents in terms of a "socially mediated textual performance in which there are norms of interconnectedness between texts, their authors, and readers" (Kaplan 2002, 347).[15] From this perspective, he looks to documentation as the ground for a new set of questions about how academics and their bureaucratic subjects both make knowledge together.

Two caveats are necessary here. First, in common usage, the concept of response has an unfortunate aura of passivity. It will be apparent from the ethnographic materials in the chapters that follow that there is nothing inherently passive or automatic about actors' responses to documents. Some of the responses to documents are pro forma, so to speak; others are creative and destabilizing of the form itself. Most responses the authors describe are interesting precisely because the agency of the form and the form-filler are not neatly circumscribed.

Second, the authors entertain no utopian fantasies about the responses documents demand of both the ethnographer and the bureaucratic subject. In her chapter, Strathern sharply critiques the excesses of "responsiveness" within which the university mission statement she describes is drafted. Institutions have taken to producing documents like the mission statement largely "in response to demands," she points out. Calls for the production of particular kinds of documents are demands that people describe themselves, and that they do so in certain bureaucratically circumscribed ways. Her usage of metaphors of pitifully unequal warfare to describe document drafting casts responses to documents as a dangerous and often hopeless game of deflecting the power of others by reflecting it back onto themselves.

However, what is interesting about documents and the responses they enable and compel, as ethnographic subjects, is that a straightforward critique of responsiveness will not do. Oppositional thinking about a contest between bureaucratic agents and their subjects obscures the way in which, as Reed powerfully demonstrates in his ethnography of prisoners' uses of prison documents, completion is effectuated only through and because of both sides' shared appreciation or "empathy" for the aesthetics of completion (Miyazaki 2004, 105). We will need some alternative to the critique of technocracy if we are to come to terms with this empathy—and indeed engage and redeploy this empathy for other purposes.

The notion that at its best, ethnography should be responsive or empathetic to its subject is of course nothing new. Neither is there anything particularly shocking about the claim that an ethically engaged ethnography would entail not just a responsiveness to one's informants as social persons, but also a response to the artifacts—the knowledge, the commitments, the practices—others introduce to us in the ethnographic encounter. But I want to suggest that thinking of ethnography as a response to artifacts is a particularly helpful way of understanding ethnographic work in conditions where the artifacts at issue already interpolate us into their practices on their own terms, where they *already demand a response*, as for example in the case of mission statements, UN documents on gender, scientific articles, or fellowship reference forms.

Audit practices are particularly pernicious, Strathern writes, because they exploit a "fundamental human capacity—responsiveness to others." Her comment invites reflection on the final section of Miyazaki's chapter in which he describes how indigenous Fijian gift-givers and gift-receivers complete the gift-giving ritual by turning together to dedicate their gifts to God. In Miyazaki's interpretation, this second act of gift-giving replicates the first on another terrain. Replication on another terrain, that is, in another register, for another purpose, is one modality of response, in other words, and one that Miyazaki explicitly adopts as his own ethnographic response to the gift-giving rituals he observed.[16]

The suggestion in Miyazaki's chapter, in light of Strathern's critique of responsiveness, then, is that one hard-nosed response to the document, including its demands of responsiveness, might be to borrow a method from the document itself (Holmes 2000; Maurer 2002; Rosga 2005). Of course, this is not to suggest that academic work actually emulate bureaucratic work—no one is proposing that ethnographers start drafting UN documents, or producing mission statements, or writing recommendation letters, or tracking valuables in exchange settings *as academic work*. Thankfully, as Strathern points out, this is not possible anyway: when bureaucratic documents translate academic language into bullet points, academic language becomes no more than unformed data, bits of information. As my chapter on academic feminist engagement with the usage of the word *gender* in UN documents illustrates, although academics increasingly take on bureaucratic tasks, the words and the authors are no longer the same entities.

Rather, these chapters show how ethnographers might respond powerfully to the mundane practices that interpolate them, by borrowing responses from the ethnographic artifact itself (here, documents and documentary practices) *onto the ethnographer's own terrain*. Strathern's essay takes the form of a series of bullet points, and in this way, far from becoming bureaucratic knowledge, it reflects and deflects the bureaucratic power to compel responsiveness. My essay responds to a specific problem in the humanistic sciences and in critical theory—a condition in which academic analytical tools such as "political analysis" or "gender analysis" are already incorporated into the object to be analyzed—by thinking about these problems as if with bureaucrats' tools for accessing the analytically inaccessible. Miyazaki borrows the device of replication in order to address the philosophical question of how to access a present moment. For Reed, the abbreviations of warrant covers, and the extensions they in turn enable, become the form of his own analysis. Collectively, then, these chapters fashion an alternative response to form filling, one that is appreciative and empathetic of the knowledge practices at issue, including perhaps most of all the propensities for violence they contain.

This then raises a further question: where lie the ethical commitments of such an ethnography? How should those commitments be defined and defended? This brings me, finally, to the ultimate surprise of this project—the emergence of the question of scholarly collaboration, and of the creative work and ethical commitment it demands.

....

Conclusion: Response as a Modality of Collaboration

Taken as a whole, this collection of essays is a somewhat odd-looking artifact. Unlike most collective academic projects, in which each of the chapters can be read as an instantiation or empirical elaboration of a singular theoretical stance—different facts under the rubric of a singular theory—this collection gathers together the artifacts of a series of particular and situated borrowings, extensions, replications—responses to—the artifacts the authors encountered ethnographically. By definition, our particular responses to abbreviations, bullet points, and brackets are not local versions of a singular global theory. Nor are they representations of a singular set of factual phenomena. To the extent that the chapters are comparable, it is in the unpredictable resonances that emerge from setting the artifacts of our responses side by side—from the comparison of responses, rather than of factual findings on the one hand or theoretical positions on the other.

In other words, the reformulation of ethnography as a modality of response gives rise to a larger descriptive and interpretive problem: the problem that the artifacts of ethnographic knowledge *cease to be comparable*, and hence open to evaluation, in a conventional disciplinary way. Because each ethnographic artifact is the outcome of a specific analytical interaction with the knowledge practices of a particular subject—the borrowing of a particular method—the results are no longer instances or exemplifications of a singular stylistic genre. Ethnography can no longer be defined and evaluated by the degree to which it conforms to a given form or positions itself within a given debate. This opens up new questions about what kind of response the artifacts of such ethnography would in turn demand of colleagues, as readers of ethnographic texts or interlocutors at academic talks and conferences. Perhaps before we need new and creative ways of "doing" the fieldwork and writing of ethnography, we need a new set of means of responding to one another's artifacts.

On the whole, ethnographers give surprisingly little attention to the task of receiving one another's artifacts and the commitments it demands. Here ironically there is a model in the very documentary practices many of the contributors to this project would in other ways revile. As Brenneis recently has put it: "I am at times surprised that many anthropologists who are extraordinarily subtle and sophisticated in their analyses of field situations are considerably less analytical about the institutional webs that we daily inhabit here at home" (2004, 581). Peership, Brenneis writes of the peer review system, is crucially "review with as well as of peers" (2004, 583). Brenneis enacts the point in a recent article that takes the form of an interview with a colleague, and in which the subject is precisely collaborative relations among specific anthropologists, artists, and activists (Feld and Brenneis 2004).

We need more subtle, creative, and careful genres of empathy and intellectual appreciation among colleagues. Traces of this empathy are on display in this volume in the way the authors speak across chapters, and find resonances in one another's work. But most intellectual appreciation does not leave overt markers in this way, as the creative work of producing texts by definition does. That is its nature—it erases its traces. Rather, the artifact of this creative work is the very existence of this book, as a totality: indeed, the effort and efficacy of collegial response became real for me as the central theme of our project in the commitment the contributors to this project maintained, over the years from our initial meeting, as we struggled at once to define new terms for ethnographic practice and to communicate them to various academic audiences accustomed to hearing problems framed in other vocabularies. This book is in a very concrete way the artifact of that commitment.

One place where response has been valued as ethical and creative work alongside production and representation is feminist debate. Marilyn Strathern has written, "Feminist debate is characterized by a compatibility that does not require comparability between the persons who engage in it, bar their engaging in it" (1991, 35). As she elaborates in another context, "One position evokes others" and hence, "The positions are created as dependent upon one another. . . . Feminism lies in the debate itself" (Strathern 1988, 24). To put the point in a different way, perhaps ethnography, like Fijian ritual (Miyazaki, this volume), is a form that cannot complete itself without others' response. I want to conclude by suggesting that one terrain for the completion of ethnographic work through response is the terrain of collegial relations.

Collaboration is both a means and an end of most projects of document production (Riles 2000). The experience of academics working together on a university committee, or of United Nations bureaucrats working together to draft the language of a UN document, is premised on the understanding that the only coherence to the project lies in the thin and surface-level identity of the subject itself (the particular UN document or committee decision at issue). This point of contact is explicitly understood as provisional: the document is just a means; it points to an end beyond itself—even as what captivates participants is the means of document production (Riles 2004). In much the same way, the participants in this project have met on the thin and provisional terrain of the document, as ethnographic artifact, while keeping firmly in mind that what was important was precisely not the document per se. This almost instrumental appreciation of the way our questions both were and were not the same, were and were not disposable, enabled other resonances to emerge. We began to compare not documents but responses to documents—our subjects' and our own. Documents became the self-consciously expendable ground of our reception of one another's work. One might think of it as ethnography's (overdue) concomitant to the replications of scientific studies performed as responses to innovative "results" in differently empirical social sciences.

The subtle appreciation ethnographers have for their relations with the people they encounter in the field, then, now is poised to serve as a model for collegial reception and response among humanistic social scientists themselves. Ethnography of course always demands evaluation and critical judgment of our subjects' practices; ethnographic empathy has never meant naive acceptance of what informants say or do. But that judgment takes place in the context of the ethnographer's careful appreciation of the way the subject's problems both are and are not the ethnographer's own. The subject's problems and solutions, the starting points and ending points, are analogous in interesting ways but also different. Appreciating these similarities and differences is the *work* of ethnography, whatever one's concept of "the field," "the informant," or "the ethnographic subject." The same subtle modality of critical appreciation is surely required of the collegial reception of one another's ethnographic artifacts.

The example of collegiality I have had the privilege of encountering in the experience of working toward this volume, and also of the documentary practices captured in these ethnographies, suggests that ethnographers might devote the kind of ethical commitment they routinely show toward their social relations with their subjects, and the creativity they display in writing about these relations, to the act of ethnographic response. This would involve both responding to the artifacts one encounters in the course of ethnographic work, and also in analogous ways, responding to the artifacts of one another's ethnographic work.

....

NOTES

1. One of the most exhaustive debates of the documentation movement concerned what should properly count as a document. There were a myriad positions and counterpositions, but all shared a commitment to two key categories, the ideal and the material, and to an instrumental relationship between the two: A document was an idea committed to material form such that it could be used—it could become a technology of its own. Walter Shurmeyer wrote in 1935 that a document included "any material basis for extending our knowledge which is available for study or comparison" (quoted in Buckland 1997, 805). The functional view of documents promoted by Paul Otlet and others suggested that documents were "objects

to which the techniques of documentation could be applied" (Buckland 1997, 805). Thus the philosopher and information specialist Suzanne Briet described documents as organized physical "evidence in support of a fact" (quoted in Buckland 1997, 806) of any kind—a wild animal was not a document, but an animal in the zoo was.

2. As George Marcus comments, this argument for the discipline is instantiated institutionally in the midcentury Human Relations Area files project, and the publication of *Notes and Queries* (1951), the massive checklist of information every ethnographer was expected to collect in the field (Marcus 1998, 50).

3. "The fiction is that the authority comes from the documents themselves, as well as the historian's obeisance to the limits they impose on any account that employs them" (Steedman 2001, par. 39).

4. Historian Roger Chartier, likewise, considers the history of the production, inventorying, and circulation of books and manuscripts and of the effects of printing on the formation of "communities of readers" (1994, 2), and he compares different forms of classifications of texts—physical libraries that arrange texts in space, anthologies that arrange texts by classes of knowledge, bibliographies, book lists, and publishing series—according to their instrumental uses and effects.

5. Questions include, how can information technologies produce institutional change? And under what organizational conditions are new information technologies productively integrated into organizational environments (Orlikowski et al. 1995)? Orlikowski and Yates (1994) track the evolution of genre rules for long-term communication between a group of scientists over e-mail. Richard Harper argues that hypertext liberates the reader from the dominating effects of documents by allowing them to gain control over the form of information (1997, 41). In contrast, Nigel Thrift queries what is new about these "new forms" of electronic communication (1996, 1464). Thrift argues that grand claims about historical shifts associated with electronic communication—claims that electronic technologies engender new forms of temporality, subjectivity, and economy—derive from a view of technology dating to the industrial revolution that he terms "technological determinism" (1996, 1466). What is new, he suggests, is that such deterministic accounts have encountered their own limits.

6. Against this view of the document, Foucault provocatively proposed "not the interpretation of the document, nor the attempt to decide whether it is telling the truth or what is its expressive value, but to work on it from within and to develop it" (1972, 6), a move he termed the transformation of documents into "monuments" deserving of "intrinsic description" (7).

7. Scott Sprenger emphasizes the political dangers of a realism that "silence(s) others by obliterating the space for adjudicating differences of interpretation" (2001, 28)—a danger he terms terrorism—through a close reading of Robespierre's uses of documentary evidence in arguments for the execution of Louis XVI during the Terror.

8. These scholars have foregrounded the rehearsal process that goes into the making of documentary dialogue, the interactional dynamics between filmmaker and subject (e.g., McAuley 1998), and the aesthetic techniques deployed by directors (e.g., Shapiro and Godmilow 1997) that allow the news to emerge as some-

thing in the world, documented by the film crew, rather than created in the news-room (Baker 1989). In theater studies, likewise, critical attention has been devoted to the limits of documenting live performance and hence the politics at play in what gets documented, by whom, and how (e.g., Cutler 1998).

One interesting trend in film studies is the emergence of forged, or faux, realism as a creative genre of scholarship—the production of fictional films that parody or replicate the documentary genre precisely in order to foreground debates surrounding the documentary's realist claims (Feldman 1998). In something of the same spirit, Hillel Schwartz takes on "the culture of the copy" to ask,

> How has it come to be that the most perplexing moral dilemmas of this era are dilemmas posed by our skill at the creation of likenesses of ourselves, our world, our times? The more adroit we are at carbon copies, the more confused we are about the unique, the original, the Real McCoy. (1996, 11)

9. Natalie Davis, for example, proposes that the historian pay attention to the "fictional" aspects of documents, "their forming, shaping, and molding elements: the crafting of a narrative" (1987, 3). In Davis's study of sixteenth-century French letters of remission, letters serve as sources of narratives "from the lips of the lower orders" (1987, 5). Peter Burke, likewise, in his bid to convince historians to treat visual images as seriously as textual ones, considers images a kind of text, with interpretable meanings (Burke 2001).

10. For example, Richard Kroll (1986) considers the effect of conceptions of physical space on the organization of mental categories in the design of title pages, tables, and other graphic elements of late-seventeenth-century printed books. The literary historian Richard Helgerson (1986) has traced the influence of cartography on Elizabethan conceptions of nationhood and sovereign authority. Attention is given to the images the maps contain and to their interpretive meanings (Fisher 1988; Sherman 2001; Vidler 1993).

11. "The function of literary inscription is the successful persuasion of readers, but the readers are only fully convinced when all sources of persuasion seem to have disappeared" (Latour 1986, 76).

12. Garfinkel (1967) began by examining clinical records as sources of "data" about clinical practices but eventually revisited his own frustrations with the incompleteness of those records, understanding patterns of completeness or incompleteness in terms of the uses of the records within the clinic.

13. George Marcus writes, "This kind of circumstantial activism is indeed the surrogate of the old sense of 'being there' in some focused place or site with its own attendant politics and ethics" (1999a, 18).

14. These arguments have analogs in applied social science focusing on the character of documentation and its effect on the structure of thought in clinical settings (e.g., Rivas-Vazquez et al. 2001; Schumock, Hutchinson, and Bilek 1992) or accounting practices (e.g., Cushing and Ahlawat 1996; Purvis 1989). The question of how people think with documents has received some attention in the field of cognitive psychology, for example, where studies contrast the "analogical reasoning" elicited by time tables with conventional forms of reading. There is also an extensive practitioner-oriented sociological literature concerning the impact of the

design of documents on their use by their intended audience (e.g., Frohlich 1986; Kempson and Rowlands 1994). The skills necessary for using documents, these authors suggest, center on the comparison of elements in the document (Guthrie 1988), for example. Building on these instrumentalist insights, reformers have sought to alter the language and format of bureaucratic documents so as to make them more accessible to the general public. Lawyers and linguists have argued that, in terms of due process, so-called paper hearings (the presentation of documents to a bureaucracy) cannot substitute for a live hearing (Shuy 1998). And marketing specialists have taken interest in how technical documentation shapes consumers' perceptions of products (Smart, Madrigal, and Seawright 1996).

15. In a similar vein, William Hanks's analysis of the discourse of Maya nobles in a series of letters to the Spanish Crown critiques colonial historians' treatment of the repetitions from one letter to the next as signs of inauthenticity and finds instead in the subtle pattern of repetition and divergences between letters, rather, evidence of "intertextuality":

> Two texts may be linked to one another by concrete shared features, for instance, by reference to each other, by amplification (where one text elaborates on the other), by contradiction, or by reinforcement. They may also be related by common membership in a single genre within a given literary tradition. . . . Interpretation of the discourse cannot treat it as an isolate, but rather as part of a series of texts situated within a larger network. The intertextual context is also a key part of the field of action insofar as it provides objective resources for intelligible communicative performance. (Hanks 2000, 111; cf. Witte 1992)

16. Miyazaki purposely collapses collegial relations, theoretical relations, and relations with his ethnographic material, treating his work as a response to the hope others have shown in his project, to the writings of philosopher Ernst Bloch on hope, and to Fijian gift-giving practices all at once (2004, 7).

....

REFERENCES

Aho, James A. 1985. Rhetoric and the Invention of Double Entry Bookkeeping. *Rhetorica* 3:21–43.

Axel, Brian K., ed. 2002. *From the Margins: Historical Anthropology and Its Futures.* Durham, NC: Duke University Press.

Baker, Carolyn D. 1989. Knowing Things and Saying Things—How a Natural World Is Discursively Fabricated on a Documentary Film Set. *Journal of Pragmatics* 13:381–93.

Bateson, Gregory. 1972. Style, Grace, and Information in Primitive Art. In *Steps to an Ecology of Mind,* 128–52. Northvale, N.J.: Jason Aronson.

Bloomfield, Brian P., and Theo Vurdubakis. 1994. Re-presenting Technology: IT Consultancy Reports as Textual Reality Constructions. *Journal of the British Sociological Association* 28:455–77.

Bowker, Geoffrey C., and Susan Leigh Star. 1999. *Sorting Things Out: Classification and Its Consequences.* Cambridge: MIT Press.

Brenneis, Donald. 1994. Discourse and Discipline at the National Research Council: A Bureaucratic *Bildungsroman. Cultural Anthropology* 9:23–36.

———. 1999. New Lexicon, Old Language: Negotiating the "Global" at the National Science Foundation. In *Critical Anthropology Now: Unexpected Contexts, Shifting Constituencies, Changing Agendas,* ed. G. E. Marcus, 123–46. Santa Fe: School of American Research Press.

———. 2004. A Partial View of Contemporary Anthropology. *American Anthropologist* 106:580–88.

Brown, John Seely, and Paul Duguid. 2000. *The Social Life of Information.* Boston: Harvard Business School Press.

Buckland, Michael K. 1997. What Is a Document? *Journal of the American Society for Information Science* 48:804–9.

Burke, Peter, ed. 2001. *New Perspectives on Historical Writing.* University Park: Pennsylvania State University Press.

Chartier, Roger. 1994. *The Order of Books: Readers, Authors, and Libraries in Europe Between the Fourteenth and Eighteenth Centuries.* Trans. Lydia G. Cochrane. Stanford, CA: Stanford University Press.

Clarke, Lee. 1999. *Mission Improbable: Using Fantasy Documents to Tame Disaster.* Chicago: University of Chicago Press.

Clifford, James. 1988. *The Predicament of Culture: Twentieth-Century Ethnography, Literature, and Art.* Cambridge: Harvard University Press.

Clifford, James, and George E. Marcus, eds. 1986. *Writing Culture: The Poetics and Politics of Ethnography.* Berkeley and Los Angeles: University of California Press.

Cohn, Bernard. S. 1987. *An Anthropologist among the Historians and Other Essays.* New York: Oxford University Press.

Comaroff, John, and Jean Comaroff. 1991. *Of Revelation and Revolution: Christianity, Colonialism, and Consciousness in South Africa.* Chicago: University of Chicago Press.

———. 1992. *Ethnography and the Historical Imagination.* Boulder, CO: Westview Press.

Cushing, Barry E., and Sunita S. Ahlawat. 1996. Mitigation of Recency Bias in Audit Judgment: The Effect of Documentation. *Auditing* 15:110–22.

Cutler, Anne. 1998. Abstract Body Language: Documenting Women's Bodies in Theatre. *New Theatre Quarterly* 14:111–18.

Danet, Brenda. 1997. Books, Letters, Documents: The Changing Aesthetics of Texts in Late Print Culture. *Journal of Material Culture* 2:5–38.

Davis, Natalie Zemon. 1987. *Fiction in the Archives: Pardon Tales and Their Tellers in Sixteenth-Century France.* Stanford, CA: Stanford University Press.

Day, Ronald E. 2001. Totality and Representation: A History of Knowledge Management through European Documentation, Critical Modernity, and Post-Fordism. *Journal of the American Society for Information Science and Technology* 53(9): 725–35.

Dery, David. 1998. "Papereality" and Learning in Bureaucratic Organizations. *Administration and Society* 29(6):677–89.

Di Leonardo, Micaela. 1998. *Exotics at Home: Anthropologies, Others, American Modernity.* Chicago: University of Chicago Press.

Dirks, Nicholas B. 2001. *Castes of Mind: Colonialism and the Making of Modern India.* Princeton, NJ: Princeton University Press.

———. 2002. Annals of the Archive: Ethnographic Notes on the Sources of History. In *From the Margins: Historical Anthropology and Its Futures,* ed. Brian K. Axel, 47–65. Durham, NC: Duke University Press.

Ealy, Jonathan B., and Aaron M. Schutt. 2002. What—If Anything—Is an E-mail? Applying Alaska's Civil Discovery Rules to E-mail Production. *Alaska Law Review* 19:119–40.

Farkas-Conn, Irene. 1990. *From Documentation to Information Science: The Beginnings and Early Development of the American Documentation Institute—American Society for Information Science.* New York: Greenwood Press.

Feld, Steven, and Donald Brenneis. 2004. Doing Anthropology in Sound. *American Ethnologist* 31:461–74.

Feldman, Allen. 1998. Faux Documentary and the Memory of Realism. *American Anthropologist* 100(2):494–509.

Ferguson, James. 1990. *The Anti-Politics Machine: Development, Depoliticization, and Bureaucratic Power in Lesotho.* Cambridge: Cambridge University Press.

Fisher, Philip. 1988. Democratic Social Space: Whitman, Melville, and the Promise of American Transparency. *Representations* 24:60–101.

Foster, R. J. 1995. *Social Reproduction and History in Melanesia: Mortuary Ritual, Gift Exchange, and Custom in the Tanga Islands.* Cambridge: Cambridge University Press.

Foucault, Michel. 1972. *The Archaeology of Knowledge.* Trans. A. M. S. Smith. New York: Harper and Row.

———. 1991. Governmentality. In *The Foucault Effect: Studies in Governmentality,* ed. Graham Burchell, Colin Gordon, and Peter Miller, 87–104. London: Harvester Wheatsheaf.

Franklin, Sarah, and Susan McKinnon. 2001. *Relative Values: Reconfiguring Kinship Studies.* Durham, NC: Duke University Press.

Frohlich, David M. 1986. On the Organisation of Form-Filling Behaviour. *Information Design* 5:43–59.

Garfinkel, Harold. 1967. *Studies in Ethnomethodology.* New York: Polity Press.

Giddens, Anthony. 1990. *The Consequences of Modernity.* Cambridge: Polity Press.

Ginzburg, Carlo. 1989. *Clues, Myths, and the Historical Method.* Baltimore: Johns Hopkins University Press.

———. 1999. *History, Rhetoric, and Proof.* Hanover, NH: University Press of New England.

Goody, Jack. 2000. *The Power of the Written Tradition.* Washington, DC: Smithsonian Institution Press.

Greenhouse, Carol J. 2002. Introduction: Altered States, Altered Lives. In *Ethnography in Unstable Places: Everyday Lives in Contexts of Dramatic Political Change,* ed. Carol J. Greenhouse, Elizabeth Mertz, and Kay B. Warren, 1–34. Durham, NC: Duke University Press.

Greenhouse, Carol J., Elizabeth Mertz, and Kay B. Warren. 2002. *Ethnography in Unstable Places: Everyday Lives in Contexts of Dramatic Political Change*. Durham, NC: Duke University Press.

Gupta, Akhil, and James Ferguson. 1997a. Discipline and Practice: "The Field" as Site, Method, and Location in Anthropology. In *Anthropological Locations: Boundaries and Grounds of a Field Science*, ed. Akhil Gupta and James Ferguson, 1–46. Berkeley and Los Angeles: University of California Press.

———, eds. 1997b. *Anthropological Locations: Boundaries and Grounds of a Field Science*. Berkeley and Los Angeles: University of California Press.

———, eds. 1997c. *Culture, Power, Place: Explorations in Critical Anthropology*. Durham, NC: Duke University Press.

Guthrie, John T. 1988. Locating Information in Documents: Examination of a Cognitive Model. *Reading Research Quarterly* 23:178–99.

Hanks, William F. 2000. *Intertexts: Writings on Language, Utterance, and Context*. Lanham, MD: Rowman and Littlefield.

Hargadon, Andrew, and Robert I. Sutton. 1997. Technology Brokering and Innovation in a Product Development Firm. *Administrative Science Quarterly* 42:716–49.

Harper, Richard. 1998. *Inside the IMF: An Ethnography of Documents, Technology and Organisational Action*. San Diego: Academic Press.

Helgerson, Richard 1986. The Land Speaks: Cartography, Chorography, and Subversion in Renaissance England. *Representations* 16:50–85.

Henderson, Kathryn. 1999. *On Line and on Paper: Visual Representations, Visual Culture, and Computer Graphics in Design Engineering*. Cambridge: MIT Press.

Hevier, James L. 1998. The Archive State and the Fear of Pollution: From the Opium Wars to Fu-Manchu. *Cultural Studies* 12(2): 234–64.

Hodder, Ian. 2000. The Interpretation of Documents and Material Culture. In *Handbook of Qualitative Research*, ed. Norman K. Denzin and Yvonna S. Lincoln, 703–15. Thousand Oaks, CA: Sage.

Holmes, Douglas R. 2000. *Integral Europe: Fast Capitalism, Multiculturalism, Neofascism*. Princeton, NJ: Princeton University Press.

Holmes, Douglas R., and George E. Marcus. 2005. Cultures of Expertise and the Management of Globalization: Toward the Refunctioning of Ethnography. In *Global Assemblages: Technology, Politics, and Ethics as Anthropological Problems*, ed. Aihwa Ong and Stephen J. Collier, 235–62. Oxford: Blackwell.

Inoue, Kyoko. 1991. *MacArthur's Japanese Constitution: A Linguistic and Cultural Study of Its Making*. Chicago: University of Chicago Press.

Ivy, Marilyn. 1998. Mourning the Japanese Thing. In *In Near Ruins: Cultural Theory at the End of the Century*, ed. Nicholas B. Dirks, 93–118. Minneapolis: University of Minnesota Press.

Jean-Klein, Iris, and Annelise Riles. 2005. Introducing Discipline. *Political and Legal Anthropology Review* 28(2): 173–202.

Joyce, Patrick. 1999. The Politics of the Liberal Archive. *History of the Human Sciences* 12:35–49.

Kaplan, Sam. 2002. Documenting History, Historicizing Documentation: French Military Officials' Ethnological Reports on Cicilia. *Comparative Studies in Society and History* 44:344–69.

Kempson, Elaine, and Ian Rowlands. 1994. *Designing Public Documents*. London: Policy Studies Institute.

Kinross, Robin. 1989. The Rhetoric of Neutrality. In *Design Discourse: History, Theory, Criticism*, ed. Victor Margolin, 131–43. Chicago: University of Chicago Press.

Kroll, Richard. 1986. Mise-en-Page, Biblical Criticism, and Inference during the Restoration. In *Studies in Eighteenth-Century Culture*, ed. J. O. M. Brack. Madison: University of Wisconsin Press.

Lass, Andrew. 1988. Romantic Documents and Political Monuments: The Meaning-Fulfillment of History in 19th-Century Czech Nationalism. *American Ethnologist* 15: 456–71.

Latour, Bruno. 1988. Drawing Things Together. In *Representation in Scientific Practice*, ed. Michael Lynch and Steve Woolgar, 19–68. Cambridge: MIT Press.

Latour, Bruno, and Steve Woolgar. 1986. *Laboratory Life: The Construction of Scientific Facts*. Princeton: Princeton University Press.

Laurier, Eric, and Angus Whyte. 2001. "I Saw You": Searching for Lost Love via Practices of Reading, Writing and Responding. *Sociological Research Online* 6(1). http://www.socresonline.org.uk/6/1/laurier.html.

Leach, Edmund R. 1986. *Political Systems of Highland Burma: A Study of Kachin Social Structure*. London: Athlone Press.

Lynch, Michael. 1993. *Scientific Practice and Ordinary Action: Ethnomethodology and Social Studies of Science*. Cambridge: Cambridge University Press.

Marcus, George E. 1998. *Ethnography through Thick and Thin*. Princeton, NJ: Princeton University Press.

———. 1999a. Critical Anthropology Now: An Introduction. In *Critical Anthropology Now: Unexpected Contexts, Shifting Constituencies, Changing Agendas*, ed. George E. Marcus, 3–28. Santa Fe: School of American Research Press.

———, ed. 1995. *Technoscientific Imaginaries*. Chicago: University of Chicago Press.

———, ed. 1996. *Connected: Engagements with Media*. Chicago: University of Chicago Press.

———, ed. 1999b. *Critical Anthropology Now: Unexpected Contexts, Shifting Constituencies, Changing Agendas*. Santa Fe: School of American Research Press.

Maurer, Bill. 2002. Anthropological Accounting and Knowledge in Islamic Banking and Finance: Rethinking Critical Accounts. *Journal of the Royal Anthropological Institute* 8:645–67.

McAuley, Gay. 1998. Towards an Ethnography of Rehearsal. *New Theatre Quarterly* 14:75–85.

Megill, Kenneth A. 1997. *The Corporate Memory: Information Management in the Electronic Age*. East Grinstead: Bowker-Saur.

Meehan, Albert. 1997. Record-keeping Practices in the Policing of Juveniles. In *Law in Action: Ethnomethodological and Conversation Analytic Approaches to Law*, ed. M. Travers and J. F. Manzo, 183–208. Brookfield, VT: Ashgate.

Miller, D. A. 1984. Under Capricorn. *Representations* 6:124–29.

Miyazaki, Hirokazu. 2004. *The Method of Hope: Anthropology, Philosophy, and Fijian Knowledge.* Stanford, CA: Stanford University Press.

Moore, Sally Falk 1993. *Moralizing States and the Ethnography of the Present.* Arlington, VA: American Anthropological Association.

Morris, Rosalind C. 2000. *In the Place of Origins: Modernity and Its Mediums in Northern Thailand.* Durham, NC: Duke University Press.

Nader, Laura. 2001. Anthropology! Distinguished Lecture—2000. *American Anthropologist* 103(3): 609–20.

Ong, Aihwa, and Stephen J. Collier. 2005. *Global Assemblages: Technology, Politics, and Ethics as Anthropological Problems.* Malden, MA: Blackwell.

Ong, Walter J. 2002. *Orality and Literacy: The Technologizing of the Word.* London: Routledge.

Orlikowski, Wanda J., and JoAnne Yates. 1994. Genre Repertoire: The Structuring of Communicative Practices in Organizations. *Administrative Science Quarterly* 39(4): 541–74.

Orlikowski, Wanda J., JoAnne Yates, Kazuo Okamura, and Masayo Fujimoto. 1995. Shaping Electronic Communication: The Metastructuring of Technology in the Context of Use. *Organization Science* 6(4):423–44.

Osborne, Thomas. 1994. Bureaucracy as a Vocation: Governmentality and Administration in Nineteenth-Century Britain. *Journal of Historical Sociology* 7(3): 289–313.

Otlet, Paul. 1934. *Traité sur la Documentation: Le Livre sur le Livre.* Brussels: Van Keerberghen.

Ouchi, William G., and Alan L. Wilkins. 1985. Organizational Culture. *Annual Review of Sociology* 11:457–83.

Purvis, S. E. C. 1989. The Effect of Audit Documentation Format on Data Collection. *Accounting Organizations and Society* 14:551–63.

Raffel, Stanley. 1979. *Matters of Fact: A Sociological Inquiry.* London: Routledge.

Raffles, Hugh. 2002. *In Amazonia: A Natural History.* Princeton, NJ: Princeton University Press.

Rappaport, Joanne. 1994. *Cumbe Reborn: An Andean Ethnography of History.* Chicago: University of Chicago.

Riles, Annelise. 2000. *The Network Inside Out.* Ann Arbor: University of Michigan Press.

———. 2004. Property as Legal Knowledge: Means and Ends. *Journal of the Royal Anthropological Institute,* n.s. 10:775–95.

Rivas-Vazquez, Rafael A., Mark A. Blais, Gustavo J. Rey, and Ana A. Rivas-Vazquez. 2001. A Brief Reminder about Documenting the Psychological Consultation. *Professional Psychology-Research and Practice* 32:194–99.

Rosga, AnnJanette. 2005. Transparency and Accountability: Trafficking in the Rule of Law. Paper presented at Cornell Law School, 7 February 2005.

Royal Anthropological Institute of Great Britain and Ireland. 1951. *Notes and Queries on Anthropology.* 6th ed. London: Routledge and K. Paul.

Ruby, Jay. 1992. Speaking For, Speaking About, and Speaking With, or Speaking Alongside:·An Anthropological and Documentary Dilemma. *Journal of Film and Video* 44(1–2): 42–66.

Sarat, Austin, and Stuart A. Scheingold. 2001. *Cause Lawyering and the State in a Global Era*. New York: Oxford University Press.

Scarry, Elaine. 1987 [1985]. *The Body in Pain: The Making and Unmaking of the World*. New York: Oxford University Press.

Schumock, G. T., R. A. Hutchinson, and B. A. Bilek. 1992. Comparison of Two Systems for Documenting Pharmacist Interventions in Patient Care. *American Journal of Hospital Pharmacy* 49:2211–14.

Schwartz, Hillel. 1996. *The Culture of the Copy: Striking Likenesses, Unreasonable Facsimiles*. New York: Zone Books.

Shapiro Ann-Louise, and Jill Godmilow. 1997. How Real Is the Reality in Documentary Film? *History and Theory* 36:80–101.

Shaw, Harry E. 1999. *Narrating Reality: Austen, Scott, Eliot*. Ithaca, NY: Cornell University Press.

Sherman, Sandra. 2001. *Imagining Poverty: Quantification and the Decline of Paternalism*. Columbus: Ohio State University Press.

Shuy, Roger W. 1998. *Bureaucratic Language in Government and Business*. Washington, DC: Georgetown University Press.

Siegel, James T. 1997. *Fetish, Recognition, Revolution*. Princeton, NJ: Princeton University Press.

Silverstein, Michael, and Greg Urban. 1996. *Natural Histories of Discourse*. Chicago: University of Chicago Press.

Smart, Karl L., J. L. Madrigal, and Kristie K. Seawright. 1996. The Effect of Documentation on Customer Perception of Product Quality. *IEEE Transactions on Professional Communication* 39:157–62.

Smith, Dorothy E. 1990. *Texts, Facts, and Femininity*. London: Routledge.

Sprenger, Scott. 2001. Off with His Head: Robespierre and the Terror of the Ideal Document. In *The Documentary Impulse in French Literature*, ed. Buford Norman, 27–38. Amsterdam: Editions Rodopi.

Steedman, Carolyn. 2001. Something She Called a Fever: Michelet, Derrida, and Dust. *American Historical Review* 106:1159–80.

Stinchcombe, Arthur L. 2001. *When Formality Works: Authority and Abstraction in Law and Organizations*. Chicago: University of Chicago Press.

Stoler, Ann L. 2002. Developing Historical Negatives: Race and the (Modernist) Visions of a Colonial State. In *From the Margins: Historical Anthropology and Its Futures*, ed. Brian K. Axel, 156–85. Durham, NC: Duke University Press.

Strathern, Marilyn. 1988. *The Gender of the Gift: Problems with Women and Problems with Society in Melanesia*. Berkeley and Los Angeles: University of California Press.

———. 1990. Artefacts of History: Events and the Interpretation of Images. In *Culture and History in the Pacific*, ed. Jukka Siikala, 25–44. Helsinki: Finnish Anthropological Society.

———. 1991. *Partial Connections*. Savage, MD: Rowman and Littlefield.

———. 1992. *After Nature: English Kinship in the Late Twentieth Century*. Cambridge: Cambridge University Press.

———. 1995. *The Relation: Issues in Complexity and Scale*. Prickly Pear Pamphlet 6. Cambridge: Prickly Pear Press.

———, ed. 2000. *Audit Cultures: Anthropological Studies in Accountability, Ethics, and the Academy.* London: Routledge.

Taussig, Michael. 1997. *The Magic of the State.* New York: Routledge.

Thomas, Nicholas. 1990. Sanitation and Seeing: The Creation of State Power in Early Colonial Fiji. *Comparative Studies in Society and History* 32:149–70.

———. 1992. Material Culture and Colonial Power: Ethnological Collecting and the Establishment of Colonial Rule in Fiji. *Man* 24:41–56.

Thrift, Nigel. 1996. New Urban Eras and Old Technological Fears: Reconfiguring the Goodwill of Electronic Things. *Urban Studies* 33:1463–93.

Tsing, Anna L. 2005. *Friction: An Ethnography of Global Connection.* Princeton, NJ: Princeton University Press.

Turner, Terence. 1997. Human Rights, Human Difference: Anthropology's Contribution to an Emancipatory Cultural Politics. *Journal of Anthropological Research* 53:273–91.

Vaihinger, Hans 1924. *The Philosophy of As If: A System of the Theoretical, Practical, and Religious Fictions of Mankind.* Trans. C. K. Ogden. London: K. Paul, Trench, Trubner; New York: Harcourt, Brace.

Vidler, Anthony. 1993. Books in Space: Tradition and Transparency in the Bibliotheque de France. *Representations* 42:115–34.

Voss, Paul J., and Marta L. Werner. 1999. Toward a Poetics of the Archive. *Studies in Literary Imagination* 32:i–viii.

Wagner, Roy. 1986. *Symbols That Stand for Themselves.* Chicago: University of Chicago Press.

———. 2001. *An Anthropology of the Subject: Holographic Worldview in New Guinea and Its Meanings and Significance for the World of Anthropology.* Berkeley and Los Angeles: University of California Press.

Weber, Max. 1968. Bureaucracy. In *On Charisma and Institution Building,* 66–77. Chicago: Chicago University Press.

Weston, Kath. 2002. *Gender in Real Time: Power and Transcience in a Visual Age.* New York: Routledge.

Wheeler, Stanton, ed. 1969. *On Record: Files and Dossiers in American Life.* New York: Russell Sage Foundation.

Whitman, Dale A. 1999. Digital Recording of Real Estate Conveyances. *John Marshall Law Review* 32:227–68.

Witte, Stephen P. 1992. Context, Text, Intertext: Toward a Constructivist Semiotic of Writing. *Written Communication* 9:237–308.

Part One **Academic and**

Bureaucratic

Knowledge

Reforming Promise

Don Brenneis

Comment specifically on the applicant's strengths and limitations for
graduate study in his or her own field. Descriptions of significant
accomplishments, contributions, and any qualities related to scholarly
achievement are particularly helpful. Your comments should support
your assessment on page 1.

— NSF Graduate Research Fellowships Reference Report Form
(NSF Form 299, August 1998)

Please attach a separate sheet(s) with your evaluation of this proposal
with respect to each of the above criteria per instructions on the previous page. Your specific comments on the proposal's strengths and weaknesses are critical.

— NSF Proposal Review Form (NSF Form 1 [10/97])

CENTRAL TO THE WORK of federal funding agencies, and
inevitable if perhaps more peripheral in the lives of most American academics, is the filling out of forms, of documents evaluating the accomplishment and promise of students and the likely significance, creativity, and
rigor of colleagues' research proposals. Read with varying degrees of
energy and attention; completed off-the-cuff or with considerable care;
acerbic, tactful, or enthusiastic; such references and reviews are part of the
characteristic routine of scholarly life. Being asked for letters of recommendation is a recurring feature of academic autumns; whether specific
requests are welcome or grudgingly granted, they are taken as part of the
job. The less frequent but usually more demanding requests to review
research grant proposals come with less predictability. They also, however,
are usually assumed to come with the territory and often—to extend the

idiom—are moments of mapping both the applicants' and one's own place in that territory.

At the same time routine and consequential, such professional practices and the documentary forms that demand them are moments of broad participation in the complex institutional processes that allocate federal money for research and graduate training. Many of us are often, for the nonce at least, bureaucratic actors, our role both invited and shaped by printed forms. Such documents, ones of which we become variably disciplined coauthors, are a critical nexus, the focus of considerable study and design work within the relevant agencies but rarely taken as other than ordinary by those completing them. To use Harper's (1998) term, these are "mundane" documents, and they engender routine responses, both from those filling them out and from later readers. They also directly link histories of broad policymaking and detailed planning with subsequent decisions shaping the course of scholarly knowledge and of individual scholarly lives. These documents are born in the work of staff and the recommendations of committees, circulate among and are given specific substance by individual scholars, and go on to figure centrally in the decisions made at other meetings. At the same time they and their consequences remain, in large part because of their very ordinariness, analytically invisible.

My goal in this essay is to examine this documentary nexus in some detail, focusing upon two kinds of forms commonly used within the National Science Foundation (NSF), forms that in their differences and their shared histories illuminate some of the broader bureaucratic practices in which they figure. One of these is the Reference Report Form, four of which are required as part of the application packet for the highly competitive NSF Graduate Research Fellowship program. The other is the Proposal Review Form used by both ad hoc external reviewers and panel members in evaluating research proposals submitted to NSF. I will also be comparing these two forms as they appeared in the early 1990s and their more recent versions, adopted in 1998 to reflect new priorities and practices within NSF.

This essay is intended as a contribution to an emerging ethnography of documents and clearly draws upon the work of my colleagues in this collection and particularly on the pathbreaking studies by Harper (1998) and Riles (2000). The forms in question, however, are artifacts of a particular sort, as they are necessarily interactive, their general features designed to elicit responses that they can shape but not wholly control. They further necessarily involve subsequent readers of many types. Such literally coauthored documents are read and evaluated by subsequent reviewers, administrators, and, occasionally, congressional oversight committees. Great care and considerable strategy have gone into planning the framework, but the authorship of the final documents is always shared—and often contested in terms of the fit between the literal framers' intentions and the respondents' texts. Similarly, how these documents are subsequently read is at the same time constrained by form and potentially subject to heterodox readings. The transformation of these forms in the mid-1990s and the institutional discussions shaping and recontextualizing these changes provide a particularly revelatory intersection for examining institutional ideologies and interests, as well as their unintended consequences.

Central to the following discussion is my concern as a linguistic anthropologist with the relationships among form and meaning, language as social practice, and the broader ideological frameworks—or ways of thinking about language and, more broadly, communicative form—within which such relationships take shape. A first striking feature of these documents *and* of the ways in which they are discussed and written about is the centrality of visual imagery. Paired terms, especially *transparency/opacity* and *visibility/invisibility*, infuse both institutional considerations of such documents and scholarly attempts to understand them. The documents in question here, for example, were reshaped in large part in response to the Government Performance and Results Act of 1993, where "clarity" is directly linked to notions of accountability and "customer satisfaction" (Department of Education 2000), and the reworking of the forms represents in part an attempt to force transparency. Moreover, my own characterization of the "analytical invisibility" of documentary practices draws upon similar visual imagery.

Such pervasive visuality, whether lucid or obscured, is more than idiomatic; it is directly linked to a cultural view of language as principally a system for conveying semantic meaning. Idiom and ideology are deeply embrangled. The mundane documents at the core of my discussion represent the working out of practical, culturally specific theories of how language works and of how different authors, respondents, and readers might best be taken into account. They crystallize in several ways recurrent though somewhat contradictory themes in contemporary ideologies of language in the United States: the assumption of the primacy of transparency as a communicative goal noted previously (see also Silverstein 1987; Brenneis 1994, 1999; Strathern 2000a) matched by the recognition of the rhetorical intentions of some respondents; increasingly specific and technical strategies for eliciting "information" with assumedly greater exactness within a broad framework that is actually described in vague and in some ways empty terms; and a further ongoing tension between a language of absolutes and one of comparison.

One way of thinking about the changes in the forms I'll be considering—and certainly one way of thinking about the much broader adoption of techniques for operationalizing accountability in American and British scholarship—is in terms of the importation and translation of terms from one domain into another, in these instances from the managerial to the academic. I'd like to suggest one way in which such translation is accomplished. Crucial to the increasing salience of managerial and business frameworks within science funding bureaucracies, a transformation underlying the documentary histories discussed here, has been the rise of particular points of articulation between what had once been fairly distinct domains.

I want to draw here on a recent essay by Bonnie Urciuoli (2000) in which she analyzes the language of liberal arts college recruiting literature, arguing that certain key phrases serve not only as "shifters" (in the sense elaborated by Silverstein 1976) but also as powerful rhetorical devices, strategically deployed and often very effective with those audiences. Perhaps most striking about such recruiting language is its generality and nonspecificity; terms such as *skills, leadership,* and *multiculturalism* (in a totally ungrounded sense) figure recurrently. In pursuing these terms, she makes a compelling case for the consequentiality of such semantically vacuous terms, extending the arguments made by Silverstein (1976) and Parmentier (1997) that those terms most deeply embedded in—and taken as central to or definitive of—particular cultural communities are often denotatively empty. Such terms draw their force, rather, from the indexical roles that they play in articulating—or *suggesting* the articulation of—different discursive fields. The terms central to Urciuoli's study serve as such shifters. Further, she demonstrates the ways in which college administrators use these terms as key strategic elements in their marketing, specifically linking liberal arts education and its supposed intellectual outcomes with values specific to the business and management world (see also Brenneis 2000).

A relevant text here is the late Bill Readings's (1996) *The University in Ruins.* Readings starts his critique of contemporary higher education with a tour through the nearly omnipresent but empty and unmoored notion of "excellence" in the discourse of academic administrators and, at times, of teaching academics themselves. He then goes on to argue that this is one symptom of the dissolution of an earlier, often unspoken, consensus on the values of higher education, ideologies often linked with specific nation-states, and of the increasing salience of a global, dislocated, and flexible political economy. In the case of NSF, the broad frame within which quite specific and explicit documentary and policy changes have been made is defined very vaguely indeed. Perhaps, following Readings at least part of the way, the repeated articulation of such guiding notions as excellence in foundational documents might function to replace what had in earlier years been an unspoken agreement as to the values underlying NSF's—or any institution's—work.

I want to suggest the analytical force of considering not only *excellence* but other terms that figure subsequently such as *accountability, stakeholders,* and *benefit* as shifters. As *skills* and its kin in Urciuoli's paper speak to the desired qualities of future managers, so *benefit* and *accountability* articulate with patterns of organizational control and power. Such shifters make the critical contact between previously disparate spheres. With such recurring articulation established, the translation of technique from one domain to the other can be effected. Marilyn Strathern has argued that the develop-ment of academic audit procedures encourages the generation of too much information of a particular, decontextualized type, as they make "transfer-able skills an objective . . . reduc[ing] what makes a skill work, its embed-dedness" (1997, 14). Within the new semantic space established by the adoption of such highly recognizable if indefinable notions as "excellence," the importance of technique—and of its increasing refinement and devel-opment—becomes unquestionable. The tension mentioned previously between nebulous orienting notions and highly specific terms and definitions for practice is perhaps not ironic; it may rather be the case that the one makes the other possible.

These concerns obviously resonate with recurrent themes in critiques of "audit culture" in contemporary Britain—and especially of the implica-tions of ongoing formal assessment for teaching, research, and the funding of higher education. The work of Power (1994, 1997), Strathern (1991, 1997, 2000a, 2000b, n.d.), and Shore and Wright (1999, 2000), to which I will return, is both revelatory and challenging. While the specific situa-tions differ in many respects, such shared issues as the rise of formalized management and assessment practices, the salience of highly technical models of accountability, and the increasing involvement of academics themselves in such activities are striking.

A further body of research at play here is the provocatively renascent consideration of classification as a central practice in contemporary society. Bowker and Star, for example, suggest that "[a] 'classification system' is a set of boxes (metaphorical or literal) into which things can be put to then do some kind of work—bureaucratic or knowledge production" (1999, 10). As they subsequently argue, "The work of making, maintaining, and analyzing classification systems is richly textured. It is one of the central works of modernity, including science and medicine. It is, we argue, central to social life" (1999, 13). Certainly it is work central to such knowledge-producing bureaucracies as NSF. But the system here is somewhat different from those Bowker and Star examine, ranging from the ICD (International Classification of Diseases) to racial categories under apartheid in South Africa. First, the elements of those schemes they consider are generally taken by their users to be natural—or naturalized—types, reflecting preexisting distinctions. In the evaluation of applications and proposals, however, the "boxes" are relative rather than absolute, placement following from comparative consideration and negotiation. Further, while most classification systems are almost necessarily composed of nouns, the language central to classificatory work of the NSF is primarily adjectival, in a quite literal sense.

This chapter represents part of a broader project, a language-focused ethnographic study of the research grant proposal as a particularly consequential genre of academic writing and of the reading practices and events through which such proposals are evaluated (Brenneis 1988, 1994, 1999). My principal methodology has been that of participant turned observer (with the informed and invaluable help of program officers and fellow panelists, and drawing upon three years of NSF interdisciplinary panel service). I have also participated for six years (three in the early 1990s and three in the late 1990s) as a member and occasional chair of the NSF Graduate Research Fellowship Panel for Anthropology, Sociology, and Linguistics and have been a panel member and ad hoc reviewer for other agencies. I have also become an increasingly self-conscious filler-in of these forms. The chapter further draws upon interviews and upon other public NSF documents and memoranda, both in print and on the Web.

The core of my ethnographic discussion here has three sections. First is a consideration of the forms themselves as texts and frames: how do they appear visually, what questions do they encourage respondents to address, and how—through both form and language—do they shape the ways in which one can respond? A second section is guided by Harper's instructive notion of a document's "career": what kinds of "doings with documents" (1998, 3) recurrently take place within an institution, and how do the documents both derive from and help constitute the work of that institution? Finally, the changes made to these forms in 1998 provide an opportunity to complement a consideration of these documentary careers with analytical accounts of their broader histories: why and how were they transformed, and what consequences for writers, readers, and staff—both anticipated and unexpected—have followed? I will then turn to a broader if brief discussion of the documents, linking them to some of the theoretical issues invoked already, and then conclude with a consideration of how such texts and practices might speak to broad issues of "audit, policy, and ethics" (Strathern 2000b, 5) and to the particular role that language-focused ethnography might play in pursuing them.

....

Forms and Frames

The form shown in figure 1.1, first approved in 1987 and in use in the NSF Graduate Research Fellowship competition for the following eleven years, was to be given to four faculty or other references by each applicant for the program. Several things are visually striking about the form: the heterogeneity of typefaces, fonts, and sizes; the small boxes to check off choices and dotted lines to fill in; the minuscule space for narrative commentary; and the diagonal array of numbered summary evaluative terms, with bold-face phrases followed by brief glosses translating the terms.[1] This both is and even more, looks like, a product of the era before word processing; it would even be difficult, although it is requested, to complete the form on a typewriter. It is also—in many ways—a form for which a close reading is not expected.

Several elements of the document index but do not explore both its history and its subsequent organizational destinations. From the perspective of the person filling in the form, many of these features do not figure; they provide little guidance or concrete explanation of the process. Such aspects of the form both bespeak and address audiences other than the immediate respondent. What might appear to some readers to be mere boilerplate may well in other contexts be quite consequential (see also Strathern 1997, 2000b, n.d.; Shore and Wright 1999, 2000). They point to an underlying question in the practical and analytical reading of such documents: which parts of the forms can be read as the frame and which as the content?

Bateson's (1972) notion of "frame" is particularly helpful here. In

NATIONAL SCIENCE FOUNDATION
GRADUATE RESEARCH FELLOWSHIPS
NSF Graduate Fellowships • NSF Minority Graduate Fellowships

Form Approved
OMB No. 3145-0023

**Reference Report
on Applicant**

Applicants' Qualifications Evaluated for the National Science Foundation
by Panels of Scientists Appointed by the National Research Council.
Awardees Selected by the National Science Foundation

Please type or print all information requested on this form.

Name of Respondent ....

Title ....

Respondent's
Department ....

Respondent's
Institution ....

To be completed by applicant:
Name of Applicant

....
last   first   middle   maiden

Field ....
e.g., Microbiology, Theoretical Physics, etc.

Date Due ....
(See Application Instructions)

ACQUAINTANCE WITH APPLICANT:

1. I have known the applicant for a period of .... years and/or .... months.

2. I have known the applicant as
   - ☐ an undergraduate
   - ☐ a graduate student
   - ☐ a research assistant
   - ☐ a teaching assistant
   - ☐ other (specify) ....

3. I have served as the applicant's
   - ☐ research adviser
   - ☐ major adviser
   - ☐ teacher in several classes
   - ☐ teacher in only one class
   - ☐ department chairman
   - ☐ other (specify) ....

COMMENTS: In the space below, please describe in some detail the applicant's abilities, and comment on his/her potential as a scientist, elaborating, where appropriate, on such matters as versatility; ability to make sound, scientific judgments; major academic weaknesses, if any; performance by the applicant, as an undergraduate, in independent study or in research-participation programs; and any other characteristics you deem pertinent. (Continue on reverse side if necessary.)

APPLICANT'S OVERALL SCIENTIFIC ABILITY: In comparison with a representative group (☐ College Seniors ☐ First Year Graduate Students) of students in the same field who have had approximately the same amount of experience and training, how do you rate the applicant in GENERAL ALL-AROUND SCIENTIFIC ABILITY?

1 ☐ **Truly Exceptional.** Equivalent to the very best you have known—a person who, in your experience, appears once every few years.

2 ☐ **Outstanding.** Comparable to the best student in a current class. Highest 5%.

3 ☐ **Unusual.** Next highest 5%.

4 ☐ **Above Average.** Ability easily identifiable, but not in upper 10%. Probably upper 15%. Certainly upper 25%.

5 ☐ **Average.** Probably able to complete work to the Ph.D. degree. Upper 50%.

6 ☐ **Below Average.** Lower 50%.

IMPORTANT——CONFIDENTIALITY: Before signing this report, you should check one of the two blocks at the right as applicable. If you wish to have your comments held in confidence so as not to reveal your identity as the author of these comments, you should check block A. If block A is checked, the Foundation will honor your request to the extent permitted by law. If you fail to check either block, the Foundation will treat your comments as confidential, but warns that your failure to check block A may result in a requirement to provide these comments to the applicant under the Privacy Act of 1974.

☐ A. My preparation of this Reference Report is conditioned on the promise of the Foundation to hold my identity as the author of these comments in confidence.

☐ B. My preparation of this Reference Report *is not* conditioned on the promise of the Foundation to hold my comments in confidence.

Signature of Respondent .... Date ....

NSF FORM 299, August 1987

**Return to the Fellowship Office, National Research Council,
2101 Constitution Avenue, N. W., Washington, D. C. 20418**

1.1. National Science Foundation Form OMB No. 3145–0023

discussing face-to-face interaction, Bateson argues that "a frame is meta-communicative. Any message, which either explicitly or implicitly defines a frame, *ipso facto* gives the receiver instructions or aids in his attempt to understand the messages included within the frame" (Bateson 1972, 188, quoted in Duranti 1984, 240; see also Goffman 1974). Forms such as the one shown in figure 1.1 represent a particular kind of document, one requiring an interlocutor's participation to be fully animated. They provide, in effect, frameworks for guided response. What is striking about these forms, however, is the relative ease with which one can fall into the frame. The metacommunicative focus on instructing the respondent is quite clear; at the same time, because of their mundane, routine, and often literally unintelligible character, many other consequential features of the form are effaced.

The core of the document solicits both narrative description and quite specific information from the respondent. Without overtly referring to this narrative, the reference is then asked to summarize the "applicant's overall scientific ability"; this involves both choosing the appropriate descriptive phrase and checking the adjacent numbered box. To assist the recommender, the phrases are matched with quite clear if, again, some-what internally contradictory definitional paraphrases; someone who is "outstanding," for example, is "[c]omparable to the best student in a current class. Highest 5%." What is particularly important is *how* the descriptors are defined. These appear to be classic referential definitions, that is, X (for example, "Unusual") *means* Y ("Next highest 5%). Such defining practice seems to conform clearly to Ewald's characterization of the language of contemporary institutions as one "of precision and certainty" (1991, 151). And such defining practice does not strike us as particularly unexpected, as it is much like a dictionary; how else could it be? It is crucial to note that the respondents themselves are assumed to be interested parties vis-à-vis the applicants; definitional rigor may serve as a way of reining in their more partisan impulses.

In moving to the second kind of document considered here, the Proposal Review Form sent with grant proposals to both external and panel reviewers by NSF prior to October 1997, some features remain generally similar, but several differences are also evident. On the front side of the sheet (not shown here) are listed the proposal name and file number as well as the name of the proposer. More significant is the reverse page (fig. 1.2). At the top of the page is a brief discussion of NSF's "statutory responsibilities" and its goal of funding the "most meritorious research, whether basic

NATIONAL SCIENCE FOUNDATION
INFORMATION FOR REVIEWERS

In meeting its statutory responsibilities, the National Science Foundation seeks to support the most meritorious research, whether basic or applied. Mail reviews play a key role in the National Science Foundation's evaluation of the merit of research proposals. Please provide both written comments and a summary rating on this Proposal Evaluation Form using the criteria provided below.

PROPOSAL EVALUATION CRITERIA

1. *Research performance competence*—Capability of the investigator(s), the technical soundness of the proposed approach, and the adequacy of the institutional resources available. Please include comments on the proposer's recent research performance.

2. *Intrinsic merit of the research*—Likelihood that the research will lead to new discoveries or fundamental advances within its field of science or engineering, or have substantial impact on progress in that field or in other scientific and engineering fields.

3. *Utility or relevance of the research*—Likelihood that the research can contribute to the achievement of a goal that is extrinsic or in addition to that of the research field itself, and thereby serve as the basis for new or improved technology or assist in the solution of societal problems.

4. *Effect of the research on the infrastructure of science and engineering*—Potential of the proposed research to contribute to better understanding or improvement of the quality, distribution, or effectiveness of the Nation's scientific and engineering research, education, and human resources base.

Criteria 1, 2, and 3 constitute an integral set that should be applied in a balanced way to all research proposals in accordance with the objectives and content of each proposal. Criterion 1, research performance competence,
is essential to the evaluation of the quality of every research proposal; all three aspects should be addressed. The relative weight given Criteria 2 and 3 depends on the nature of the proposed research: Criterion 2, intrinsic merit, is emphasized in the evaluation of basic research proposals, while Criterion 3, utility or relevance, is emphasized in the evaluation of applied research proposals. Criterion 4, effect on the infrastructure of science and engineering, permits the evaluation of research proposals in terms of their potential for improving the scientific and engineering enterprise and its educational activities in ways other than those encompassed by the first three criteria.

SUMMARY RATINGS

Excellent: Probably will fall among top 10% of proposals in this subfield; highest priority for support. This category should be used only for truly outstanding proposals.

Very Good: Probably will fall among *top 1/3* of proposals in this subfield; should be supported.

Good: Probably will fall among *middle 1/3* of proposals in this subfield; worthy of support.

Fair: Probably will fall among *lowest 1/3* of proposals in this subfield.

Poor: Proposal has serious deficiencies; should not be supported.

CONFLICT OF INTERESTS

If you have an affiliation or financial connection with the institution or the person submitting this proposal that might be construed as creating a conflict of interests, please describe those affiliations or interests on a separate page and attach it to your review. Regardless of any such affiliations or interests, unless you believe you cannot be objective, we would like to have your review. If you do not attach a statement we shall assume that you have no conflicting affiliations or interests.

CONFIDENTIALITY OF PROPOSALS AND PEER REVIEWS

The Foundation receives proposals in confidence and is responsible for protecting the confidentiality of their contents. For this reason, please do not copy, quote, or otherwise use material from this proposal. If you believe that a colleague can make a substantial contribution to the review, please consult the NSF Program Officer before disclosing either the contents of the proposal or the applicant's name. When you have completed your review, please destroy the proposal.

It is the policy of the Foundation that reviews will not be disclosed to persons outside the Government, except that verbatim copies without the name and affiliation of the reviewer will be sent to the principal investigator. The Foundation considers reviews to be exempt from disclosure under the Freedom of Information Act (5 USC 552) but cannot guarantee that it will not be forced to release reviews under FOIA or other laws.

1.2. National Science Foundation: Information for Reviewers

or applied." Those to whom the proposals and evaluation forms have been sent are asked to "provide both written comments and a summary rating . . . using the criteria provided below." The four criteria include "[r]esearch performance competence," which has been referred to as the "threshold criterion" or sine qua non for funding, and the functionally paired criteria of the "[i]ntrinsic merit of the research" and the "[u]tility or relevance of the research," to be emphasized in the case of basic research and applied proposals respectively. The fourth criterion is to make possible the evaluation of proposals having to do with broader programmatic and educational support not necessarily involving research in the strict sense. Past accomplishment and the strength of the proposed research strategies are critical for funding, with the merit and significance of the questions addressed playing a secondary role.

A second point to note is the way in which the terms for "Summary Ratings" are defined. In contrast to the dictionary-like definitions in the reference forms, the terms here are discussed in terms of their likelihood for funding. While "Outstanding" should be used in a reference report to characterize only those in the highest 5% of one's usual student group, an "Excellent" rating is normed to the pool of present applications. Such comparative judgment is particularly tricky if one is, as with most ad hoc reviewers, only reading one or two proposals during any funding cycle. Reviewers are, in effect, advised to select "Excellent" if they want to see a project emerge in the "top 10% of proposals . . . [with the] highest priority for support." The gloss continues that "[t]his category should be used only for truly outstanding proposals." This is not a primarily referential style of defining terms; reviewers are rather given a much more rhetorical range of choices—and are asked to compare proposals with a broader range that they can, in almost all cases, only imagine. Here, where those filling in the form are presumptively neutral or disinterested parties, rhetorical choices are possible.

Beginning with the 1999 applications year a new form has come into use (fig. 1.3). Visually, it is strikingly different from its predecessor—stylistically much cleaner, with much more homogeneous typography and design, the irritating boxes replaced by underlines, a gridlike array of specific categories and evaluative choices, and considerably more space for narrative comments. While this form cannot in fact be submitted electronically, it certainly appears computer ready. The general sequence of elements within the document has also changed. The "Scholarly Characteristics" section is new, consisting of a grid of eight qualities (for example,

NSF Graduate Research Fellowships

REFERENCE REPORT FORM

Receipt date: December 10, 1998

Name of
Applicant: _____
           last   first   middle   Jr, II, etc

Name of
Respondent: _____
            last   first   MI

Title: _____ Department: _____ Institution: _____

Telephone Number: _____ Electronic Mail Address: _____

To the Respondent: Your thoughtful evaluation of the applicant's strengths and weaknesses is an essential part of the fellowship application and is greatly appreciated.

1. ACQUAINTANCE WITH APPLICANT:

I have known the applicant for a period of _____ years and/or _____ months.

I have known the applicant when he/she was _____ an undergraduate _____ a graduate student _____ a research assistant
                                              _____ a teaching assistant _____ other (specify) _____

I have served as the applicant's _____ research adviser _____ teacher in several classes _____ department chair
                                _____ major adviser _____ teacher in only one class _____ other (specify) _____

2. APPLICANT'S SCHOLARLY CHARACTERISTICS:

Please rate the applicant in comparison with other students whom you have known in similar stages of their academic careers by placing an "X" on one of the lines.

	Truly Exceptional (Top 1%)	Outstanding (Top 5%)	Excellent (Top 10%)	Very Good (Top 25%)	Satisfactory (Top 50%)	Below Average (Lower 50%)	No Basis for Judgment
Knowledge in chosen field							
Motivation and perseverance toward educational goals							
Ability to work Independently							
Ability to work as a member of a research team							
Ability to plan and conduct research							
Ability in: Oral expression							
Written expression							
Imagination and probable creativity							

3. APPLICANT'S OVERALL SCIENTIFIC ABILITY:

Please indicate the strength of your overall endorsement of this applicant for an NSF Graduate Research Fellowship by placing an "X" on one of the lines.

Truly Exceptional (Top 1%)	Outstanding (Top 5%)	Excellent (Top 10%)	Very Good (Top 25%)	Satisfactory (Top 50%)	Below Average (Lower 50%)	No Basis for Judgment
1	2	3	4	5	6	

Page 1 of 2

NSF Form 299, August 1998
Form Approved OMB No. 3145-0023

1.3. NSF Form 299 (August 1998): Reference Report Form, p. 1

motivation and persistence, imagination and potential creativity) and a range of rating categories from "truly exceptional" to "below average." These are the same options as in the earlier form, but the prose definitions have vanished, and the descriptors are solely linked to percentages, for example, "Truly Exceptional (Top 1%)." The respondent is then asked to evaluate the "Applicant's overall scientific ability," using the same evaluative terms as in the preceding grid, and the opaque but still consequential numbers are now placed under the relevant lines.

On the reverse of the form, narrative commentary is requested, in contrast to the earlier form, where the "Comments" section was squeezed in between an informational section and the overall rating. Most strikingly, the recommender is told that his or her commentary "should support [the] assessment on page 1," a much more straightforward move to direct referee's behavior; NSF makes its expectations and standards for appropriate texts quite clear. The more thoroughly designed character of the new form is striking. The recommender is guided from considering the applicant's specific qualities through an overall characterization to prose that, to be effective, must reflect those earlier judgments.

The new Proposal Review Form shows some similar features to the reference sheet, including a reduced number of typefaces and generally cleaner design (figs. 1.4, 1.5). Most striking, however, is the transformed organization of the form. One page is all text, beginning with what is now "Instructions for Proposal Review" rather than "Information for Reviewers." These new instructions move straight to the qualities desired for a useful review. As with the new recommendation form, this document is much more explicit about what a good review should include and provides many more specific suggestions for what "potential considerations" could be usefully addressed. The new forms are much more directive and move to shift the responsibility for the forms to the respondents, whether recommenders or reviewers.

Perhaps most important, however, has been the change in the criteria for review. The four criteria discussed on the earlier form are now two:

Criterion 1. What is the intellectual merit of the proposed activity?
Criterion 2. What are the broader impacts of the proposed activity?

In the earlier set of criteria, the quality of the applicant's scientific research and the rigor of the proposed study were central, with "intrinsic merit" and "utility or relevance" as secondary elements depending on

INSTRUCTIONS FOR PROPOSAL REVIEW

Please provide detailed comments on the quality of this proposal with respect to each of the two NSF Merit review Criteria below, noting specifically the proposal's strengths and weaknesses. As guidance, a list of potential considerations that you might employ in your evaluation follow each criterion. These are suggestions and not all will apply to any given proposal. Please comment on only those that are relevant to this proposal and for which you feel qualified to make a judgement.

Criterion 1. What is the intellectual merit of the proposed activity?

Potential considerations: How important is the proposed activity to advancing knowledge and understanding within its own field or across different fields? How well qualified is the proposer (individual or team) to conduct the project? (If appropriate, please comment on the quality of prior work.) To what extent does the proposed activity suggest and explore creative and original concepts? How well conceived and organized is the proposed activity? Is there sufficient access to the necessary resources?

Criterion 2. What are the broader impacts of the proposed activity?

Potential considerations: How well does the activity advance discovery and understanding while promoting teaching, training, and learning? How well does the proposed activity broaden the participation of underrepresented groups (e.g., gender, ethnicity, disability, geographic, etc.)? To what extent will it enhance the infrastructure for research and education, such as facilities, instrumentation, networks, and partnerships? Will the results be disseminated broadly to enhance scientific and technological understanding? What may be the benefits of the proposed activity to society?

Please provide an overall rating and summary statement which includes comments on the relative importance of the two criteria in assigning your rating. Please note that the criteria need not be weighted equally.

YOUR POTENTIAL CONFLICTS OF INTEREST

If you have an affiliation or financial connection with the institution or person submitting this proposal that might be construed as creating a conflict of interest, please descibe those affiliations or interests on a separate page and attach it to your review. Regardless of any such affiliations or interests, we would like to have your review unless you believe you cannot be objective. An NSF program official will examine any statement of affiliations or interests for the existence of conflicts. If you do not attach a statement we shall assume that you have no conflicting affiliations or interests.

YOUR OBLIGATION TO KEEP PROPOSALS CONFIDENTIAL

The Foundation receives proposals in confidence and protects the confidentiality of their contents. For this reason, you must not copy, quote from, or otherwise use or disclose to anyone, including your graduate students or post-doctoral or research associates, any material from any proposal you are asked to review. Unathorized disclosure of confidential information could subject you to administrative sanctions. If you believe a colleague can make a substantial contribution to this review, please obtain permission from the NSF program officer before disclosing either the contents of the proposal or the name of any applicant or principal investigator. When you have completed your review, please be certain to destroy the proposal.

PRIVACY ACT PUBLIC BURDEN STATEMENTS

The information requested on this reviewer form is solicited under the authority of the National Science Foundation Act of 1950, as amended. It will be used in connection with the selection of qualified proposal and may be disclosed to qualified reviewers as part of the review process, to government contractors, experts, volunteers and researchers as necessary to complete assigned work, to other goverment agencies needing information as part of the review process or in order to coordinate programs, and to another Federal agency, court or party in a court or Federal administrative proceeding if the government is a party. See Systems of Records, NSF-50 'Principal/Investigator/Proposal File and Associated Records', 60 8031 (February 17, 1994). The Foundation does not otherwise disclose reviews and identities of reviewers who reviewed specific proposals to persons outside the government, except that verbatim copies of reviews without the name, affiliation or other identifying information of the reviewer will be sent to the principal investigator. Submissions of the requested information is voluntary.

Public reporting burden for this collection of information is estimated to average 5 hours per response, including the time for reviewing instructions. Send comments regarding this burden estimate or any other aspect of this collection of information including suggestions for reducing this burden to:

Gail A. McHenry
Report Clearance Officer
Information Dissemination Branch
National Science Foundation, Suite 245
4201 Wilson Boulevard
Arlington, VA 22230

1.4. NSF Instructions for Proposal Review (10/97)

| PROPOSAL NO: | INSTITUTION: |

| PRINCIPAL INVESTIGATOR: | NSF PROGRAM: |

PROPOSAL TITLE:

* Criterion 1: What is the intellectual merit of the proposed activity?

* Criterion 2: What are the broader impacts of the proposed activity?

Please attach a separate sheet(s) with your evaluation of this proposal with respect to each of the above criteria per instructions on the previous page. Your specific comments on the proposal's strengths and weaknesses are critical. Do not share, copy, quote or otherwise use or disclose material from this proposal. Destroy it after you complete your review.

Summary Statement: (Include comments on the relative importance of the two criteria in assigning your rating. Continue on an additional page, if necessary.)

Overall Rating (check one):

☐ Excellent: Outstanding proposal in all respects; deserves highest priority for support.

☐ Very Good: High quality proposal in nearly all respects; should be supported if at all possible.

☐ Good: A quality proposal worthy of support.

☐ Fair: Proposal lacking in one or more critical aspects; key issues need to be addressed.

☐ Poor: Proposal has serious deficiencies.

YOUR IDENTITY WILL BE KEPT CONFIDENTIAL

NSF keeps reviews and your identity as a reviewer of specific proposals confidential to the maximum extent possible. We will, however, send the Principal Investigator(s) a copy of this review without your name and affiliation.

REVIEWER'S
SIGNATURE:

REVIEWER'S NAME AND ADDRESS (TYPED):

OTHER SUGGESTED REVIEWERS (OPTIONAL)

FASTLANE PIN:

PLEASE RETURN BY: 2/27/1999

FILE IN PROPOSAL FILE

1.5. NSF Form 1: Proposal Review Form (10/97)

whether the proposal focused on basic or applied research. While elements of the earlier criteria are evident among the "potential considerations," the new criteria focus equally on "intellectual merit" and "broader impacts." There is also no longer an explicit threshold criterion, and the relative weighting of the two criteria can vary.

....

Careers

In order to understand these changes it is crucial to locate the forms in the specific annual administrative processes within which they figure, that is, to follow their "careers"—the "doings with documents" (Harper 1998, 3) in which they are routinely involved—and to trace the subsequent events in which they take particular kinds of evaluative life. A brief consideration of the broader administrative history of policy at NSF in the mid-1990s and the changed institutional goals that set the context for the new forms is also necessary. In the next two sections I will first address the question of documentary careers and then turn to the context of new NSF policies, especially as articulated in a range of statements, reports, and resolutions, all of which shaped the new documents.

Four reference reports are routinely requested as part of the application materials for the Graduate Research Fellowship. These letters are sent to the contract organization managing the fellowship review process for NSF (the National Research Council [NRC], a branch of the National Academy of Sciences, in the early 1990s and Oak Ridge Associated Universities [ORAU], a regional consortium based in Tennessee, since the mid-1990s). When they are received, the numerical equivalents of reviewers' summary evaluations are entered as part of each applicant's quantitative profile. The reports are then read by panel participants as part of the evaluative process. I have discussed panel proceedings in detail elsewhere (Brenneis 1994), but several aspects of the process deserve highlighting here. First, the numbers associated with summary evaluations, the implications of which are not wholly evident to those filling out the form, actually play an important role in the quantitative profile developed for each applicant and in the preparation of a roster of preliminary rankings.

The panel meetings in which recommendations were considered in the early 1990s had several marked features. The earliest—and potentially quite consequential—appearance of the recommendation forms was in a quantitatively reduced form, the salience and nature of which would be difficult to determine from the form itself. Further, the range of variation in how seriously reference letters were considered was obviously quite considerable across disciplinary panels. Third, the outcomes of panel discussions took the forms of a different kind of document, a list of ranked names with specific numerical scores, which was then forwarded to NSF. It was, most importantly, often not clear in panel discussions what criteria were employed by NSF in the allocation algorithm it would apply to those applicants ranked in Quality Group 2, the classification within which approximately half of the applicants would receive awards. Finally, there was a strong, if at times implicit, assumption on the part of NRC that panelists' evaluations were not merely opinions but, in the aggregate, could be taken to represent the objective promise of the applicants under consideration, even if such promise must be represented relatively. This premise informed a highly disciplined set of reading and evaluative practices.

In turning briefly to the careers of proposal review forms, more variation is evident along several lines. First, in any particular funding cycle different kinds of panels solicit and evaluate such reviews in different ways. On the interdisciplinary panel on which I served, for example, such proposal reviews were solicited only from, in most cases, about half of the panel members themselves; no ad hoc reviews were requested from external scholars. In our panel discussions, then, written evaluations were discussed as part of the peer review process, but the peers who had written the texts were always part of the conversation. On most disciplinary panels, at least within the social sciences, a different pattern obtained. Program officers often had only one or two panel members—those whose expertise came closest to the topics in the proposal—read and write responses and would also submit a number of ad hoc external reviewers (ranging from three to eight or so) for each proposal. In the panel discussions themselves, one of the panelists who had reviewed a proposal would serve as its primary reviewer, providing not only his or her view but also glossing and evaluating the responses of the ad hoc reviewers. In such a setting texts were read quite differently; the authors of reviews themselves were in many ways part of the reviewed portfolio. Peer review with absent peers makes for somewhat different discussions than those where all the respondents are present, especially given the strong value placed on sustaining amity among fellow panelists (Brenneis 1999)—and the lessened salience of such concerns when outside reviews are being discussed and evaluated.

A second important feature has to do with the change in criteria for evaluation. Here I can only speak to the earlier situation, where, always faced with a greater number of promising research proposals than could be funded, we consistently turned to the framing documents—program description, explicit evaluative criteria, and the like—for specific ways of reducing the field of contenders. Such texts were taken very seriously—and often quite literally. Panel discussions were often shared interpretive exercises, with as much focus on the "real" meanings of such documents and of the fit between specific proposals and such meanings as on the proposals themselves in isolation. It is difficult to imagine that this underlying panel dynamic has changed dramatically; the two new criteria have most likely become central and consequential documentary foci for discussion and decision-making.

....

Histories

These documents are embedded in multiple histories, some at the very local level of subagency practice at NSF, some within the much broader ambit of federal policy and administrative review. I'll turn first to more local dimensions and then consider larger-scale aspects. In 1999, the same year that the new reference forms were introduced to the Graduate Fellowship review process, a significant change was made in the competition itself and considerable effort was made to revise panel procedures. The central change was the consolidation of the "competition for all Graduate Fellowships, combining for the first time since 1978 all processing and review for Graduate and Minority Fellowships . . . separate awards will not be made for members of underrepresented minority groups" (ORAU 1999, 3–4). As described in the "Guide for Panelists," this restructuring, "decided at the highest levels of the NSF, is consistent with the new Foundation-wide policy statement on diversity: Broadening opportunities and enabling the participation of all citizens—women and men, underrepresented minorities, and persons with disabilities—are essential to the health and vitality of science and engineering" (National Science Foundation Guide to Programs, quoted in ORAU 1999, 4).

In her briefing of panel chairs at the beginning of the 1999 sessions, Dr. Susan Duby, NSF's director of the Graduate Research Fellowship program, noted a further factor. It had been announced at the previous year's meetings that a suit had been brought against NSF challenging the legality of the Minority Fellowship Program. Dr. Duby told chairs that "NSF settled [the] lawsuit in June 1998 with no conditions put on how to structure GRFP" (Duby 1999, 1). It is important to note here that, at the same time that the previous system of a separate minority competition was under threat, a broader transformation of NSF policies made it possible to continue to take questions of diversity into serious account—and in fact to take them into more explicit account in panel meetings.

In following through on issues related to the consolidation, Dr. Duby laid out two general changes in panel procedures for 1999. First, chairs were to ask their panel members to "seek . . . a better balance between quantitative and qualitative factors in review of applications" (Duby 1999, 1); in practice, this meant that chairs were told to encourage more thorough reading of textual materials, both applicants' essays and respondents' commentaries. Second, Dr. Duby presented the revised NSF criteria discussed previously to chairs and encouraged them to discuss the new standards at some length with their panels. Judging from my own experience as a chair in previous years, the direct discussion of the general NSF criteria was a new addition to the program; we had previously operated independently of them.

A final important aspect of the 1999 changes has to do with how the rating scale, that is, the numerical scores used for rating applicants, is defined. In past competitions, the numerical terms for assessing individual candidates were defined wholly independently of the descriptions of ranked groups into which candidates were ultimately sorted. With the 1999 competition, however, "the definitions of the rating scale and the Quality Groups are directly linked" (ORAU 1999, 12). The manual then notes that this change should make it more difficult for "an individual panelist [to] unduly influenc[e] the final rankings by placing a disproportionate number of applicants high on the rating scale" (ORAU 1999, 12), that is, that panelists will be forced to monitor their own rankings more closely because of the new definitional structure.

These new definitions link characterizations of individual quality with the likely subsequent fate of applications, tying them directly to ranked group designation. There is a marked tension here between the descriptive labels themselves, which are cast in absolute terms—for example, "A truly exceptional or outstanding applicant" (ORAU 1999, 12), but always with a necessarily relative sense of ranking ("outstanding" vis-à-vis whom?)—and the definitions of the ranked groups, which are both directive and based on a more rhetorical theory of how the categorization should "mean."

The overt introduction of the two new criteria, especially the new emphasis given to "broader impacts," and the encouragement to panelists to "consider factors that will produce a diverse pool" but definitely *not* "to use any quota system" led to very different reading practices on the part of panelists than those in previous years. One was licensed, indeed encouraged, to consider, among other factors, to "what extent . . . this applicant [would] broaden the participation of underrepresented groups" (fig. 1.5). Moreover, again on the Social Sciences B panel, this criterion shaped very different discussions than in the previous years on the last day of meetings, when the difficult questions of boundary points and final scores were being negotiated. Apart from substantive changes in the criteria at the center of panel considerations, the last day's discussions tended much more to be conversations of the whole rather than of the immediately concerned panelists alone.

To understand the development of these new evaluation forms it is also necessary to examine, however briefly, the general administrative context and concerns of NSF in the early 1990s. Several contextual features are particularly relevant. The federal government was in a budgetarily weak position, both because of the state of the general United States economy and because of an often antipathetic Congress. Concerns about the fairness of the peer review process—and especially about the relatively low participation of younger scholars, women, and members of underrepresented minorities—were strong. A number of highly visible scandals, both actual and somewhat exaggerated, helped create a climate suspicious of, if not directly hostile to, publicly funded research. And, on several of the congressional committees that oversee the operations to federal research, concerns about the relative importance of basic research, especially in a post–Cold War world, were considerable. Finally, the early 1990s was a period during which both new kinds of managerial models and, especially given the constrained resources and political climate, a new stress on accountability were quite evident. In Thatcherite Britain, similar concerns helped catalyze the rise of "audit culture" (Power 1994, 1997); on the United States research scene a response was to focus on developing more rigorous styles of assessment rather than audit in the strict sense.

A central piece of legislation in this regard resulted from the initiative to reinvent government chaired by Vice President Al Gore. Formally known as "The Government Performance and Results Act of 1993 (GPRA)" this was defined as "a straightforward statute that requires all federal agencies to manage their activities with attention to the consequences of those activities. Each agency is to clearly state what it intends to accomplish, identify the resources required, and periodically report their progress to the Congress. In so doing, it is expected that the GPRA will contribute to improvements in accountability for the expenditures of public funds, improve congressional decision-making through more objective information on the effectiveness of federal programs, and promote a new government focus on results, service delivery, and customer satisfaction" (Department of Education 2000). NSF's first published report under this mandate was its "GPRA Performance Report FY 1999" (NSF 1999b), but the 1993 act catalyzed significant discussions and changes almost immediately.

A further pivotal document during this period was *Peer Review: Reforms Needed to Ensure Fairness in Federal Agency Grant Selection*, a report from the General Accounting Office (GAO 1994) to Senator John Glenn, chairman of the Committee on Governmental Affairs of the Senate. The report noted that, while peer review "appeared to be working reasonably well," several concerns were raised. First was the relatively low degree of participation as reviewers by junior scholars and women, whether on panels or as ad hoc evaluators. In regard to how proposals had been rated, various analyses showed that the "intrinsic qualities of a proposal" were the crucial factors in reviewers' scorings, rather than any "measured characteristics of reviewers or applicants" (GAO 1994, 2). Recommendations here included the ongoing monitoring of reviewing for possible discrimination in scoring.

Most directly relevant to the development of the new forms here, however, was the finding that there were "some problems in how review criteria were applied. "Reviewers were inconsistent in considering agency criteria and, especially at NSF and NEH, in applying agency criteria and rating scales. Finally, the report further cited difficulties in the socialization of reviewers; "[a]ll agencies do little to ensure that the reviewers have an accurate and similar understanding of the agency's criteria and rating scales" (GAO 1994, 56). The report and its recommendations played a central role in the agencies evaluating their policies and developing new strategies and techniques for evaluation.

A further significant document developed in response the GPRA was "NSF in a Changing World: The National Science Foundation's Strategic Plan" (NSF 1995). Strategic plans and their associated mission and vision statements were emergent documentary genres in the early 1990s, seen in part as documents for representing organizations and their goals to external audiences and in part for providing more apparently clear internal representations of and standards for evaluation within the institutions themselves (cf. Strathern's essay in this collection).

Among the "core strategies" outlined for pursuing NSF's stated stewardship vision was the importance of "Develop[ing] intellectual capital: [to s]eek out and support excellent activities among groups and regions that traditionally have not participated as full stake holders [*sic*] in science, mathematics, and engineering, including women, minorities, and individuals with disabilities" (NSF 1995, Executive Summary 2). The emphasis on greater inclusiveness within science, mathematics, and engineering is strongly highlighted in the plan. In a subsequent section, a more detailed argument for the importance of diversity is laid out: "In a democratic society that is highly dependent upon science, mathematics, and engineering for its well-being and place in the world, the scientific enterprise cannot thrive unless it is open to all segments of the population. Diversifying the workforce to create a more inclusive and robust scientific enterprise is necessary to assure excellence. Bringing the benefits of a diverse population to science, mathematics, and engineering requires that NSF work with its partners toward the assignment and acceptance of responsibility for assuring that the full range of talents in the population is engaged" (NSF 1995, Meeting Our Goals 2). The goal of increasing diversity is clearly praiseworthy—and all the more valuable because of its recurrent salience in the plan. The grounds for making diversity important, however, deserve some attention: the value of diversity is cast much more in terms of aggregate, societal gain rather than drawing upon the older language of rights and equal individual opportunity. It is, after all, science to which the "benefits of a diverse population" are brought. In many ways the rhetorical field is reversed from that of previous decades. A second rhetorical feature of both the preceding citations is the salience of "excellence" without any specification of what it implies or how it might be measured and evaluated.

That the goal of diversity is expressed in terms of underrepresented groups becoming *stakeholders* is also particularly striking; the word is borrowed from contemporary managerial literature and practices, as, indeed, were the notions of mission and vision statements. Stakeholders are taken as those who share an interest in an institution. The connotations of the word, however, suggest not a language of rights and individual access but a more narrowly defined, quasi-economic relationship, a sense borne out in a subsequent strategy concerning partnerships, in which a broad range of interested parties is delineated, and the nature of their "interest" is defined in quite business-like terms. As with the genre itself, these choices in language reveal the clear influence of broader managerial theory and practice.

The notion of stakeholders is also evident in another document from 1995, a report from a "NSF stakeholders' panel in Linguistics." As "[t]he National Science Foundation must respond to new legal requirements to develop a meaningful set of performance measures that can be used in future years to evaluate the effectiveness of NSF activities" (Bachenko et al. 1995, 2), an ad hoc committee was convened to evaluate the linguistic program at NSF as a prototype of how such review might take place. The committee members were defined as stakeholders, that is, representing "those who have a beneficial interest in the results of some activity; they are not necessarily performers of the activity but their own work is affected in some way by its outcome" (Bachenko et al. 1995, 2).

One quite specific consequence of the 1995 strategic plan was the appointment by the National Science Board (NSB), the oversight and policy group for NSF, of, first, an NSF Staff Task Group and then a joint NSB/NSF Staff Task Force to suggest improvements in NSF peer review practices. In its "Discussion Report" of November 1996 (NSF 1996), the task force concurred with the staff group's conclusion, that "[t]he NSB criteria are in need of clarification and should be rewritten with consideration given to: (a) making the criteria clearer to evaluators; (b) emphasizing important attributes such as innovation, clarity of thought and soundness of approach; and (c) encouraging substantive comments on the quality of proposals" (NSF 1998, 5). The task force further endorsed two new criteria to replace the earlier four. The task force argued that "NSF is increasingly asked to connect its investments to societal value, while preserving the ability of the merit review system to select excellence within a portfolio that is rich and diverse. Having two criteria, one for intellectual quality and the other for societal impact, should serve to reveal the situations where proposals have high quality but minimal potential impact (and viceversa). Quality will continue to be the threshold criterion but will come to be seen as not sufficient in itself for making an award" (NSF 1996, 6). "Societal impact" is far from a clear or unequivocal phrase; for some readers it might centrally imply issues of diversity and equal opportunity, for others it might connote industrial or defense applications. At the same time, the task force was concerned to refine the instructions given to reviewers, noting that the new criteria should be "defined for reviewers and proposers by a set of suggested contextual elements. Reviewers [should be] asked to describe the proposal's 'strengths and weaknesses' with respect to each criterion using only those contextual elements that they consider relevant to the proposal at hand" (NSF 1996, 6).

After wide consultation, final recommendations were presented to the National Science Board and led to a resolution on March 27–28, 1997 (NSF 1997a, 1997b). The resolution approved the two new criteria and authorized the director of the NSF to move forward with implementing the requisite changes, reporting back in November 1997. The new reference and evaluation forms already discussed are among the products of this implementation.

It is critical to note several summary points, not so much about the practical political dimensions of these changes as about the language of the documents through which those changes can be charted—and in which they leave their traces. A first point is the semantic vacuousness of terms with which NSF defines its mission. A central term here is *excellence* as both goal and hallmark of practice. It is never clear what the term means—or how we might recognize the success of the institution in achieving it. This is not to say that NSF does not do very good or important work indeed, nor is it to claim that NSF is alone using terms that are so definitionally ungrounded that they could not be regarded even as ambiguous. In fact, the very widespread invocation of excellence in corporate, educational, and administrative organizations contributes directly to its semantic inutility— which suggests that something other than the usual sense of meaning is at play here.

A further point has to do with the very specificity of the changes that have flowed from the strategic plan—and the assumptions about evaluation and evaluators that underlie them. The work of the task force focuses directly on how best to elicit the most useful, comprehensible, and comparable information from reviewers: how might the clearest instructions leading to the most desirable kinds of responses be framed? And how might the gap between institutional intentions and requirements and individual respondents' private criteria and apparently idiosyncratic responses best be bridged? Not only, however, must there be greater clarity as to what is desired by NSF; reviewers, references, and other participants need to learn how to respond appropriately—and to discipline themselves to act upon that learning. The shift from "Information" to "Instructions," the restructuring of reference forms so particular kinds of narratives might more likely be elicited, and the increased specificity as to how evaluations must be justified and supported all point to a much greater concern with controlling and standardizing responses, not in content per se but in the kinds of issues that must be addressed.

....

Conclusions

Writing recommendations and evaluating research proposals are part of everyday academic life, work squeezed into the occasional odd moments, often completed on the run and a bit late, and, perhaps, without much attention to the forms on which such texts take shape. If we do read the forms with some care, we often attend only to the very practical question: what do they want to read? And rarely would we be likely to turn to the upper-right and lower-left corners in which the marks of the administrative past of the form itself usually lie. As this chapter suggests, such forms have very real presents, moments in which they are filled out and subsequent moments in which they are read, cited, and evaluated. As they move from one reading and writing event to the next, these forms have, as Harper (1998) suggests, careers, being animated by and animating meetings, contributing to specific and consequential outcomes for individuals and for scholarship. Beyond these specific careers, such forms have histories of how and why they have taken their particular shapes; to adapt Riles's phrase (2000, 70), such histories lie in the margins, where, for example, agency approval is noted and dated. For the complying academic, the problematic aspect of a proposal review would most likely lie in what he or she is to write; for the funding program administrator, the problematic aspect of the review might primarily surface in such apparent marginalia, the usually taken-for-granted framework.

Even the simplest of forms speaks to multiple audiences and is produced by multiple hands, with often quite different interests and concerns at play. Any single reader is unlikely to be able fully to "read" all that is represented or indexed on a single page, as this perhaps overly detailed but nonetheless far from exhaustive examination should make clear. And this is not solely a matter of the past. In those subsequent readings and rereadings characteristic of the careers of such documents, what might be taken initially as unproblematic framework might become the central point of contention or re-analysis. Figure and ground can often reverse.

The documents and practices at the heart of this chapter are essentially instruments for assessment rather than audit in the strict sense, but some similar issues underlie both these doings and the range of audit practices now critical in British academic culture. Certainly the public concern for accountability—in both the literal sense and its metaphoric extensions—is central to both. Power (1994, 1997) has tracked the rise of what is now generally termed "audit culture" in the United Kingdom, following the penetration, first, of models of financial audit into systems of broader managerial evaluation and, then, of such managerial models into organizations of quite disparate types. I can only touch briefly upon two of Power's insights here. First is his observation that, even within its most traditional role within business, "the knowledge base of the financial audit process is fundamentally obscure" (1997, 30). Even when only financial matters are being examined, in other words, auditors necessarily rely upon partial measures, developing proxies or other kinds of indicators that are taken somehow to map the fiscal well-being of an organization. The accountability of organizations is measured in terms of such mappings. What a financial auditor "knows" is inherently obscure and partial, but she or he acts upon it as if it provided a full, adequate, and explicit account. And the techniques that audits develop as strategies for pursuing such indicators then become in themselves both technically refined and taken as broadly applicable to a range of financial situations—and very rarely are reexamined (cf. O'Barr and Conley 1992). With the extension of financial audit practices as a strategy for insuring accountability in broader administrative practices, the "knowledge base" issue becomes even trickier, as techniques are adapted—and generalized—to assess increasingly more complex kinds of phenomena. Following her earlier discussion of the decontextualization of skills inherent in audit procedures, Strathern makes the compelling suggestion that what is "needed" is not the development of such transferable (and inherently partial) skills but "the very ability to embed oneself in diverse contexts . . . that can only be learned one context at a time" (1997, 14).

Power's second crucial point for this discussion is that, for "auditing practitioners, 'making things auditable' is a deeply practical issue. It is what they do when they apply various techniques to an organization" (1997, 87). Developing the classificatory and analytical techniques that translate the specifics of any organization or setting into comparable, critically available terms is crucial. In the United Kingdom the "research tradition [that] has been developed to analyze and evaluate these judgment processes and to develop new methods which might improve them" (Power 1997, 87) is auditing; in the United States other disciplines such as psychometrics clearly play a similar role. Beyond "making things auditable," however, Power argues that the extension of audit practices to educational and other nonfinancial institutions requires "making auditees" (1997, 98) of such actors as researchers and teachers. As Woolgar notes in writing of British academic assessment practices, "the new relations of accountability entail new categories of identity and audience. The first appearance of these categories can engender uncertainty and confusion, but their subsequent congealment can tempt us into taking for granted the sets of relations and the moral order they imply" (1997, 30–31). Not only terms are translated across domains—from the academic to the managerial; so also are persons and their activities. And these redefinitions can, with time, be taken as the way things just are, concealing both their histories and their implications. My own work suggests that a third kind of transformation also takes place: institutions are made auditable, actors are made into auditees, and often the very same actors are also made into auditors, for the nonce—or, at the least, into increasingly disciplined evaluators and participants in assessment. As I have argued elsewhere, it is not so much that we "become" bureaucrats as that we have learned how to "do bureaucratic things" (1994, 33)—and that we are willing, and at times eager, to do them. As Strathern (1997, 2000a, 2000b, n.d., and this collection) and Shore and Wright (1999, 2000) compellingly argue, our own participation as actors in these processes raises a range of ethical and political issues. We are not somehow outside such systems of evaluation and audit.

Finally, I want to pull back to a broader view of the current funding scene in the United States. The changes discussed in this chapter came out of a period of economic uncertainty and deep federal budget deficits. The move toward increasingly regulated and managed practices of evaluation took place as fewer resources were available for allocation. In neither of the types of funding competitions previously mentioned was there a shortage of strong candidates; selecting from among a range of good possibilities was the problem. The economy, the federal budget situation, and the perceived centrality of science, if not social science, had changed dramatically by the time the new criteria and forms were put into place. Policy takes time to move from inception to practice, and times had changed remarkably. More significant, however, has been the decreasing relative importance of such peer-reviewed funding processes for research, even within the federal government. Literally partnered research jointly undertaken by universities and corporations, extensive research operations within commercial enterprises, and a return to what, in the federal surplus year of 2000, was recurrently referred to as "pork barrel" funding for major research projects and institutions have all reshaped the sources of research money. One way of reading this chapter is as an account of the move toward greater attempted standardization and control within a particular range of agencies—as a study of Foucauldian "governmentality" at work in primarily invisible but consequential ways. At the same time, it can also be seen as an account of the increasing refinement of administrative technique within organizations whose importance may be, for the present at least, be on the wane—and in a context in which a more visible traditional politics plays an increasingly important role.

68 ☐ DOCUMENTS

NOTES

I would like to thank Annelise Riles for organizing the conference in which these essays were first presented, colleagues participating in that remarkable conversation for their stimulating presentations and lively commentary, and the Center for Law, Culture, and Social Thought at Northwestern University for its hospitality. I very much appreciate the insight and candor of fellow panelists and staff at NSF, the National Research Council, and Oak Ridge Associated Universities, especially of Susan Duby, Stuart Plattner, Michael Musheno, and Paul Chapin. Dan Segal, Wynne Furth, and Annelise Riles have provided invaluable advice on subsequent drafts.

1. I would like to thank Steven Eisenman, Professor of Art History at Northwestern University and chair for my session at the conference, for his insightful and provocative comments on visual aspects of these forms.

REFERENCES

Bachenko, Joan, David Balota, Roy d'Andrade, James Hoard, Sandra Hutchins, C. Raymond Perrault, and Louise C. Wilkinson. 1995. Report of NSF Stakeholders' Panel in Linguistics. Submitted to Dr. Paul Chapin, Program Director, Linguistics Program.

Bateson, Gregory. 1972. *Steps to an Ecology of Mind.* New York: Ballantine.

Bowker, Geoffrey C., and Susan Leigh Star. 1999. *Sorting Things Out: Classification and Its Consequences.* Cambridge: MIT Press.

Brenneis, Donald. 1988. A Propos de *Research Proposals. Actes de la Recherche en Sciences Sociales* 74:82.

———. 1994. Discourse and Discipline at the National Research Council: A Bureaucratic *Bildungsroman. Cultural Anthropology* 9(1): 23–36.

———. 1999. New Lexicon, Old Language: Negotiating the "Global" at the National Science Foundation. In *Critical Anthropology Now: Unexpected Contexts, Shifting Constituencies, Changing Agendas,* ed. George F. Marcus, 123–46. Santa Fe: School of American Research Press.

———. 2000. Sympathetic Vibrations and the Neo-Liberal Arts College: Response to Bonnie Urciuoli, "Strategically Deployable Shifters in College Marketing, or Just What Do They Mean by 'Skills' and 'Leadership' and 'Multiculturalism?'" *Language and Culture: Symposium* 5. Electronic document, http://www.language-culture.org.

Department of Education. 2000. The Government Performance and Results Act. Electronic document, http://www.ed.gov/offices/OPE/HEP/iegps/is-grpa .html (accessed June 2002).

Duby, Susan (Division Director, DGE/HER, Acting Program Director, NSF Graduate Fellowship Program). 1999. Notes for briefing of GRFP panel chairs.

Duranti, Alessandro. 1984. *Lāuga* and *talanoaga:* Two Speech Genres in a Samoan Political Event. In *Dangerous Words: Language and Politics in the Pacific,* ed. Donald L. Brenneis and Fred R. Myers, 217–42. New York: New York University Press.

Ewald, François. 1991. Norms, Discipline, and the Law. In *Law and the Order of Culture*, ed. Robert Post, 138–62. Berkeley and Los Angeles: University of California Press.

General Accounting Office (GAO). 1994. *Peer Review: Reforms Needed to Insure Fairness in Federal Agency Grant Selection.* Report to the Chairman. Committee on Governmental Affairs, U.S. Senate.

Goffman, Erving. 1974. *Frame Analysis: An Essay on the Organization of Experience.* Cambridge: Harvard University Press.

Harper, Richard. 1998. *Inside the IMF: An Ethnography of Documents, Technology, and Organizational Action.* San Diego: Academic Press.

National Science Foundation (NSF). 1987a. Proposal Review Form. Washington, DC: National Science Foundation.

———. 1987b. Reference Report on Applicant. Washington, DC: National Science Foundation.

———. 1988. Reference Report Form. Washington, DC: National Science Foundation.

———. 1995. NSF in a Changing World: The National Science Foundation's Strategic Plan.

———. 1996. Discussion Report of the National Science Board and National Science Foundation Staff Task Force on Merit Review.

———. 1997a. Final Recommendations of the National Science Board and National Science Foundation Staff Task Force on Merit Review.

———. 1997b. New General Criteria for Merit Review of Proposals. Resolution adopted by the National Science Board at its 342nd Meeting, March 27–28, 1997.

———. 1999a. National Science Foundation Graduate Research Fellowships: Application Forms and General Instructions for Completing a Fellowship Application.

———. 1999b. GPRA Performance Report FY 1999. Electronic document, http://www.nsf.gov/pubs/2000/nsf0064/nsf0064_2.html (accessed June 2002).

Oak Ridge Associated Universities (ORAU). 1999. *Guide for Panelists in the Review and Rating of National Science Foundation Graduate Research Fellowship Applications.* Oak Ridge, TN: Oak Ridge Associated Universities.

O'Barr, William M., and John Conley. 1992. *Fortune and Folly: The Wealth and Power of Institutional Investing.* Homewood, IL: Business One Irwin.

Parmentier, Richard. 1997. The Pragmatic Semiotics of Culture. *Semiotica* 116(1): 1–115.

Power, Michael. 1994. *The Audit Explosion.* London: Demos.

———. 1997. *The Audit Society: Rituals of Verification.* Oxford: Oxford University Press.

Readings, Bill. 1996. *The University in Ruins.* Cambridge: Harvard University Press.

Riles, Annelise. 2000. *The Network Inside Out.* Ann Arbor: University of Michigan Press.

Shore, Cris, and Susan Wright. 1999. Audit Culture and Anthropology: Neo-Liberalism in British Higher Education. *Journal of the Royal Anthropological Institute* 5(4): 557–75.

———. 2000. Coercive Accountability: The Rise of Audit Culture in Higher Education. In *Audit Cultures: Anthropological Studies in Accountability, Ethics, and the Academy*, ed. Marilyn Strathern, 57–89. London: Routledge.

Silverstein, Michael. 1976. Shifters, Linguistic Categories, and Cultural Description. In *Meaning in Anthropology*, ed. Keith Basso and Henry Selby, 11–55. Albuquerque: University of New Mexico Press.

———. 1987. Monoglot "Standard" in America. Working Papers of the Center for Psychosocial Studies, 13. Chicago: Center for Psychosocial Studies.

Strathern, Marilyn. 1991. *Partial Connections*. Lanham, MD: Rowman and Littlefield.

———. 1997. From Improvement to Enhancement: An Anthropological Comment on the Audit Culture. Founder's Memorial Lecture, Girton College, Cambridge, March 11.

———. 2000a. The Tyranny of Transparency. *British Educational Research Journal* 26(3): 309–21.

———. 2000b. Introduction: New Accountabilities. In *Audit Cultures: Anthropological Studies in Accountability, Ethics, and the Academy*, ed. Marilyn Strathern, 1–18. London: Routledge.

———. N.d. A Case of Self-Organization. Unpublished ms.

Urciuoli, Bonnie. 2000. Strategically Deployed Shifters in College Marketing, or Just What Do They Mean by "Skills" and "Leadership" and "Multiculturalism"? *Language and Culture: Symposium 5*. Electronic document, http://www.language-culture.org.

Woolgar, Steve. 1997. Accountability and Identity in the Age of UABs. CRICT Discussion Paper 60, Brunel University, February.

2 [Deadlines]

Removing the Brackets on Politics in Bureaucratic and Anthropological Analysis

Annelise Riles

IN SEPTEMBER 1995, the United Nations (UN) convened in Beijing the "Fourth World Conference on Women," an event that brought together delegates from 189 member states with the purpose of negotiating and signing a "document" known as the "Global Platform for Action" (United Nations Fourth World Conference on Women 1995a).[1] One of the odd features of these proceedings, given the conference's stated objectives, was that attempts to talk about gender in terms someone schooled in the academic feminist debates of the last ten years would recognize failed miserably. Feminist academics present at the conference complained that gender analysis was effectively drowned out by right-wing critics of feminism, but they also felt confused by the language and objectives of the activists and bureaucrats with whom they had expected to share a great deal. One ethnographic puzzle the knowledge practices surrounding the Beijing proceedings raised, therefore, was the following: How was it possible that gender was quite literally bracketed out of the proceedings?

The subject of this chapter is the bracketing of gender in this particular episode of bureaucratic knowledge production. But in a more general sense, I want to suggest that the best way to make ethnographic sense of what is bracketed in bureaucratic knowledge is to understand what is also bracketed in the ethnographic study of bureaucratic practice. Most anthropologists invited to reflect on bureaucratic or legal documents like the Platform for Action would seek to understand the text's meanings by uncovering the politics latent in the drafting and words of the text. They would be suspicious of the way the uses of formal language impoverished the political conversation at the conference and hence served certain interests at the expense of others (e.g., Bloch 1975). Where were the points of contention about the character of gender, academics might want to ask, and how was that politics reflected in the language, the meaning of the document—or was that meaning and politics deflected, bracketed only to be recuperated through critical academic inquiry (Otto 1999)?

This focus is one that in the past I have bracketed out. My problem with this approach was not a disagreement with the impetus for the critique, but rather a sense that the critique was anticipated, and even already appropriated, by the very bureaucratic practices it targeted (Riles 2000). But for many anthropological readers, my approach by definition left the "meaning" and the "politics" of the document bracketed.

In this chapter, I want to return to politics and meaning. But following efforts in feminist anthropological accounts of bureaucratic practices to treat the proximity of anthropological and technocratic knowledge practices as a kind of methodological opportunity (e.g., Dahl 2004; Riles 2004a; Tsing 2004; Rosga 2005; Maurer n.d.),[2] I will define "politics" and "meaning" not only as events in the document and on the conference floor but also as markers of anthropological analysis. Politics and meaning, in this sense, are also what anthropologists appeal to in order to transform ethnographic data into anthropological analysis and what anthropological readers look for in order to know that data has been so transformed—the recognized artifacts of anthropological analysis.

My task, then, will be to work with the politics of the making of the Platform for Action and the meaning it was given in order to treat the "politics" and "meaning" of anthropological work ethnographically also, that is, to make what is so proximate that it eclipses anthropological knowledge newly accessible. In other words, I want to see whether thinking alongside bureaucrats' own tools for recuperating what is bracketed from their own documents might help an academic observer of bureaucratic knowledge such as myself to recuperate what is bracketed in academic accounts of documents such as the Beijing Platform for Action.

....

The Bracketing of Gender (I): The Bureaucrats

In order to bring the question into sharper focus, I will concentrate on a rare moment of the conference proceedings at which "politics" came into full view, from participants' point of view, as negotiations stumbled precisely over the "meaning" of the word *gender*. The word produced a moment of high drama in otherwise staid and laborious proceedings; it framed a period in which participants struggled under conditions of heightened tensions to find a solution in time for the denouement—the production of a document, on deadline.[3] As we will see, however, gender emerged not as a marker of an academic debate but as a barrier to the bureaucratic completion of the document.

During the preliminary negotiations for the Beijing Conference held at UN headquarters in New York in March 1995, a nongovernmental group began circulating leaflets to the delegates stating that *gender* was a code word for homosexuality. According to delegates with whom I was working, the leaflets stated that *gender* meant that there are "five genders and not two," where the five "genders" were "male," "female," "lesbian," "gay," and "transsexual." It was reported in the press that this "five genders" claim was also made among Latin American religious leaders in the months before the Beijing Conference (e.g., Inter Press Service 1995). In the corridors of the conference hall, delegates from Argentina, Guatemala, Honduras, and a handful of other states demanded of their counterparts a clear definition of gender and an explanation of why the term was different from and preferable to *sex* or *women*. Flyers that appeared on delegates' desks read:

> THE PLATFORM FOR ACTION uses the terminology of "Gender," i.e., "Gender Issues" throughout the Document. Why??
>
> Is this not the Commission on the Status of Women in preparation for the Fourth World Conference on Women. Then why the term— "gender." In fact, using the term "gender" dilutes the strength of Women. The aim of this conference is to address concerns of the Women! Let's keep the language of this Document focused on WOMEN.
>
> The term "gender" in the Document should be replaced with the word "Women."
>
> —"Proud to Be a Woman" Coalition

This challenge caught the majority of delegates and NGO representatives off-guard. From their point of view, gender was a common, "technical" term in development policy documents, hardly the sort of word that might be expected to generate controversy. Yet the majority found it hard to respond to a demand for a definition. As it turned out, gender was a bit different from other "technical" UN terms. As delegates readily pointed out, there was a history to the emergence of gender as a part of UN vocabulary. A product and distillation of academic debates, gender referenced the tools of those debates. Guatemala's delegate seized on the slippage between academic and bureaucratic worlds encapsulated in this word when she presented reporters with copies of academic articles and syllabi for "gender" courses taught at American universities as evidence that a "gender perspective" condoned and even "meant" homosexuality. If her assertion was a confused reductionism, it was one made possible by delegates' explicit acknowledgment of the proximity of academic and bureaucratic knowledge practices.

When no satisfactory definition of gender was forthcoming, the Guatemalan delegate proposed an amendment: "The word 'gender' in this document means the existence of woman and man as the two sexes of the human being" (cf. Archibald 1995). Rising to a point of order, however, the United States refused to allow the resolution officially to be read on the floor. What happened next was the bracketing of gender. Several states exercised their prerogative to "bracket" the word—to mark the word as in contention—each time it appeared in the text.

To understand the implications of this move requires some background on the process of negotiation at UN conferences. Because the goal is to produce a document that can gain the assent of every national government, a complicated organizational process has been devised to allow each delegation input into every word of the text. A draft text is first prepared by the Secretariat and is tabled for discussion at the opening of the meeting. Delegates then propose amendments to this draft, sentence by sentence. This string of proposed amendments—and there are often dozens of alternatives offered for a singular paragraph—is placed in brackets. The document is then divided into sections, and the delegations are divided into corresponding "working groups," such that France might send one of its diplomatic team to the working group for the chapter on health and another to the working group for the chapter on human rights. These working groups then work to whittle away at the bracketed text in the paragraphs in their respective sections by withdrawing proposals here, or redrafting alternatives there. Only near the close of the conference is the document and the delegation put back together again.

It is in this organizational sense that gender was "different" from other technical UN terms from delegates' point of view. Because of its special quality as a cross-cutting distillation of decades of feminist debate, gender defied the jurisdiction of any particular committee. In this context, the move to bracket gender had cross-committee implications: unlike abortion, or torture, for example, which appeared primarily in certain sections of the document, gender appeared throughout the text and hence was the responsibility of every working group. To bracket gender was to instigate an organizational nightmare. It would require coordination among the members of each delegation, among working groups, and within the Secretariat. Activists accurately termed the proposal to bracket gender an assault on the entire endeavor of the conference. The form that such an assault took, however, was organizational.

In this light, the conference chair ruled that the word *gender* would not be placed in brackets throughout the document because to do so would set the process back too far. If the meaning of gender had engaged only a handful of delegations' interest or concern, however, this procedural move unleashed a collective fury. To overrule the dissenters' demand that gender be placed in brackets was to create an issue of process—what the Moroccan ambassador termed a "very serious jurisprudential question" of the sovereignty of states. After the ambassador of Benin described the chair's decision in fiery terms as illegal "game playing," the chair proposed to mediate this concern with the appointment of a "contact group with a mandate to seek agreement on common usage and understanding of the word gender in the context of the Platform." Delegates then turned their attention to the procedures to govern the activities of the "contact group."

....

The Bracketing of Gender (II): The Academics

At the outset, this moment of politics made evident a problem of incongruity: the document could not accommodate an analytical perspective such as gender. And yet, throughout the three-year preparatory process for the Beijing Conference,[4] there had been many references to gender. In speeches and private conversations, among nongovernmental organizations (NGOs) in Fiji, where I conducted fieldwork, and at Beijing, "gender analysis" referenced a new approach to development at once more technically sophisticated and politically progressive than an older generation of "woman-centered" development projects. One of my earliest and most embarrassing fieldwork gaffes was a careless attempt to articulate to a meeting of representatives of aid agencies and international organizations what was wrong with the sociological assumptions inherent in a "gender perspective." This intervention was received as a regressive, even reactionary attempt to "hold back progress," and I was rebuked in terms usually reserved for aging male directors of suspicious First World institutions. On another occasion, the staff member of an aid agency privately disparaged Fiji's NGO community with the comment that "most of them don't even have a gender perspective."

What did participants intend by the word? At first glance, its meaning seemed familiar. In a speech on the floor of the Beijing Conference, the head of the Gender in Development Programme of the United Nations Development Programme (UNDP) urged the plenary to take up a "gender approach," which she described as a "fundamental rethinking of development" (United Nations Department of Public Information 1995). The characteristics of the approach, she said, were that it focused not only on women but on men, and that it looked at women as a question of the development of society as a whole. Anthropologists can readily recognize the concepts at play in this definition—society seen as a whole, or relations between men and women—as the familiar fruits of our own twentieth-century academic enterprise (Strathern 1995).

But in this bureaucratic context, these familiar academic concepts were rendered in a quite different key. Gender was principally a matter of *projects*, of procedures and programs for bureaucratic action. The secretary general's report to the Beijing Conference, drafted by a "gender specialist" (an American political scientist), was devoted to "mainstreaming" the concept of gender by making organizational changes within the UN bureaucracy and the structure of development organizations (UN ECOSOC 1995). Other conference participants defined "gender analysis" as the task of creating development projects on topics outside the traditional scope of "women's rights," such as torture or IMF lending policies, or of reorganizing bureaucratic practices so that "women's issues" were addressed in all projects and at all levels rather than by a separate bureau.

Along with this focus on projects came a refusal of a certain style of analysis. The following typical exchange at the preparatory meetings illustrates the mundane way in which some kinds of knowledge were foreclosed in the work of drafting:

> Chair: So we have taken all the proposals for [paragraph] twenty-two? Kenya?
> Kenyan delegate: Thank you Madam Chair. I have a problem with what the Holy See [the Vatican] is proposing, because I see the role of the

woman going beyond the family. Because, the . . . the . . . from what I'm understanding, we're confining this role specifically within the family and I think it's broader than that. So I have a problem.

Chair: We are just noting these suggestions and we will try to settle them later. Does EU have their flag up? No? G-77, paragraph twenty-two still.

As this exchange illustrates, efforts to take a perspective, to point to underlying principles or issues, were not rejected outright, nor did they generate contention. They were simply passed over in favor of the next proposed amendment.

This problem was a source of frustration for many feminist academics observing the Beijing process from the sidelines. Vivienne Wee, a sociologist and founding member of DAWN, a network of feminist academics from developing countries, critiqued this aspect of bureaucratic practice in a speech at the NGO forum held in tandem with the Beijing Conference:

We would like to consult with all of you for your input for a document that goes beyond paragraph substitution and word insertion. (Applause) An enormous amount of energy has gone to such things and that is also important. . . . But we cannot just do that and that alone, because we need to *analyze* what kind of development paradigm underlies those documents, and that's what we're trying to do.

The question of what was lacking in the Beijing document then led her directly to her own understanding of gender:

because of the gendered perspective that the women's movement has introduced into these conferences, linkages are now being seen between the different topics themselves: between environment, between rights, between population, between poverty.

In Wee's understanding, gender was a marker for "linkages" among disparate "topics," for a kind of thinking that generated its meaning not through projects, but through analytical relationality.

But as Wee suggested, the process of drafting documents seemed to block such relational thinking before it could even get started. Indeed, the gender dispute ultimately was resolved not by arguments over meaning, but by the formation of a committee to draft a further document indicating that the dispute was so resolved. Academics interested in the ultimate definition of gender produced by the "contact group" after several weeks of meetings at UN headquarters will be disappointed by its reference only to settled procedure. The statement reads, in its entirety:

> Having considered the issue thoroughly, the contact group noted that: (1) the word "gender" had been commonly used and understood in its ordinary, generally accepted usage in numerous other United Nations forums and conferences; (2) there was no indication that any new meaning or connotation of the term, different from accepted prior usage, was intended in the Platform for Action.
>
> Accordingly, the contact group reaffirmed that the word "gender" as used in the Platform for Action of the Fourth World Conference on Women was intended to be interpreted and understood as it was in ordinary, generally accepted usage. (United Nations Fourth World Conference on Women 1995b)[5]

The "meaning" of gender, then, was rendered as a matter of settled history, and that history was the history of the documents, and of procedure. Gender was documented in this statement as itself a matter of settled documentation, rather than a definitional question.

Even this rare moment of explicit conflict over the meaning of a word, then, is liable to leave anthropological observers dissatisfied with the blindness both the proponents and opponents of *gender* showed toward the term's multiple and complex meanings. There was more to this than simply a sociological divide between academics and bureaucrats. Many of the delegates, consultants, and lobbyists were highly schooled in academic debates about gender. The conference roster included numerous academics who, in another setting, would have deployed *gender* in a very different way (cf. Brenneis, this collection). And indeed, the premise of the dispute over gender was precisely the acknowledgment that gender was not just a "technical" term but also an "academic" one. One important ethnographic insight that can be drawn from this account is that "politics," in this instance, was an artifact of an uncomfortable proximity between academic and bureaucratic modalities.

From one point of view, what I have just given is an account of the bracketing of academic knowledge by bureaucratic knowledge. In this view, bureaucratic knowledge and academic knowledge are distant, different ways of knowing, and the one—bureaucratic—in this instance crowded out the other—academic. But these events also draw attention to the proximity of anthropological and bureaucratic practices that delegates themselves recognized as the premise of the gender dispute (Riles 2004a, 2004b). At the Beijing Conference, one of the important end points or outcomes of academic and feminist knowledge—the concept of gender—had become a beginning point for bureaucratic knowledge—the basis for the production of a gender document. And it was widely understood that this conversion of one kind of end into another kind of means created problems for the workings of both knowledges. It locked them in a relationship in which it was difficult to define either in relation to the other.

What is bracketed in anthropological accounts of bureaucracy, in other words, are the special problems posed for anthropology by the very proximity of anthropological knowledge to subjects like "gender." As numerous anthropologists have shown, anthropological knowledge works upon and against a certain precondition of distance between analyst and object of study, between "our" knowledge practices and "theirs." The existence of an "outside" to anthropological knowledge—difference—is the precondition of anthropological work. The immense creativity of anthropological knowledge has consisted largely in finding ways of innovating upon this distance—for example, by drawing surprising but illuminating analogies between "their" practices and "ours." But the problem of making documents a subject of ethnographic inquiry is a problem of studying knowledge practices that draw upon and overlap with the anthropologist's own rather than serving as a point of analogy or comparison for the anthropologist's questions as ethnographic subjects usually do. "Their" discussions cannot usefully illuminate ours because bureaucratic and academic vocabularies are already so intertwined. It may seem in such conditions that ethnography loses the ground of its own effectiveness—indeed it is no wonder that in such conditions many anthropologists seem to abandon their commitments to ethnography altogether. What anthropologists would wish to call the "politics" of the Beijing document, in other words, indexes the way an artifact such as the Beijing document forecloses anthropological tools of analysis. From this point of view, the methodological problem becomes how one form of knowledge, such as academic feminism, can encounter analytically an artifact produced by others who take our own artifacts as their ground.

....

Gridlock

One way to recuperate what is bracketed out of anthropological accounts of bureaucracy is to return to anthropology's own analytical practices as ethnographic subjects, and, conversely, to turn to bureaucratic practices as sources of methodological inspiration for anthropological knowledge. From this point of view, the solutions delegates found to their problem may prove comparatively interesting to anthropologists. But first we will need to understand what was truly at stake in the gender dispute for the delegates.

When they described gender as a "code word," the critics had not been entirely wrong. In UN document-drafting, the meaning of terms is often hidden, known only to insiders, but it is never indeterminate. What the word actually encoded, however, was an institutional *history*. Spurred by the past twenty years of feminist debates, activists, governments, and aid agencies had taken a step forward, had *progressed*, by moving from a "woman-centered perspective" to a "gender perspective." As one of Fiji's negotiators confided to me, those Pacific Island delegations that did not support the use of the term *gender* in the Platform for Action were simply a little *behind*, and it was up to the more developed states in the Pacific to bring them up to speed on UN technicalities. The NGO delegates I worked with took it as given that "gender" referenced progress.

This particular form of progress was itself part of a larger progressive trajectory. For the delegates and NGO representatives seasoned in UN conferences, conferences and documents form a kind of chain. The history of documents is created through the unfolding of one conference from the materials produced at another, the incorporation of one document into the next (cf. Wagner 1986, 81). The steps that led to the making of this particular document—the preparatory conferences and documents—constituted a trajectory of work, and this trajectory encompassed this document's relationship to future conferences and documents.

If the meaning of the word gender could not be articulated clearly, then, the *bracketing* of gender could be rendered simply and powerfully as a barrier to progress. NGO representatives asserted that in its very opposition to the view that "biology is destiny," "gender" embodied a progressive history. The social constructionism[6] that anthropologists and academic feminists might associate with the critique of the notion that "biology is destiny" was rendered in a different modality, as a historical subject of its own. In response to a question from a member of the press pleading for a more precise definition of gender, Bella Abzug, a renowned woman's rights activist and founder of the Women's Environment and Development Organization, offered the following institutional explanation:

the concept of gender has been embedded in all kinds of contemporary, social, political and legal and economic discourse. It's already been integrated into the planning and the language of the documents and the programs of the UN system. So putting that in brackets shows a real attempt to retrogress.

It was this historical trajectory of conferences and meetings, not social constructionism per se, that had to be defended within the brackets. At a demonstration in the conference hall at which representatives of NGOs held up pink signs sporting a singular word, *gender* or *gendre*, Bella Abzug read a statement asserting that the brackets around the word gender were "an insulting and demeaning attempt to reverse the gains made by women, to intimidate us and to block our progress." In the next twenty-four hours, it was repeated again and again, in private conversations and in speeches on the conference floor, that the word gender had appeared in many UN documents and therefore was settled text. To "reopen" it would be "going back," or "to retrogress." Buttons began to appear on delegates' lapels that read "no going back." What had been bracketed, the delegates seemed to agree, was institutional progress itself.

But this barrier to institutional progress took a particular form in the moment of the conflict: it took the form of a dispute over how to spend a highly valuable unit of time. In fact, the critics of the inclusion of *gender* in the document were vocal, but they represented only a small minority of delegates. The real danger, as it emerged in the minds of most delegates and activists, was that the debate would "waste precious time," as Abzug put it, that is, that the ensuing procedural gridlock would impede the completion of a host of other imperative tasks. In framing a problem, the brackets also framed a unit of time, then, a bounded moment in which delegates were forced to address this issue, and hence were impeded from addressing other issues.

Delegates experienced negotiations within the brackets as a torturous gridlock, a kind of interminable present. Again and again, colleagues remarked that the several days we had spent together felt like months. In the windowless conference halls there were no outside indicators of the passage of time and sessions habitually began and ended several hours behind schedule. Built into the premise that every delegation had a right to be heard on every point was a lack of a sense of narrative—of a beginning, middle, or end to the proceedings—as participants wondered again and again if *this* would be the last comment on a particular point or whether there might be many more to come.[7] It was as if within the brackets, time stopped.

The deliberation over the creation of a contact group to handle the problem of gender, for example, dragged on for several hours. As the customary ending time for the afternoon session, and then the dinner hour, came and went and still there was no end in sight, the frustration among the weary delegates became increasingly evident. In side conversations, delegates grumbled about the length of one another's speeches. Even in their formal statements, delegates began to reveal their irritation:

> Pakistan: Madam Chair, I would again propose that the *main* business before us now is to establish the contact group. You have *proposed* it and in fact, I'd suggest that you should *insist* on a response from the Commission,[8] and when we have that from the Commission then we can formally endorse that decision. Thank you Madam Chair. . . .
>
> Australia: I do think that we are far closer together than these ten minutes may have suggested. . . .
>
> Norway: Thank you Madam. I've a strong feeling that we are now *absolutely* ready to move to a final decision. After the last statement from Benin there seems to be clear agreement in the room as to how to proceed. Could we now proceed on that given the sense of agreement on that in this room now, thank you.

Of course, this sense of gridlock was perceptible only from the perspective of one caught in the moment: Once the brackets were lifted and gender was once again seamlessly incorporated into the text, it was all but forgotten (cf. Miyazaki, this collection). Despite the interminable complaints during the conference, I never heard any recollection of the experience of gridlock among the Fiji delegates after the close of the conference. Gender became just a word in the document, a unit of settled text rather than a unit of temporal and analytical gridlock.

But at the moment, within the brackets, delegates experienced a particular kind of problem. For the delegates working within the brackets, time and institutional progress (bureaucratic analysis) were bound together like partners in a three-legged race. The bracket was both a unit of time and a unit of organizational gridlock. And here is where I see an analogy to the anthropologist's problem of proximity between anthropological knowledge and its object, gender: What caused gridlock for the delegates was the collapse of time and institutional progress, two key parameters of their work, such that no measurement of one against the other was possible. There was no way of measuring the passing of time until the institutional problem was solved, and likewise no means of measuring progress against the passing of time. Hence any problem required a seemingly infinite amount of time, and any moment of time could generate a seemingly intractable bureaucratic problem.

There is an analogy here also, I think, to the problem of how to bring ethnographic objects such as gender into view. The bracketing off of the question of the meaning of gender, and of the time for its discussion, forecloses the possibility of an appeal to something "outside," as anthropologists might appeal to history, politics, or social context to make sense of their material, or might take time to work through a problem. The only possibility then is what is internal to the document and its forms of knowledge itself. The ethnographic interest of the gender debate for anthropology, then, becomes, where time and analysis are bound together, how do delegates see progress for themselves? How do bureaucrats find the means to move their process forward? And is there anything to be learned for anthropology's own means?

············

Steps

Thankfully for the delegates, the document embodies its own internal progressive trajectory. A participant in UN negotiations would offer something close to the following overview of what Richard Harper (1998) terms a document's career: A document comes to exist when a conference is convened to reach an agreement on a certain set of issues. This is a matter of a series of well-defined stages or steps. After initial speeches and discussion, the text is negotiated section by section. At the close of the conference, the document is adopted by the delegates in a formal resolution.

Documents only emerged as concrete printed objects when a stage in the analysis was complete. The emergence of the printed document is a moment at which it becomes possible to perceive of one's work as a step in a wider progressive trajectory (a "great chain of conferences," as delegates were fond of saying), to return to origins (to "take the document back to Fiji"), and to take the analysis apart again (to pinpoint key "language" from the document to be included in the next document). To lift the brackets and render the document "readable" in this way was also to erase the memory of gridlock and the trace of the steps delegates had made in their work inside the brackets (cf. Miyazaki, this collection).

The steps in this progressive trajectory were highly formalized. The debate over the proposal to form a contact group to determine the meaning of gender, for example, generated a further dispute about procedure: Should the contact group report to the chair of the Commission, who in turn would report to the Conference, or should the chair of the contact group write directly to national delegations, or should she instead deliver the report to the Conference as a whole when it reconvened in Beijing in several months' time? What preoccupied the delegates was the necessity of adherence to proper form. The Australian delegate's proposal captured many of the collective concerns:

> I would now like to put to you and to the Commission the proposal on which we should take a decision and it has several parts. First of all that you should propose that we establish the contact group on gender, with the mandate that you've already stated. I'm sure you will want to read it again. And that you should propose that its initial meeting time should be the dates that you stated, from the 15th of May to the 15th of June. Now that has an important element which is reporting, but I'll come back to that. But you should propose that the chair of this contact group be the rapporteur, the distinguished representative of Namibia, and that, in order for all interested states to participate, that notice would be given straight away, here in New York of this decision, to all permanent missions, of this decision, mandate and time. The next important point is that these decisions be fully recorded in the report that we will be adopting tonight, so that all will see what we have done. . . . The reporting procedure, for the work of the contact group, should be the same as what we adopt for the Platform and for all of the documentation, because this issue must be considered in the same way as that documentation. It is an important part of it. . . . If it is decided that all our documentation goes direct to Beijing, then I'd say so be it with the report of the contact group. So surely we should state that we do the same with this as we do with the other documentation. That would show that it is being treated as an important part of all of the documents for Beijing and that it is being treated in the same way. Now unless there is some technical reason why that shouldn't occur, I ask wouldn't that be logical.

This effort to think in stages extended also to the work of making the decision at hand:

> Pakistan: Madam Chair, I am proposing that you as the chairperson of the Commission on the Status of Women submit your proposal to

this commission for the establishment of the contact group on gender, and seek the approval of this commission. If this commission endorses it, you formally adopt it as a decision. And hence we will complete the first part of the business. Of course, when you would announce that decision, you will also say that Namibia has been designated as the chair of that working group, that contact group. After that business has been completed, we shall proceed to the modalities. And the modalities are: one is the responsibility, whether it should be responsible to the Commission on the Status of Women; or two, the Commission on the Status of Women to the ECOSOC, or directly to the countries. That decision can be taken separately after we have taken the decision on the establishment of the contact group.

As the delegates here made plain, the form of deliberations entails steps—it is sequential. It is also consequential: when properly produced, the form moves from the initiation of a conference to its conclusion, and it is anticipated that a product—a successful document—will result.

To anthropological observers, delegates' interest in procedural matters may seem to border on the obsessive. But I want to suggest that this obsession is ethnographically instructive: in the absence of outside meters, the only internal measure and engine of progress was this formal *process*—the elaboration of the steps the body should take. This is possible because the steps are both a "part" of the document and the context of the document's making: Later, the document will be imagined as one "step" of its own in the chain of UN women's conferences (Mexico City 1975, Copenhagen 1980, Nairobi 1985) that were referenced as the "history" of the women's movement at most meetings I attended. Indeed, this internal history was the only "background" I ever heard discussed among NGOs, bureaucrats, and aid agency staff members in Fiji.

The evidence that this process of laying out steps "works" to create a forward momentum to the conference proceedings is the following: Once the steps have been laboriously hammered out, something important and surprising, given the interminable present within the brackets, happens— the passing of time intrudes. In the course of laying out the requisite steps to be taken, the constraint of time emerged as an external reality such that it became possible once again to think of one's analytical progress in light of the constraints of time. At least for that bracketed moment, it was simply a fact that the session was ending the following day and delegates would have to return to their capitals regardless of whether the work was completed or not.[9] Some points of contention in the negotiations had to be passed over, some work left undone, simply because of lack of time. "I am literally pushing, and pushing," the chair repeatedly said of her activities, and indeed, in the negotiations her comments were like a drumbeat: "All right, can we move on? . . . OK, let's move on. . . . Can we turn our attention to page three, please. . . . We can't afford to spend any more time on this." A sense of racing against the clock emerged in the way the passing of time made formality yield to the exigencies of time. Whatever differences separated them, participants shared a collective anxiety about being forced to abandon proper procedures because of limitations of time. This is made explicit in the procedural vocabulary of UN conferences: As time runs short, delegates break into so-called informals—smaller and less procedurally elaborate committees—and then if necessary yet again into "informal informals" that dispense with even more essential elements of the process such as translation and NGO access. At every turn, there was a collective awareness of the cost of doing so.

Indeed, the chair skillfully exploited this sense that time was an outside constraint on bureaucratic form to push for progress. If the chair's authority was always contentious, the authority of time went unquestioned. Consider the following interchange between NGO leaders who challenged the lack of transparency in informal informal sessions, and the vice-chairperson of the commission, concerning the shortcomings of the informal informals:

> Vice-Chair: That may be, but the fact of the matter is, that it took us until Thursday evening to finish two sections of Chapter Four. And we didn't have more time.
> Audience member: I appreciate that. All I'm saying is that the method of operation needs to . . .
> Vice-Chair: So the decision we had to take is, do we continue with [formal procedures] at the risk of not having any text that is readable at the end of this meeting, or we would move into a different way of operating. . . . But, see, I don't want to defend the procedure which holds, I don't want to say whether it's democratic or not, I'm just laying before you the time constraints.

Assertions of this kind always elicited at least tacit understanding and sympathy even when, as in this case, an interchange had begun as a confrontation. Unlike the lack of information, for example, the lack of time was no one's fault; it was just a fact of the proceedings, an outside constraint. The chair makes it plain in this exchange that she is not the cause (Strathern 1988) of the political problem, that her own political agency is in abeyance (Miyazaki 2000).

In sum, although within the brackets bureaucratic progress and time were so tightly bound together that neither could serve as ground, as external meter for the other, the participants in the Beijing Conference were skilled in the uses of formality—of their own internally mandated steps—in making both progress and the passing of time come into view. Progress was internal to the document—it was effectuated through the elaboration and taking of steps. And because the procedures were borrowed or adapted from previous conferences, their elaboration made the participants aware of the wider progressive scale of their endeavor—that the document they were drafting was a step in a larger progression of conferences and documents. But in order for progress to unfold, formality also had to be abandoned (cf. Humphrey and Laidlaw 1994, 128). Indeed, it is through the abandonment of the steps that "progress," in the sense of the lifting of brackets and the completion of the document, ultimately is made. Despite the vice-chairperson's laments, it was also widely acknowledged that nothing ever got accomplished at UN conferences in the formal sessions that adhered to proper form; that progress only occurred in the "informals." Only by having a shared form in mind, and ultimately abandoning it, did the delegates escape from the gridlock of the brackets to the fleeting of time, in other words. And like "gender," when time came into view, it was as an organizational problem, a quantity of the same order as other problems faced at the conference. What was achieved in the process of destroying the formalities of the process, in other words, was an external vantage point from which to view progress.

Recreating Distance

It is perhaps less than surprising that the attention of a meeting of bureaucrats is devoted to matters of process. What would interest most anthropologists, rather, is what lies "behind" that process—for example, how the politics of gender were obscured or diverted as it was proceduralized (Rappaport 1979, 174). But I want to suggest that here we have another example of how the proximity of academic and bureaucratic knowledge causes each to eclipse the other: It is not that a political analysis of process would be incorrect from the delegates' point of view; rather, it would simply be mundane, self-evident, unsurprising in precisely the way that a discovery of the centrality of process in bureaucratic contexts is mundane to anthropologists. When anthropologists search for the "politics" behind the procedure, we are searching for an engine of analysis, for how to *do something* with the ethnographic subject. But in the case of the UN conference, the engine of analytical work is located elsewhere, in the steps delegates set out for themselves. Hence politics cannot do the work anthropologists expect it to do.

So what stands in the place of politics in anthropological analyses, in the knowledge practices of negotiators? What is the engine of their progress? An ethnographic answer, as we have seen, would have to be procedural form. Steps "work" for the delegates as politics works in the anthropological account: It comes to be perceived, once the analysis is complete, as an entity outside of analysis but it also is the internal engine of analysis itself.[10]

This brings us back to the question of how anthropological knowledge is obviated by ethnographic objects like the Beijing document, and what might be done about it. If asked why they failed to intervene in the debate about gender at the Beijing Conference, I suspect that many academics would say that there simply was no time to explain themselves in that context. Yet where time and analysis are bound together in bracketed units, as we have seen, to say that one does not have time is also to refer to the displacement of the steps in one's analysis.

What I aimed to show in this chapter was that the very proximity of academic work to the work of negotiators made the differences imperceptible; that like time and analysis for the delegates, which were bound together like partners in a three-legged race, academic and bureaucratic knowledge, when applied to one another, eclipsed the most central dimensions of each. In other words, each could not provide the ground or material for the other to work on. The difference between, for example, gender as a set of organizational practices and gender as a critical analytical perspective is not immediately accessible to those who produce either form of gender. Academic knowledge is eclipsed by this ethnographic object, then, not because it is utterly foreign to the conference, but because the two forms of knowledge work with the end points of one another's knowledge. And thus to analyze this material as if ethnographic distance in its traditional form was available would be as absurd as for delegates simply to declare that they would take a year to complete the document.

The problem of ethnographic subjects such as UN conferences, then, is that the productive analytical distance between anthropology's theoretical categories and what we used to term the "folk categories" must be created in the ethnographic act. The difference between an academic modality of gender analysis and a bureaucratic one, for example, becomes the ethnographic artifact itself. If there is an analogy to be found between the anthropologist's politics and the bureaucrat's procedural form, this analogy would point toward the necessity of *both* a commitment to anthropology's analytical devices and a willingness to eschew them as the means of recreating the ground for those devices to work. My response to the question of the politics of the document, then, has been to render accessible an alternative "outside" to the document from the standpoint of the "inside." I am proposing, in other words, that anthropologists begin to think of what we share with our subjects as a source of the very conceptual distance that makes analytical progress possible.

....

NOTES

I am grateful to the government of the Fiji Islands and to Fiji's many participants in Beijing-related activities for making this research possible, to Andy Adede and Ming-ya Teng for arranging my access to the intergovernmental deliberations, and to Jane Campion and Beth Olds for their research assistance. I thank Robert Burns, Tony Crook, Ulrika Dahl, Bonnie Honig, Iris Jean-Klein, Hirokazu Miyazaki, George Marcus, Kunal Parker and Adam Reed for their comments. I also thank John Comaroff and James Ferguson for taking time to show me what was bracketed out of my earlier analyses of UN conferences. Unless otherwise indicated, all quotations are taken from my own tape recordings of UN proceedings and where necessary have been translated by me.

 1. As its name indicates, the conference was the fourth global conference on women's issues convened by the UN since 1975. The document ratified at the conference is a text of 150 pages consisting of twelve "critical areas of concern" and a series of "strategic objectives" that respond to them. The document was drafted through an elaborate structure of tiered conferences at national and regional levels that each produced their own platforms for action. Much of the text was negotiated at a final preparatory meeting at UN headquarters in New York in March 1995, which is the subject of this chapter. I have written about this process more extensively elsewhere (e.g., Riles 1999, 2000, 2002).

 2. Mario Biagioli (this collection) makes a parallel observation with respect to the way authorship in scientific articles is rendered as a matter of good management technique.

 3. Given the explicit debate over questions of meaning and politics, it is no surprise that this moment has been the subject of considerable academic writing (e.g., Otto 1996; Baden and Goetz 1997).

 4. The negotiations began several years prior to the conference with the

drafting of numerous "regional documents," whose texts ultimately were used as the building blocks of the final Platform for Action.

5. At the opening of the Beijing Conference, the Main Committee of the Fourth World Conference in Beijing ratified the text produced by the contact group. As reported in a daily newspaper for delegates at the Beijing Conference, the winning argument was again a procedural and progressive one. When the Guatemalan delegate again objected to the contact group's conclusions, the delegate of Malta "received applause when he said, 'this issue has been resolved. The language was agreed upon. Governments gave their promises. We must not disrupt the work that was done in New York'" (Shepard 1995).

6. Statements by some opponents of the use of the word *gender* indicated that at least part of what was at stake were the merits of social constructionism. The Guatemalan delegate told reporters, "[Feminists] object to the biological determination toward being wives and mothers, which the word 'sex' implies" (Archibald 1995).

7. Several anthropological observers of meetings have commented on this problem of a lack of narrative structure. Paul Rabinow, for example, describes the extreme boredom and irritation produced by the interminability of successive panel presentations at academic conferences as "constitutive elements of such events" (1996, 5; cf. Schwartzman 1989).

8. "The Commission" is the Commission on the Status of Women, a suborganization of the UN Economic and Social Council (ECOSOC) created in 1946 to address "the advancement of women." Member states are elected on a rotating basis to two-year terms from the wider membership of ECOSOC.

9. In practice, of course, this externality is open to reconstitution from within the document: The following day the chair announced that the conference would be extended, and the delegates simply continued with their work.

10. Although the moment of the conference proceedings seems to be constrained by time, as if it were "external" to and independent of the activities of the negotiators, later the "internal" progression of conference documents will seem to encompass, to be external to, momentary time constraints.

....

REFERENCES

Archibald, George. 1995. Groups Coalesce to Fight "Gender" Agenda: UN Platform Called Divisive. *Washington Times*, June 23, A6.

Baden, Sally, and Anne Marie Goetz. 1997. Who Needs [Sex] When You Can Have [Gender]? Conflicting Discourses on Gender at Beijing. *Feminist Review* 56:3–25.

Bloch, Maurice, ed. 1975. *Political Language and Oratory in Traditional Society.* London: Academic Press.

Dahl, Ulrika. 2004. Progressive Women, Traditional Men: The Politics of Knowledge and Gendered Stories of Development in the Rural Northern Periphery of the EU. Ph.D. diss., Department of Anthropology, University of California, Santa Cruz.

Harper, Richard. 1998. *Inside the IMF: An Ethnography of Documents, Technology, and Organizational Action.* San Diego: Academic Press.

Humphrey, Caroline, and James Laidlaw. 1994. *The Archetypal Actions of Ritual.* Oxford: Oxford University Press.

Inter Press Service. 1995. Church Women: Bishop Declares War on Beijing Conference. May 9.

Maurer, Bill. 2005. Due Diligence and "Reasonable Man" Offshore. *Cultural Anthropology* 20(4): 474–505.

Miyazaki, Hirokazu. 2000. Faith and Its Fulfillment: Agency, Exchange, and the Fijian Aesthetics of Completion. *American Ethnologist* 27(1): 31–51.

Otto, Dianne. 1999. A Post-Beijing Reflection on the Limitations and Potential of Human Rights Discourse for Women. In *Women and International Human Rights Law*, ed. Kelly Dawn Askin and Dorean Marguerite Koenig, 115–35. Ardsley, NY: Transnational.

Rabinow, Paul. 1996. *Essays on the Anthropology of Reason.* Princeton, NJ: Princeton University Press.

Rappaport, Roy A. 1979. *Ecology, Meaning, and Religion.* Richmond, CA: North Atlantic.

Riles, Annelise. 1999. Models and Documents: Artifacts of International Legal Knowledge. *International and Comparative Law Quarterly* 48:809–30.

———. 2000. *The Network Inside Out.* Ann Arbor: University of Michigan Press.

———. 2002. The Virtual Sociality of Rights: The Case of "Women's Rights Are Human Rights." In *Transnational Legal Processes: Globalization and Power Disparities*, ed. Michael Likosky, William Twining, and Christopher McCrudden, 420–39. Cambridge: Cambridge University Press.

———. 2004a. Real Time: Governing the Market after the Failure of Knowledge. *American Ethnologist* 31(3): 1–14.

———. 2004b. Property as Legal Knowledge: Means and Ends. *Journal of the Royal Anthropological Institute.* 10(4):775–95.

Rosga, AnnJanette. 2005. The Traffic in Children: The Funding of Translation and the Translation of Funding. *Political and Legal Anthropology Review* 28(2): 258–81.

Schwartzman, Helen B. 1989. *The Meeting: Gatherings in Organizations and Communities.* New York: Plenum Press.

Shepard, Daniel J. 1995. Contentious Preparatory Meeting for the Beijing Conference Is Extended by a Day. *Earth Times* 8(6): 16.

Strathern, Marilyn. 1988. *The Gender of the Gift.* Berkeley and Los Angeles: University of California Press.

———. 1995. *The Relation: Issues in Complexity and Scale.* Prickly Pear Pamphlet 6. Cambridge: Prickly Pear Press.

Tsing, Anna L. 2004. Keynote address presented at the Cornell University Southeast Asia Program's Sixth Annual Graduate Student Symposium, Ithaca, April 2–3.

United Nations Department of Public Information. 1995. Economic Difficulties Impede Implementation of Strategies for Advancement of Women, Speakers

Tell Commission on Status of Women. Economic and Social Council Press Release. WCM/821 21 March 2.

United Nations Economic and Social Council (UN ECOSOC). 1995. *Second Review and Appraisal of the Implementation of the Nairobi Forward-Looking Strategies for the Advancement of Women.* Report of the Secretary-General to the Commission on the Status of Women, E/CN. New York: United Nations.

United Nations Fourth World Conference on Women. 1995a. Platform for Action. In *Report of the Fourth World Conference on Women,* A/Conf. 177/20.

———. 1995b. *Report of the Informal Contact Group on Gender.* A/CONF.177/L.2. New York: United Nations.

Wagner, Roy. 1986. *Symbols That Stand for Themselves.* Chicago: University of Chicago Press.

Part Two Authorship

and Agency

3

Conceiving Children

How Documents Support Case versus Biographical Analyses

Carol A. Heimer

HERE IS A TEXT ON assessment of gestational age by ultrasonography (Greene 1991, 35):

> During the second and third trimesters, measurements of the biparietal diameter (BPD) of the fetal skull and of the fetal femur length are useful in estimating gestational age. Strict criteria must be observed in making and measuring the cross-sectional images through the fetal head in order to ensure accuracy. Nonetheless, due to biologic variability in fetal growth and head shape, the accuracy with which the gestational age can be estimated decreases with increasing gestational age. For measurements made at 16 weeks of gestation the variation is ±10 to 11 days; at 27 to 28 weeks, it is ±14 days; and at 29 to 40 weeks, the variation is ±21 days. The length of the calcified fetal femur can be measured and may be useful in cross-checking BPD measurements. Femur length may provide a significantly more accurate estimate of gestational age in the third trimester than the BPD, with an error of only 5 days at 25 to 35 weeks and 6 days at 40 weeks. Under circumstances where the BPD may be technically difficult to measure, e.g., a deeply engaged fetal head, or where there is pathologic anatomy of the fetal head, e.g., hydrocephalus, the femur length may be the only accurate measurement available.

Here is a text from a card holding an ultrasound print given to expectant parents:

[On outside of card:] *Our **Welcome** Addition* [On inside of card:] *My Picture Taken On:* ____ *My Expected Arrival Date:* ____ *Possible Girl Names:* _____ *Possible Boy Names:* _____ PLACE ULTRASOUND PRINTOUT HERE

Although as Gertrude Stein famously asserted, "a rose is a rose is a rose," it is much less clear that "an ultrasound is an ultrasound is an ultrasound" even though the creators of many such documents rather clearly intended to create uniformity. Concurring with Weber that written files are a core feature of bureaucracy, Dorothy Smith observes that "the formality, the designed, planned and *organized* character of formal organizations depends heavily on documentary practices, which co-ordinate, order, provide continuity, monitor and *organize* relations between different segments and phases of organizational courses of action" (1984, 66). Although the work of documents seems to depend on their capacity to produce uniformity and to make actors interchangeable, we know that we cannot take organizational records as objective accounts; they are instead accounts that are locally produced and used. Both the universal and the local are present simultaneously. As Stefan Timmermans and Marc Berg (1997) discover, although medical protocols produce only a local universal, the attempt at universality remains important. Despite this tension between the locally historic and the timeless universal, there is little doubt that documents and organizational routines deeply affect what we see and therefore what we do.

But if much of the work on documents, routines, and schemas has investigated the relation between universal and local, another accomplishment of documents remains to be examined. In documentary practices, the "deliberate stripping away of context detaches and obliterates social relationships" and erases human agents (Espeland 1993, 299). But this feature of documentary practices is not quite as universal as has been imagined. Some uses of documents, even documents created by organizations for official purposes, do just the opposite. So just as Viviana Zelizer's (1989) account of "special monies" examines what at first blush seems to be a quaint anomaly, so I here examine another countertrend, the persistence of another social form in a process often considered to be the hallmark of the modern bureaucratic project. Just as people continue to earmark money, the most liquid of assets, giving it a social as well as an economic meaning, so people use the documents and categories of bureaucracies for very unbureaucratic purposes. And just as many organizations collaborate in the creation and protection of special monies, so organizations participate in this nonbureaucratic use of their documents and forms, a clue that this alternative social form may not be an anomaly. Rather, I would argue, the bureaucratic uses of documents often assume that someone outside the organization will have a rather different relation to the subjects of their documents.

Smith is absolutely right that something important has happened when a "young man" roughed up by the police comes to be categorized as a "juvenile" and to have a police record. As she notes, "This is a form of social consciousness that is a property of organization rather than of the meeting of individuals in local historical settings" (1984, 62). But however it is transformed in the official record, for family, friends, and perhaps even the witness, the event retains its local, historical character, and the record becomes part of the young man's biography. The documentary practices of police and courts, including charging offenders and releasing them to family members, are intertwined with the quite different practices of families and friendship groups in which people continue to treat the offender as a "young man" who has an ongoing relationship to a social group. Likewise, as I will argue subsequently, hospital practices are intertwined with quite different family practices, and hospitals could not continue to treat critically ill infants as cases if parents did not see them as babies and ultimately take them home.

I begin by arguing that we should see routinization, indeed bureaucracy, as a variable and by noting that objects can be understood simultaneously as cases and as individuals with biographies, depending on who is doing the looking, which documents they use, and what they do with those documents.

···

Variations in Routinization

The forms, checklists, routines, scripts, organization charts, procedural requirements, and face-to-face meetings of organizations all attempt to focus the attention and activity of participants. Sociologists vary in their assessments of the effects and efficacy of these organizational efforts. Participants sometimes find routines helpful—Robin Leidner's (1993) trainees found scripts a useful crutch as they learned how to sell insurance. Sometimes participants find routines irksome—faculty are irritated by administrative routines requiring them to file annual vita updates. And sometimes routines seem counterproductive—engineers working on the O-ring problem were hindered by the "bureaupathology" of the space shuttle program

(Vaughan 1996). Although there may be some consensus that routines, protocols, and scripts provide an important template for novices and increase the likelihood that key tasks will be performed, organizational participants can be overwhelmed by routines. As Diane Vaughan (1996) demonstrates, when too many items are considered "critical" (for instance in NASA's Flight Readiness Review), the value of such a designation diminishes. After a certain point routines cease to focus attention. Apparently it is only an intermediate level of scripting or routinization that focuses attention, just as only an intermediate level of uncertainty makes games fun (Goffman 1961). Too many rules and too little uncertainty make the game boringly predictable; too few rules and too much uncertainty decrease incentives for mastery. Likewise, too much routinization is mind-numbing and dulls attention, but with insufficient routinization participants receive too few cues about where to direct their attention. These unanalyzable "numerous inpouring currents" result in the "blooming buzzing Confusion" described by William James (1984, 21).

Sociologists suggest that routines, scripts, protocols, and institutions shape attention and structure thinking (see, e.g., Berger and Luckmann 1967; DiMaggio 1997; Giddens 1984; Meyer and Rowan 1977; papers in Powell and DiMaggio 1991; Scott 1995; Zucker 1983) and that documents in particular induce selective attention, create a method for interpreting the particulars of a situation, and through the use of categories hide some facts while making others observable (see especially Smith 1984, 67; Carruthers and Espeland 1991).[1] Further, sociologists no longer think of culture as integrated and coherent but instead argue that culture is more appropriately thought of as fragmented, more like a toolkit that people draw on than a unified system that constrains them. Less attention has been given to how these two observations fit together (Bourdieu 1990; Sewell 1992; Swidler 1986; note the parallel here to Chomsky's work on the generativity of grammar). If institutionalized practices and routines are some of the "stuff" in the cultural toolkits that people might draw on, we should then be asking what about these practices and routines contributes to the fragmentary nature of culture. An examination of situations that vary in levels of routinization might tell us something about when and how routines shape cognition and behavior.

Three such situations come to mind: situations so mind-numbingly overroutinized that participants ignore routines, situations so underroutinized that participants must act without much guidance, and situations in which the conflict among institutions requires participants to decide which rules and routines are most appropriate or most compelling. Elsewhere I have shown how institutional competition reduces constraints on the behavior of organizational participants and creates the space for strategic manipulation of organizational routines (Heimer 1999).[2] Here I instead explore an example with varying levels of routinization—the activities of one group highly routinized, those of another much less shaped by routine and protocol—to show how routine and biography function as alternative ways of organizing cognition and shaping behavior. To make this argument I draw on material from a study of the social organization of responsibility for critically ill infants, a study that looks at what happens both in hospitals and in infants' homes.[3] I also show how the different uses of documents by parents and medical staff—parents sometimes treating documents as artifacts or relics, staff treating them as almost exclusively as texts—support different ways of thinking about the infants who are the subjects of the documents. In essence, I take comparison itself as my subject, asking how organizational contexts and documentary practices contribute to variations in the kinds of comparisons people routinely make.[4]

....

One Object in Two Settings

We generally think of children as being mainly the concern of their families, with increasing involvement of other bodies, such as schools, as they mature. Critically ill infants, unlike other newborns, begin their lives as the focus of attention of a team of medical experts as well as of their parents. Occasionally they also receive scrutiny from the legal system, for instance when parents and providers of medical care disagree about treatment. Critically ill infants are thus a good example to use in examining how a single object is thought about and acted upon in multiple settings. The same infant is simultaneously conceived as a patient by the medical team; as a young citizen by attorneys, court-appointed guardians, and judges; and as a child by parents (Heimer and Staffen 1998, 137–77). Further, these settings vary in the degree to which activity is governed by scripts and protocols.

Neonatal intensive care units (NICUs) specialize in caring for the very sickest newborns, including many infants transferred from other hospitals.[5] Although most NICU patients are hospitalized because they are premature, they may instead (or also) have genetically based anomalies (e.g., Down syndrome), have experienced some accident or insult during gestation (e.g., fetal alcohol syndrome), or have been injured during labor or birth (e.g., asphyxiation arising from the separation of the placenta from the uterine wall). Although most babies spend only a few days in the NICU, a few are hospitalized for much longer.

Hospitalized infants are cared for by a large team that includes residents, attending neonatologists, consulting physicians (e.g., surgeons, gastroenterologists); nurses; social workers; nutritionists; phlebotomists; physical, occupational, speech, and respiratory therapists; and X-ray and ultrasound technicians. At the beginning of the hospital stay, parents' participation may be limited to touching and sitting by the baby, discussing treatment plans, and signing consent forms. As discharge approaches, their role grows, and they are taught to administer medications and perform rudimentary therapies, recognize signs that medical help is needed, and modify routine newborn care to accommodate their child's special needs. After discharge home, the parents bear primary responsibility for the child. Depending on the child's condition, parents may be assisted by home-health nurses and may spend many hours taking the child to appointments with doctors, therapists, and child-development specialists.

Clearly the hospitalized infant and the infant who has gone home are not *identical* entities. One is well enough to be cared for at home (albeit perhaps in a home transformed into a medical outpost); the other is so sick that hospitalization is essential. Nevertheless there is substantial continuity in the object (the infant), coupled with a sharp discontinuity in the way activities are organized and documented, and this is what merits investigation.

....

Documenting Intensive Care

Even before birth a baby has a bureaucratic existence. With few exceptions, the documentary life of a contemporary American fetus begins in the obstetrician or midwife's office with the mother's prenatal visits. An expected date of birth is calculated from information about the mother's last menstrual period; data about head circumference and other skeletal features are recorded during ultrasounds; maternal blood and urine are collected and analyzed; the fundus is measured; and the condition of the cervix and the adequacy of the birth canal are assessed during episodic vaginal exams. Relevant parts of the mother's medical history (Has she had rubella? What were the outcomes of previous pregnancies?) are discussed and noted in her medical record.

The transition to a separate physical existence is marked with the creation of a separate documentary existence—a new medical record is born! When a newborn is admitted to a neonatal intensive care unit (NICU), one of the staff's first acts is to create a file. The first pieces of information for the baby's file often come from outside—from the hospital's labor and delivery ward, a perinatal service that has overseen a high-risk pregnancy, or a referring hospital. But the NICU also immediately begins to produce its own documents—the shell of the record (a binder, color-coded dividers, face sheet, identification code) and information from the admitting officer's physical examination of the baby. Almost immediately other care-givers step in. Consulting physicians investigate and treat maladies that fall into their specialty; speech therapists address difficulties with the coordi-nation of suck and swallow; social workers help family members adjust to the NICU, prepare parents to take home a "damaged" newborn, and alert staff to familial idiosyncrasies.

Each care provider documents his or her activities in the medical record kept at the nursing station, nursing notes kept at the patient's bedside, more ephemeral forms on NICU clipboards, or personal notes retained by the caregiver. The vast majority of these documents are semipublic records, boundary objects (Bowker and Star 1999) used to coordinate the activities of a large and transient team. Nurses must be informed about doctors' orders and must coordinate their activities so that babies are fed, bathed, changed, and given medical care around the clock. Physicians need access to nursing data about vital signs and patient response to medica-tions. New residents rotating onto the unit need accurate but succinct information about the patients for whom they are now responsible.

These documents help to create an understanding of a newborn as a medical problem appropriately compared with others having similar med-ical problems. Medications are prescribed according to diagnosis, cali-brated to take account of the baby's age and weight. Treatment decisions are based on comparisons of cases—maple sugar urine disease with maple sugar urine disease, Hirschprung's with Hirschprung's. Likewise, insur-ance adjusters decide on appropriate reimbursement by looking at diagno-sis, treatments, medications, and hospital days.

Creation of the documents is part of the standard operating procedures of hospitals. And indeed the documents often are quite standardized. Care providers fill in blanks and check boxes on a wide variety of forms describ-ing the patient's condition—the "Retinopathy of Prematurity Ophthalmic Examination Record," the "Observation Sheet for Neonatal Behavioral Assessment," the forms used to estimate gestational age by assessing six indicators of neuromuscular maturity and six indicators of physical maturity, and the neonatal versions of the charts commonly used by pediatricians to track height, weight, and head circumference. Forms are also used to request tests and document the times at which vital signs were read, treatments given, or medications administered. In some units, the nursing record provides space to note whether parents visited and what they did during those visits. One textbook supplies a "Bereavement Follow-Up Tool" for documenting postmortem discussions with parents.

Even when no forms give them shape, inscriptions nevertheless are quite rigidly formatted. An "off service note" by a resident moving to another rotation is quite similar to other off service notes and quite different from consulting physicians' notes. A couple of points of commonality among these inscriptions: written in formal language with the abbreviations and jargon of the writer's "discipline," they are opaque to outsiders; because damning information about staff performances is not highlighted, mistakes can be discerned only by insiders who know what *should* have happened or can recognize a subsequent action as an antidote.

The *preserved* documents on a hospitalized newborn can easily fill one or more loose-leaf binders. My *notes* on selected portions of 945 of these medical records fill three and one-half file drawers.

....

Documenting a Family Member's Life

Medical staff are not the only ones creating or using documents; family documentation often begins prenatally as well. For instance, the first photographic entry in a contemporary baby book may be an ultrasound printout, although some baby books offer a place to preserve the positive home pregnancy test. Parents may keep notes on when they first felt the baby move or save the slips of paper on which they recorded contractions. After their child's birth, parents produce and store a wide variety of documents and other artifacts: photographs, videotapes, birth announcements, records of "firsts," notes jotted on calendars, clippings of hair, the identification bracelet from the hospital. These documents and artifacts are particularly important in creating the sense of time and historicity that undergirds our understanding of how a human life unfolds.[6]

Because their child's life hangs in the balance, NICU parents may be especially likely to produce extensive documentation. Their record of their feelings and actions and the baby's responses may be a valiant effort to construct the personhood of a fragile creature too unformed or jarringly unusual to seem fully human. In discussing these matters, parents could be brutally blunt (e.g., confiding that their tiny newborn really looked like "lunchmeat"), but were just as likely to be outraged at hospital staff's callous comments (e.g., "I'd forget him if I were you"). Baby books were often pulled out during interviews; once I was pressed to take a videotape home with me. Somewhat less frequently I was shown files of correspondence with insurance companies, or hands were waved in the direction of a shelf where the voluminous records were stored.

These documents, like those of the providers of medical care, are to some degree shaped by templates. The information packet, often supplied by NICU social workers or parent support groups, may include a baby book.[7] When the baby book designates a space for the ultrasound print or early footprints and blanks to be filled in with length and weight, parental attention is directed to assembling these components. But although some elements in the medical record and the baby book are the same, the use made of them is quite different. The baby book does not direct parents to inspect the ultrasound print for evidence of a neural tube defect.[8] Rather, the ultrasound print is valued as physical evidence of a baby's existence, a trace of the earliest part of its biography, a prop that supported the beginnings of its relationship with family members. This distinction between text and artifact, tool and relic, data and memento is especially clear in the preservation of objects, such as the crib card or tape used to measure a baby's length, by those who have experienced pregnancy losses and for whom these objects serve as "proof" of the baby's existence and the woman's motherhood (Layne 2000).

Parents create and appropriate documents to construct and sustain biography and the continuity of human relationships, while medical care providers create and appropriate documents to construct and sustain a medical case. Parents often say that they are creating documents to present to their child later, sometimes simply to explain what happened, sometimes to document their unwavering commitment. Documents and other artifacts must be understood as elements of a conversation. And just as hospital documents are not transparent to outsiders unfamiliar with medical vocabulary or the hospital division of labor, so family documents must be understood in the context of their creation and use. The balance between oral and written in family life is different than in the hospital (as would be expected given legal and organizational mandates for documentation). Moreover, the production of documents and other artifacts are more extensive in some families than in others.

Interestingly, parents and staff each contribute to the other's documentary efforts. Parents supply information about their own medical history and the pregnancy, and offer their observations during and after the hospitalization. But usually parents do not believe that they can themselves make use of this quasi-medical information. The information becomes the property of the hospital, although parents can, with difficulty, get copies of the record. Similarly, staff offer parents ultrasound prints and other souvenirs of the NICU. Nurses may color cartoons to post at the infant's bedside to mark such milestones as the one-month birthday, signing these posters with affectionate greetings from the "NICU aunts." But such decorations ultimately go home with the family—they are not the property of "NICU aunts."

The use of bureaucratic documents in the creation of biography is by no means restricted to NICU patients. Bureaucracy and home collaborate in the production, refinement, and transport of school records, assignments, awards, and annual photographs whose role as the raw material for biographical collections is widely acknowledged. Later in life, expired passports (especially those with numerous visa stamps), ticket stubs, and exotic matchbooks are collected to mark the uniqueness of biography. Bureaucracies dependent on middle-class clients understand that souvenirs build *joint* biography (i.e., customer loyalty) and offer ample artifacts. An ice cream parlor whose Christmas treat comes in a dated souvenir mug hopes that children will clamor to return each year. Organizations do occasionally fail as producers of artifacts for biographical collections, and this may be especially likely when they and their clients have divergent understandings of the situation. For instance, if a picturesque church thinks of itself exclusively as a religious institution serving a local congregation, it may neglect to produce postcards for tourists. An enterprising artist or photographer may fill this void. More to the point, hospitals and governments, who see themselves as responsible for patients and citizens, produce only scant documentation on miscarriages, stillbirths, and neonatal deaths. Documents that closely mimic those that would have been produced by official sources are now supplied by others or created by parents themselves (Layne 2000). Pregnancy loss support groups advise parents on how to find sonographic images of fetuses at the same stage as their own and offer do-it-yourself baptismal and "recognition of life" certificates.[9]

Moreover, documents and artifacts are used to mark the boundary between medical and familial spheres and to remind participants to adjust to that boundary. The pink and blue crib cards inscribed with babies' names remind staff that in discussions with parents the child should be referred to as "Lindsay," not "baby girl Jones." Further from the boundary, less effort is made to conceal patienthood with an attractive veneer of personhood. "Lindsay" becomes "this product of a 27 week gestation" in the medical record or letter to the pediatrician who will care for "Lindsay" after discharge. Likewise, parents are expected to acknowledge their infant's patienthood in the NICU. Whether or not gowns reduce infection rates (and research now suggests that they do not), donning a gown reminds parents that their child is a *patient* and the NICU is not their living room. As the nurses record bath and feeding times on their charts, observant parents learn that although *babies* may get fed on demand, *patients* are fed and bathed on a schedule and parents who hope to participate must be present at the appropriate time. The clipboard and form make this official policy rather than just some nurse's whim. Many parents have trouble locating the boundary between patienthood and babyhood. They understand that medications and therapies are "medical" and so governed by hospital protocols, but often are surprised that feeding, bathing, and even cuddling may fall within the medical domain. When the elements to construct biography and relationship are so sparse, parents may feel that they need to stake a clear claim to the remaining turf.[10]

One contrast, to which I return later, is important. The connection between the creation and use of the documents of biography in the home is looser than the connection between production and use of the documents of intensive care in the NICU. Like the forms of an intensive care unit, baby books may function as templates for creating some of the documents of biography, and outside organizations routinely supply the materials (souvenirs, photographs, objects that become family relics or mementos) for these collections. But the "instructions" offer advice only on how to create the documents, not on how to use them once they've been produced. Organizations like schools, doctors' offices, and insurers may also supply copies of documents with the suggestion that they be filed "with your records." More rarely help is offered in creating forms for use in the home. Business forms can be purchased in office supply stores; computer programs can assist in creating legal forms (e.g., wills) and financial records; curriculum consultants advise home-schooling families on the creation of records that will satisfy educational bodies. But these exceptions are instructive. Routinization is most common in the intersection of biography and bureaucracy (where bureaucracies take the lead) and in the creation of some kinds of memorial documents (where the demand from families is especially strong). Although hints and fragments can be uncovered (e.g., in parenting guides), the documentary practices of biography are not very fully institutionalized.

....

Routinized NICUs and Less Routinized Homes

It may seem odd to claim that NICU life is predictable and orderly given that the tiny patients receive around-the-clock monitoring precisely because their needs and responses are *unpredictable*. NICU life is not *naturally* predictable and orderly. Its orderliness and predictability are important social achievements, produced by a stunning array of mechanisms that standardize, regulate, coordinate, and ensure the appropriateness of the health care team's activities. Given the number of discrete operations performed each day and the number of people performing them, one might expect frequent confusion. Yet such confusion only occasionally occurs. Elaborate records and charts help people track who is caring for which child, what has been accomplished, and what remains to be done.

The predictability of NICU life contrasts sharply with the unpredictability of the homes to which infants are discharged. Infants' homes are more variable than NICUs on three key dimensions. First, parents vary more than hospital staff in their preparation and willingness to care for a sick baby. NICU staff have undergone rigorous training and have chosen the work of caring for sick babies. Parents may or may not have chosen to have any baby, let alone a sick one. Parents can rarely match hospital staff in knowledge of child development or medicine, but some parents assimilate information and acquire new skills quickly and eagerly, while others become only marginally competent in caring for their child.

The social control system of a home is also more variable than that of an NICU. In NICUs a clear hierarchy governs and supervises the activity of staff. The co-presence of multiple workers sharply reduces error, and the social control infrastructure (including alarm systems that signal emergencies as well as reminding workers to change IVs or reposition monitor leads) makes social control less obtrusive and less costly and therefore probably more consistent. Moreover, the need for oversight is reduced because in conforming to requirements imposed by templates, workers discipline *themselves*.[11]

Some households are characterized by intensive "supervision" by other family members; very little supervision occurs in others. A few families post charts to help them track whether medications have been administered and temperatures taken. When an infant requires home nursing, routines that approximate those of a hospital incorporate nurses into the household and coordinate the team's work, though some of the administrative apparatus is located outside the household in a home-health agency. In contrast, households with only a single adult member may have fewer mechanisms for supervision and provide fewer incentives for doing a good job. The variance in social control is thus higher in homes than in NICUs, with families providing both the most careful monitoring on the widest variety of indicators, at the high end, and inadequate care with little monitoring and consequently little hope of corrective action, at the low end.

Finally, there is less variability in the congruence of interests between NICU care providers and infants than between parents and infants. NICU staff have only a brief and even then intermittent responsibility for their patients and are therefore less passionately concerned with their futures. Parents, in contrast, have a long-term stake in their own children. Parents and family also are more likely to find that their interests conflict with the child's. Former NICU patients are especially likely to stretch their parents to the limit. If they need special care, are unusually fussy, or become ill often, these children can cost their parents more than other babies while giving back less. NICU staff may also become exasperated with a baby, but they can leave the baby behind at the end of the day, reminding themselves that a particularly burdensome infant will leave the unit soon.

Although it wouldn't be fair to say that NICUs are identical and completely interchangeable, then, they are much more uniform than households. Such uniformity is built into the design of health care, and provides a foundation for the construction of hospital routines. In contrast, the variability of households makes it difficult to import preexisting routines (such as medical protocols) without reshaping the household in fundamental ways. Nurses are interchangeable in ways that parents are not.[12] Families' approaches to child rearing varied much more than did NICU approaches to medical treatment. For instance, I found substantial variation in levels of planning of the child's daily activities, approaches to discipline, and time spent in interaction with the parents or other adults rather than children. Parents varied in concern about growth and weight gain, language acquisition and cognitive development, social skills and relations with peers, physical coordination, and attainment of developmental milestones. Although concern was not perfectly correlated with objective indicators of illness or disability, some parents were thoroughly convinced that their child would have a tough time and need considerable medical intervention; others were intensely worried about early indications that something was amiss; and still others thought that their child would be fine.

NICUs place a premium on responsibility—on thoughtful adaptation of medical protocols to the needs of individual patients, on making sure that each tiny patient gets the care and attention he or she needs—and this responsibility is ensured by documentation, routines, protocols, and reviews. Even when they cannot be applied without modification, protocols supply a starting point for NICU activity; the information needed to adapt protocols to individual circumstances comes from the documents continually produced by NICU staff.

In contrast to responsible doctoring and nursing, responsible parenting is less dependent on a foundation of routines and (especially) documentation. During the baby's hospitalization, parents are required to fit into hospital routines and their visits, learning, and performance of childcare and medical tasks are duly assessed and recorded. After discharge, parents often discover how hard it is to get all the work done. In addition to the usual round of diapers, feeding, baths, and laundry, these parents have to give medications, do the physical therapy exercises, and take the baby to follow-up appointments (so trained medical personnel can continue to perform the more complicated medical tasks), often at distant locations. To be sure, a few families go through elaborate planning for the transition, but many households suddenly discover that those hospital charts and forms serve an important purpose and begin to create their own tracking tools. Parents have to decide for themselves—without protocols to guide them and make order out of the chaos—what to track and record. Some families modify their documentary practices so that they now serve two purposes. Although they continue to document their child's budding personhood, some parents also begin to create proto-records that mimic those of the hospital, noting details about feeding, responses to medication, or modifications in physical therapy routines that work particularly well. But although they create some infrastructure and produce some routinization, these family records are more attentive to the idiosyncrasies of a particular child than to the medical literature's suggestions about what is important, and so retain a strongly biographic character.

Case and Biography as Alternative Ways to Organize Information

How organizational participants think about and treat "cases" depends on the other cases they have encountered (see, e.g., research on social control decision-making by Emerson 1983; Gilboy 1992; Sudnow 1965). The processing of one case may set precedents for others deemed similar; the treatment of one case depends on which others compete with it for resources; and what seems normal or aberrant depends on how a case is classified and which cases have preceded it. Medical protocols and medical routines focus on infants as *patients* appropriately compared with other patients. Important aspects of care are determined by whether the baby is classified as premature or drug-exposed or is believed to have some genetically based syndrome.

At the most basic level, classification shapes the allocation of medical attention and resources. If a unit has only two ECMO (extracorporeal membrane oxygenation) machines, ECMO patients compete for these scarce resources. An ECMO patient (whose blood is oxygenated by a machine) requires the full attention of a nurse and a technician; a "feeder and grower" shares a nurse's time with several other infants. Classification also determines which specialists and therapists will consult on a case. Infants who have symptoms of necrotizing enterocolitis will be seen by a gastroenterologist. A speech therapist assesses whether and how a baby with a cleft palate can be bottle-fed. If those expert in treating a rare condition are located in another hospital, the infant may be transferred. And the advice parents receive about when and whether their baby is likely to come home depends on how the infant is classified. Some conditions are invariably fatal; other life-threatening conditions sometimes can be successfully treated.

Patients often fall into several categories (e.g., preemie with spina bifida). They may develop new symptoms and have to be reclassified. Classification is often difficult, and the staff's understanding of medical problems may be shaped by the cases they have encountered. The "normal" preemie of one unit can be quite different from the "normal" preemie of another. The preemies of a suburban NICU often are the products of multiple gestations (resulting from fertility treatments); inner-city hospitals more often receive preemies whose mothers are especially young and poor.

Classification focuses attention on some features of the case rather than others. Usually, this is good because it leads care providers to see the relation between symptoms and to deal with more serious problems first. Sometimes, though, cases are misclassified, and attention is then inappropriately focused. Symptoms that are unexpected may be misinterpreted or overlooked. Julius Roth (1972), for instance, discusses what happens when emergency room patients are perfunctorily classified as inebriated. A case orientation also tends to be associated with abstraction (so the infant is discussed as a diseased body part or congenital malformation), with privileging of some types of evidence (e.g., test results as compared to nurses' visual inspection), especially when it comes from respected sources (e.g., physicians rather than patients or family members) (Anspach 1988, 1993).

But such case-based analysis depends on an infrastructure (forms and documents, medical protocols, trained personnel to sort, analyze, and act on cases) and a stream of cases to be classified and compared. Case streams are common, in well-established areas, but do not exist in cutting-edge fields with rapid technological innovation, when an established technology is being extended to a new environment, or when something is being done or encountered for the first time. Rather than comparing quite similar cases, analysts then must work with partial precedents, reason by analogy, and splice together bits and pieces of relevant information. Social systems may not facilitate efficient use of fragmentary information; they may instead construct barriers, impose rules, or merely label or standardize information in ways that make it seem foreign in other settings.[13]

Families do not typically think of their child as a "case."[14] For almost all NICU parents, this is a new experience. Although they can sometimes draw on the experiences of other families in parent support groups, parents are one-shotters who lack the case base that allows repeat players to make comparisons. To say that families do not analyze their child as a case does not mean that they do no analysis, however. Rather than comparing their infant with other infants, parents for the most part compare the infant with itself. Rather than comparing one case with another, they compare current experiences and observations with previous experiences and observations of the *same* case. Coherence is supplied, then, by biography rather than by categorization. But what does it mean to say that coherence comes from an analysis of biography rather than an analysis of similar cases? And how is the process of creating cognitive coherence different when biography is the source of coherence?

As a first stab, let me suggest three important differences. Although both biographical and case analysis are supported by conceptual scaffolding, in biographical analysis, a larger proportion of the conceptual edifice is created by the analyst rather than being received from others. A basic understanding of childhood and child-rearing practices is meager cognitive scaffolding compared with the basic science, system of categories, diagnoses, medical data, and supporting bureaucratic forms that undergird the medical care of a hospitalized infant. Although we can assume that all parents have some cultural tools for thinking about children, some have a more elaborated and others a more restricted conceptual scheme. Such differences, not surprisingly, shape what parents see when they spend time with their child.

Second, because much of the task is to understand the unique properties of an entity (here, a child) and to interpret current events in the light of past and anticipated events, firsthand contact is more important to biographical than to case analysis. How parents think about what they experience depends on the conceptual scheme with which they start (for instance whether they think infants can communicate with their parents). Here conception and perception tend to reinforce one another. Different parents see different things when they look at infants, with the result that their conceptual schemes evolve differently.

Finally, because biographical meaning is more about relations among (different) objects than comparisons of (similar) objects, analysis is more likely to focus on how the object acts on and shapes the world than on how external forces have acted on the object. In biographical analysis, the object becomes a subject, an agent. Personalities are ascribed to infants. Some infants are described as "fighters," others "decide that it's time to go." Such attributions introduce continuity into observations of and interactions with the child, helping the parent to construct a unique relationship with the child and to sustain commitment in bleak circumstances. I illustrate these points in what follows.

Because parenthood is less bureaucratized than medical care, the relation of documents and forms to cognitive processes is somewhat different in the two. Documents are not always used for their intended purposes, of course—they may languish unused or be used for entirely different purposes. Nevertheless, in bureaucracies documents usually are created to support specific tasks, while the documents that support biographical analysis are less likely to have been assembled for analytic purposes. Of course families do keep some records for narrow tasks, and some of these records may be stored in baby books along with the locks of hair and so brought out for display and discussion at family gatherings. But it seems farfetched to suggest that biographical documents are assembled by parents with the single-mindedness that nurses and doctors evince in compiling medical records.

Cognitive Conceptions, Biography, and the Construction of
Relationships with Critically Ill Newborns

Although parents arrive at the NICU with a simpler set of concepts than
those with which the medical care-providers are equipped (many parents
are, after all, new to parenthood as well as to NICUs), their understandings
of what a child is and what their infant needs shape their interactions with
the infant. Ralph LaRossa and Maureen Mulligan LaRossa (1981) argued
that gendered patterns of childcare arose from difference in mothers' and
fathers' understandings of infants' status as persons. Although fathers were
comfortable leaving the baby in the crib for long periods while they did
other things, mothers felt compelled to interact with the child. For fathers,
they argue, the infant was an object; for mothers the infant was already a
person, capable of real interaction and entitled to many of the interactional
courtesies extended to other people. A parallel argument runs through
Alice Rossi and Peter Rossi's (1990) study of gender differences in inter-
generational contact. They show that gender differences in care-providing
are largely accounted for by differences between men and women in emotional expressiveness. Men who were more likely to discuss feelings with
other people resembled women in their patterns of contact and helping,
while women who were less emotionally expressive resembled men in having less contact and providing fewer services across generational lines. This
suggests, then, that feminine socialization in emotional expressiveness is
one, though likely not the only, route to empathetic interaction.

The mothers I interviewed were somewhat more likely than the fathers
to think of the baby as a person, able to experience pain and to interact
(Heimer and Staffen 1998, 299–305). Quite a few parents describe interaction with the child as central to their feelings of attachment. Eye contact
and touch were especially important, and they felt they communicated
when the baby met their eyes or squeezed their finger. Occasionally parents even went so far as to say what message they felt the baby was communicating. Describing the first time she saw her daughter, one mother
noted that she "had her eyes open and like looked right at me and like 'Hi,
Mommy' you know, and the one hand was even out, you know, and it was
just kind of like 'Hi, Mom, hi Mom, I'm going to be okay.'" One father
reported that right after delivery, "She looked, it's like 'Dad, what's going
on?' She was holding my finger, holding on to it real tight . . . just looking
at me, and I was looking and I was crying." A few parents also reported on
what they tried to communicate back to the child. One mother felt that her

daughter was appealing for help: "She seemed to know me, and she kept . . . trying to look at me and—this is the hardest part—she would roll her eyes back and forth, like this, desperate: 'Get me out of here.' And . . . she was begging me to help her." The mother responded by explaining to the baby that she was her mother, describing their home, and assuring her that this wasn't what life was going to be like. "I figured that for her to survive we had to make it clear to her that she had to fight and stay with it and not think that this is what she was created for." While some of this is undoubtedly parental projection, it should not be dismissed. Such projection helps parents construct the humanness of infants, and was more likely to occur among those parents who thought of the newborn as being already a person equipped with interactional skills and other human traits and capacities. Such reports are also notable for the evidence they provide about conceptions of parental duties and how these depend on the budding relationship with the child.

Although causal direction is difficult to untangle here, some parents claimed that their feeling of attachment and their sense of their child as a person arose very directly from these interactions:

> I mean I don't remember feeling like this strong attachment. I remember feeling more duty bound because like I said he was paralyzed [by drugs], he was asleep, his eyes were closed. It wasn't until that first time I saw him in the hospital and he like looked at me that, all of a sudden, it was like, "Oh my God," you know, there he is. Because I mean he just might as well have been a cardboard picture. . . . Like I said when I first saw him he was just a cardboard frog.

After this experience, she reported, her "maternal instincts" kicked in. This same woman insisted that hospital staff members use the baby's name because "I just wanted to make sure that he was a person."

How do parents learn to do biographical analysis? A middle-class parenting "curriculum" is one source of this framework. Parents who read books or magazines about pregnancy or child rearing were more likely to talk about developmental milestones, to track and sometimes record information that allowed them to assess whether their children were "behind" and needed additional stimulation to help them "catch up." Such parents heard early cries as crude attempts to communicate, connected early babbling with subsequent speech, and read the baby's reactions as signals about its state. Believing it was their job to help children with developmental tasks, they provided appropriate toys and structured situations to elicit repetitions of behaviors that would help children develop. These cognitive categorizations of infants' behavior were especially likely to occur in well-educated people and were more common among women than men. Both men and women noted that women read more about pregnancy, child development, and their child's specific condition. As the family leaders in this area, women looked for useful materials, highlighted sections for fathers to read, and kept notes about their child.

Though the middle-class "curriculum" gave people a rudimentary grasp of developmental milestones and equipped them to assess their child's progress, this basic framework could also be supplied and reinforced in other ways. Spending time in a NICU exposed parents to the talk of nurses, physicians, and therapists, who taught them how to "read" their babies. For instance, staff might comment on physical indicators of stress or relaxation in the baby, noting how these were apparently correlated with parental presence. Physical therapists, working to increase the range of an infant's movement might also point out indicators of whether the baby was "organized" or could "console" itself. With this new conceptual scheme, parents looked at their child in new ways.

Finally, this enriched understanding could arise from the obligation to report on the baby's progress (see, e.g., Layne 1996). If a child is sufficiently ill to require intensive care, a perfunctory response to parents' questions about how the child is doing—for example, that the baby is "fine"—will not satisfy most families. But the obligation to report depends on there being a partner or extended kin group that wants the news. Parents who are married and embedded in an extensive kin network are more likely to be called on to describe their own observations of the baby and to transmit physicians' and nurses' reports. In interviews, married mothers gave more detailed descriptions of the children's hospitalization than unmarried mothers. Apparently, the obligation to report to a spouse increased the acuity of parents' observations.

A cognitive framework may prime parents to notice things about the baby—to assemble the components for a biographical analysis. But a cognitive framework must be *used*. Without observation of the child, a cognitive framework can only create an abstract understanding of the infant's situation. Contact with the child is also crucial in creating the sort of positive emotional reaction that shapes our preferences (Zajonc 1980) and that seems to explain why even brief contact with a "victim" makes experimental subjects more likely to offer help (Latané and Darley 1970; see also Mynatt and Sherman 1975; Rutkowski, Gruder, and Romer 1983).

These variables that predispose parents to see infants as people rather than as objects work in tandem with variables that influence contact and the creation and use of documents. Mothers are somewhat more likely than fathers, and married somewhat more likely than unmarried parents, to visit their hospitalized infants (Heimer and Staffen 1998, 71–75). And it was mainly mothers who kept journals and collected and stored souvenirs of the baby's hospitalization. Causation is transparently circular here. Parents who visit are more likely to see things that reinforce their view of their baby as fully human. But those who already think of the baby as a person are more likely to visit—and to tell interviewers that they felt obligated to visit because their presence was crucial to the baby's well-being.

Finally, parents who felt they had a unique tie to their baby often believed that this tie gave them special obligations. Some parents (particularly mothers) said the baby "knew" them—for example, recognizing their voices from prenatal exposure—and suffered during their absence (e.g., because a source of comfort was missing). More commonly, parents worried that in their absence the baby would be treated as just another patient. By virtue of their unique attachment, parents saw themselves as having a special obligation to make up for the deficiencies of case-based understandings of their child's needs.

Although the ideologies, observations, emotional responses, and cognitions of parents may not arise from anything as concrete as prescribed organizational routines, they are rather clearly supported by the routinized practices of families or larger groups. When parents say that the mother reads the parenting books, discusses them with her husband, and highlights sections for him to read, they are telling us about a household routine that refines parents' conceptual categories and so increases the acuity of their observations of the child. Routines that bring the parents into contact with the child (e.g., visiting every evening after work), require collection of information about the child (e.g., telephoning before going to bed, keeping the baby book), or necessitate discussion of that information with others (e.g., transmitting telephoned news to the other parent) support attentiveness to the child's experience. Although many of these routines for acquiring information about child development, for reporting and assessing observations about the child, and for "creating" the child's personhood are especially common in couples, they can and do exist in other relationships.

In essence I am arguing that the construction of the child as a person undergirds parental commitment to meeting the child's needs, and that this constructive process is no more automatic than the process of constructing a medical case. Whatever one may think of its historical accuracy, Philippe Ariès's (1962) argument that childhood is a relatively recent invention provides a salutary reminder that humanness is a social product. Other scholars have also documented the historical shift in our views of children (see, e.g., Boli-Bennett and Meyer 1978; Pollock 1983; Skolnick 1975; Zelizer 1985). Contemporary and historical debates about when life begins and about alleged biological differences between the sexes and races provide similar evidence of the social construction of humanness.[15] The construction of humanness, whether it be the humanness of women, people of color, or premature babies, is supported by props that emphasize individuated responses and relationship with others. As evidence of familial ties, names, birth announcements, family pictures, clothing and other gifts from friends and relatives reconfirm precarious humanness.

The humanness of NICU babies is thus produced by uncertain and imperfect social technologies, precariously routinized, and adopted and supported by only some of the parents, their families, and friends. This particular social product—the humanness of a fragile child—takes the form of a biographical narrative of a unique person already embedded in a family. Biography is constructed in conversations with family and friends, in conferences with physicians, social workers, nurses, and discharge planners. It is in these oral conversations that the narrative of a child's life is worked out—parents talk of their desire for a child; of how this pregnancy compared with others; of siblings' sympathy, anger, or bewilderment; of the contributions of the child's unique personality to its medical course; of their hopes and plans for the child.

In these conversations, documents and artifacts bolster the construction of biography—not just by supplying evidence of the child's fragility or the nature of the illness, but also by offering a text from which glimmers of personality and relationship can be extracted. Some might see only tubes and machines in NICU photographs, but as constructors of their child's biography, parents guide naive observers to more subtle and sophisticated readings. The baby's eyes are always open in the photographs, they might point out. That's not the case with all NICU babies, but *she* always had her eyes open; she was from the beginning so interested in the other people around her. Or they might note how the child's fingers entwine the nasogastric tube. He always hated that tube, pulled it out whenever the nurse turned her back. That was characteristic of him from the beginning; always a fighter, he was, and that determination was probably what got him through. In such discussions and with such materials is the uniqueness of a child constructed.

....

Does It Matter How Coherence Is Constructed?

The contrast I have drawn between cognition and activity structured by an analysis of streams of cases versus streams of events in a biography is of course overdrawn. While physicians and nurses may think of a patient as "the product of a 28 week gestation" and so compare the infant with other preemies or as "a hypoplastic left heart" appropriately compared with other heart patients, they also look at family medical histories, information about the pregnancy, and the infant's medical course. Similarly, although parents do not mainly reflect on how their baby compares with other 28-weekers or heart patients, they do sometimes draw on such categorical schemes. "Parenting professionals" make their living reminding parents of the dangers of relying too heavily on biographical analysis. The classification of children as infants, toddlers, preadolescents, adolescents, or young adults introduces some modicum of comparison into parental thinking. Nevertheless, the dominant mode of thought is different in families than in infant intensive care units. And subsequent uses of case archives are different from the uses of archives constructed with biographical materials. The archives of a hospital are usually opened only if the patient becomes a legal case, a "mistake" to be reviewed, or a "subject" in research. Filled with props to support claims about identity and relationship and mark transitions, the archives of a biography are reopened for weddings, funerals, birthdays or other anniversaries, and holidays. They are revisited when people reflect on their commitments to each other.

I have argued that the effect of institutions decreases when people are so overloaded with routines that routines become noise rather than signal and cease to focus attention, when institutional competition undermines the capacity of institutions hegemonically to shape cognition or action, or when routines are underdeveloped or absent on the fringes or beyond the boundaries of formal organizations. Critically ill infants are "boundary objects" (Bowker and Star 1999), seen simultaneously as patients by hospital staff working in carefully structured NICUs and as children by the parents who cross the boundary into the NICU and ultimately take the babies home. Medical records and other NICU documents likewise are boundary objects, employed by both staff and parents as they strive in quite different ways to create some sort of cognitive order from the disorder (as Star 1985 argues is the case for all scientific work). Medical workers compare the infant patient to other infant patients, making causal arguments about what they know of human biology and the effects of medical and pharmacological interventions. Parents construct the causal unity of the child over time, looking to the child's past and future for explanations.

Sociologists have shown how comparing a case with other cases in a stream shapes its treatment. When a case is seen in isolation, analysis must proceed by scrutinizing the case itself. Rather than being imposed, categories emerge in conversations and attempts to act. Lacking precedents, parents treat their child as an individual. The vaunted particularism of parents may thus arise as much from the absence of the universalizing pressures of a preexisting case base as from the tendency of parents to value the uniqueness of their child.

The comparison of parents and hospital care providers also suggests that different kinds of innovation may arise from these two ways of organizing cognition. In NICUs, innovations are so plentiful as to be obvious even to casual visitors. A surgical mask might double as a diaper and Cabbage Patch doll clothes function as the layette for especially tiny preemies. More subtle, and no doubt more important, are the innovations in feeding regimes, development and adaptation of pharmacological fixes for neonates, and refinement of surgical techniques for babies weighing less than a kilo.

Major innovations also occur in homes, but because these innovations tend to be child-specific, they are less likely to be written up in a medical journal or diffused through a protocol. One mother created activities to provide sensory stimulation for her blind and ventilator-dependent daughter. Another, attempting to help her daughter overcome a tendency to tilt her head to one side (because her muscles had been stretched when her neck was used as a site for ECMO), exhibited considerable ingenuity in overcoming the child's resistance to the exercises. Exploiting the baby's natural curiosity, this mother placed her on her belly in the stroller with her head facing the direction they were walking. To see the sights the child had to hold her head up. Her neck muscles quickly became strong and the tilt disappeared.

It is in the fine-tuning of therapeutic interventions, the disciplined modification of routines to increase the odds of success, that NICUs and homes differ most. NICU research projects, facilitated by a division of labor that allows people to specialize in one set of tasks or one part of the anatomy, are the most extreme form of this disciplined search for solutions. As they repeatedly encounter the same problems, staff can see what works and what doesn't. Working as members of a team with regulatory requirements for adequate staffing, NICU personnel are encouraged to reflect on and learn from their experience and to share their discoveries with interested and informed colleagues. Adaptations of routines—within the constraints established in protocols—are thus extremely likely.

While the expertise of NICUs is *extensive* (its staff includes experts in many fields), the expertise of homes is *intensive* (parents are experts about a particular child). In a structured work setting with an elaborate division of labor, the constants are the workers and their encounters with particular *tasks*. When the division of labor is less elaborate and work is less governed by routine, continuity instead comes from *relationships* between workers and the persons or objects with which they work. In one situation, innovations are more likely to entail fine-tuned adaptations to smooth or improve performance of a specific task; in the other, they are more likely to be oriented to the particular person or object that is being worked with.

Physicians are sometimes accused of treating by the numbers. Poring over medical records and engrossed in discussions with colleagues, they may scarcely glance at the patient. In contrast, parents spend little time with the numbers and many hours with the baby. Unaware of the contents of the medical record and unable to interpret test results anyway, their best hope is to develop a parallel analysis grounded in visual and other sensory information. Structured less by a medical conceptual scheme than by an evolving understanding of the child (sometimes but not always systematized in a written record), those untutored observations occasionally pay off. And when they do, it is partly because parental observations, freed from the discipline of the bureaucratic template, are more likely to have retained some key piece of contextual information that would have been ruled irrelevant. Physicians can be as ignorant of the information available to parents as parents are of medical information. Just as ethnographers may see something that participants can't by juxtaposing information from disparate sources (Dauber 1995), so parents' observations may truly tell medical staff something new.[16]

Although NICU innovation is grounded in specialization in a particular procedure or aspect of physiology, and household innovation is based on specialization in a particular child, in both cases innovation requires specialized knowledge and careful collection of data. Recorded in medical records or parents' journals, staff and familial observations are clearly about the same events and the same child, but each may omit information that is vital to the other's understanding of the situation. Because the creation and review of medical documents are so important to the practice of medicine, medical innovation is much shaped by the nature of information included (and excluded), by the privileging of some types of data and some categories of observers. Innovation is grounded in narrow definitions of roles for health care providers. More diffuse understandings of obligations to the child undergird parental creativity. In asserting that parental innovation is based on biographical analysis, I am suggesting that parents are constructivists in two senses. They construct the infant as a person with interpersonal competence—an important step, given the motivational effects of relationships. But as innovators, parents move beyond constructing an account to constructing the life itself. The act of constructing the story shows parents that they have some small measure of control over how the story unfolds.

I have suggested that biographical analysis tends to be emergent, the result of an inductive process, while the analysis of case streams tends to be more deductive, arising from comparison of each new case with an imposed and preexisting cognitive system embodied in routines and protocols. In biographical analyses, documents supply the analytic context by fashioning an account of a person's past and hinting at a future; in case analyses, in contrast, the function of documents is to structure comparisons across cases. In addition, though, in biographical analyses, the objects under scrutiny are more likely to be permitted an active role in the creation of the cognitive edifice. To some degree this observation may be artifactual, arising from a study of cognitions about human beings. Nevertheless, because some parents expect that infants can give and not just "give off" information (to use Erving Goffman's [1969] words), they look for and attempt to interpret rudimentary communications from their child and give such data pride of place. The causal continuity of biography requires a sentient human being to be meaningful, and a first task of biographical analysis is to construct that being when it has only a precarious existence. To say that a biographical analysis focuses on and adapts to the stream of events and reactions associated with a particular case is not to say that this is always wise. Baroque adaptations to individual idiosyncrasies may lead to silly and time-consuming rituals of the sort one sees among animals adapting to the reinforcement schemes of behaviorist experiments, or, more consequentially, to ignoring serious symptoms that are "normal" for that person (as occurred with several infants in this study).

Finally, a brief note on the degree to which action is constrained or enabled. People need some cognitive structure to give them the tools to make sensible observations. Without a conception of the child as a person, parents do not look for and see the child's human response to pain or comfort. Without some understanding of neural tube defects, physicians would not know what they were seeing in a sonogram. But order is hard to impose on an unruly and evolving object such as a child. Under such circumstances, a rudimentary cognitive structure that encouraged people to reexamine the evidence would encourage deliberative rather than schematic thinking (DiMaggio 1997; D'Andrade 1995), and a strategic rather than unthinking use of cultural tools might be especially appropriate. If parents really do think that there is "never a dull moment" and that their young children "keep them hopping," it may be because schema failure is so common in parenting that biographical analysis works better than the more constraining routine-based analysis of case streams that is supported by hospital documents and forms.

....

NOTES

This chapter benefited enormously from the helpful and enthusiastic comments of Annelise Riles, the conference organizer, and other conference participants. Barry Cohen, Robert Dingwall, Jennifer Earl, Wendy Espeland, Linda Layne, Kate Linnenberg, Mitchell Stevens, and Arthur Stinchcombe also offered insightful suggestions. Rebecca Culyba was a critical reader and superb research assistant. I thank the Research School of the Social Sciences, Australian National University, where I began the paper, and the American Bar Foundation, where I finished it, for supporting my work. Warm thanks as well to the Lochinvar Society.

1. For similar observations in other fields, see work by anthropologist Mary Douglas (1986), political scientist Aaron Wildavsky (1987), and psychologist Jerome Bruner (1990).

2. Other kinds of constraints on cognitive processes also may be lessened by the give and take of social life. For instance, the powerful framing effects observed in the laboratory by psychologists such as Daniel Kahneman, Paul Slovic, and Amos Tversky (1982) may be less important in ordinary social life, where people may contest a received frame rather than just accepting it (Heimer 1988).

3. That research is reported most fully in Heimer and Staffen 1998. Other findings are presented in Heimer 1992 and Heimer and Stevens 1997. The study was based in two neonatal intensive care units where my research assistants and I observed, gathered information from medical records, and interviewed staff members and parents. Despite my use of the singular pronoun in this essay, then, it was often "we" rather than "I" who collected and analyzed the data.

4. Heimer (2001) extends this argument about comparison to markets and legal systems. In very different ways, Marilyn Strathern (this collection) and Don Brenneis (this collection) also take comparison as their subject.

5. Other social science studies of NICUs include pieces by Renée Anspach (1993), Fred Frohock (1986), and Jeanne Guillemin and Lynda Holmstrom (1986).

6. Annelise Riles (this collection) and Hirokazu Miyazaki (this collection) also point to the link between documents and our sense of time.

7. *Footsteps* (Wilson 1983), for instance, is a combination baby book and introduction to neonatal intensive care.

8. In the days before ultrasound prints were offered to parents, technicians nevertheless differentiated between what *they* and *parents* were supposed to take from the image. "He's waving to his papa!" my Norwegian midwife exclaimed as she examined the ultrasound image of my son. (The papa didn't buy the story, but shed tears nonetheless.)

9. In the example of pregnancy losses, substitutes assist the construction of selves that are not fully supported by the bureaucracy. The production of such substitutes contains a reproving suggestion that a humane organization would have supplied the documents. When the identity being constructed is an oppositional one, bureaucratic forms may still be adopted, but their use is more subversive and ironic than reproving. For instance, although the "autograph" produced by prisoners in Papua New Guinea adopts the form of an official "warrant cover," it constructs the biography rather than the case of the prisoner, emphasizing ties to family and friends (both within the prison and outside) and personal idiosyncrasies (see Reed, this collection).

10. Many parents affix family pictures to the infant's bed; a few bring in audiotapes of family members' voices. Wishing to give their premature twins the olfactory experience of home, one family put cotton balls soaked with bacon grease and lemon juice inside the isolettes.

11. See Brenneis (this collection) on the structure of reference report forms and the rhetorical devices employed by the National Science Foundation to discipline proposal reviewers.

12. It would be hard to exaggerate the variability among the families I studied. Several families had no regular income beyond welfare; other families had two employed parents. Some parents had completed only elementary school; others had postgraduate degrees. Some parents were married; others were divorced or had never married. Some families had only a single child; others had many children, not always from the same union. Some mothers did all the childcare; in other families fathers, grandmothers, or hired helpers pitched in. Families also varied in the material objects they possessed. All of the households had televisions, but some had no telephone (important for summoning emergency medical help).

13. Heimer (1985) and Diane Vaughan (1996) comment on how social barriers inhibit the importation and use of "foreign" information. In analyzing rate setting in a new area of insurance (Norwegian North Sea oil fields), Heimer shows that information can be *technically* sufficient without being *socially* sufficient. Diane Vaughan shows how "structural secrecy" made information unavailable for prob-

lem solving (in the space shuttle O-ring case) even in an organization that was conscientious about circulating information.

14. Similarly, Joseph Schneider and Peter Conrad (1983), Kathy Charmaz (1991), and Arthur Frank (1995) suggest that people who are ill or disabled do not identify themselves primarily as "patients."

15. These assertions about the humanity of various categories of people typically are arguments in support of actions (e.g., enslaving or freeing nonwhites). One could argue that in the case of NICU patients, they often also are "performative" acts in that their effect is to bring into (social) being something that did not really exist before. For an analysis of constative and performative acts in the creation of political entities, see Bonnie Honig's (1991) discussion of Hannah Arendt's and Jacques Derrida's readings of the American Declaration of Independence.

16. It is this insight about the difference between case and biographical reasoning that undergirds the individualist branch of the home-schooling movement with its attention to tailoring education to the abilities and learning styles of individual children (Stevens 2001). Homeschoolers condemn schools as organizations that manage children not as individuals but as cases. Constructing the individualism of children, Mitchell Stevens notes, requires intensive attention from others, usually mothers. Homeschoolers remind us that there is no "average child," a sentiment endorsed by many parents of NICU graduates.

....

REFERENCES

Anspach, Renée R. 1988. Notes on the Sociology of Medical Discourse. *Journal of Health and Social Behavior* 29(4): 357–75.

———. 1993. *Deciding Who Lives*. Berkeley and Los Angeles: University of California Press.

Ariès, Philippe. 1962. *Centuries of Childhood: A Social History of Family Life*. Trans. Robert Baldick. New York: Vintage.

Berger, Peter L., and Thomas Luckmann. 1967. *The Social Construction of Reality: A Treatise in the Sociology of Knowledge*. New York: Doubleday.

Boli-Bennett, John, and John Meyer. 1978. The Ideology of Childhood and the State: Rules Distinguishing Children in National Constitutions, 1870–1970. *American Sociological Review* 43:797–812.

Bourdieu, Pierre. 1990. Structures, *Habitus*, Practices. In *The Logic of Practice*, trans. Richard Nice, 52–65. Stanford: Stanford University Press.

Bowker, Geoffrey C., and Susan Leigh Star. 1999. *Sorting Things Out*. Cambridge: MIT Press.

Bruner, Jerome S. 1990. *Acts of Meaning*. Cambridge: Harvard University Press.

Carruthers, Bruce G., and Wendy Nelson Espeland. 1991. Accounting for Rationality: Double-Entry Bookkeeping and the Rhetoric of Economic Rationality. *American Journal of Sociology* 97(1): 31–69.

Charmaz, Kathy. 1991. *Good Days, Bad Days*. New Brunswick, NJ: Rutgers University Press.

D'Andrade, Roy G. 1995. *The Development of Cognitive Anthropology.* New York: Cambridge University Press.

Dauber, Kenneth. 1995. Bureaucratizing the Ethnographer's Magic. *Current Anthropology* 36(1): 75–86.

DiMaggio, Paul. 1997. Culture and Cognition. *Annual Review of Sociology* 23:263–87.

Douglas, Mary. 1986. *How Institutions Think.* Syracuse: Syracuse University Press.

Emerson, Robert M. 1983. Holistic Effects in Social Control Decision-Making. *Law and Society Review* 17(3): 425–55.

Espeland, Wendy. 1993. Power, Policy, and Paperwork: The Bureaucratic Representation of Interests. *Qualitative Sociology* 16(4): 297–317.

Frank, Arthur W. 1995. *The Wounded Storyteller: Body, Illness, and Ethics.* Chicago: University of Chicago Press.

Frohock, Fred M. 1986. *Special Care: Medical Decisions at the Beginning of Life.* Chicago: University of Chicago Press.

Giddens, Anthony. 1984. *The Constitution of Society: Outline of the Theory of Structuration.* Berkeley and Los Angeles: University of California Press.

Gilboy, Janet A. 1992. Penetrability of Administrative Systems: Political "Casework" and Immigration Inspections. *Law and Society Review* 26:273–314.

Goffman, Erving. 1961. *Encounters: Two Studies in the Sociology of Interaction.* Indianapolis: Bobbs-Merrill.

———. 1969. *Strategic Interaction.* Philadelphia: University of Pennsylvania Press.

Greene, Michael F. 1991. Fetal Assessment. In *Manual of Neonatal Care*, 3rd ed., ed. John Cloherty and Ann R. Stark, 34–46. Boston: Little, Brown.

Guillemin, Jeanne H., and Lynda L. Holmstrom. 1986. *Mixed Blessings.* New York: Oxford University Press.

Heimer, Carol A. 1985. Allocating Information Costs in a Negotiated Information Order: Interorganizational Constraints on Decision Making in Norwegian Oil Insurance. *Administrative Science Quarterly* 30(3): 395–417.

———. 1988. Social Structure, Psychology, and the Estimation of Risk. *Annual Review of Sociology* 14:491–519.

———. 1992. Your Baby's Fine, Just Fine: Certification Procedures, Meetings, and the Supply of Information in Neonatal Intensive Care Units. In *Organizations, Uncertainties, and Risk*, ed. James F. Short Jr. and Lee Clarke, 161–88. Boulder, CO: Westview.

———. 1999. Competing Institutions: Law, Medicine, and Family in Neonatal Intensive Care. *Law and Society Review* 33:17–66.

———. 2001. Cases and Biographies: An Essay on Routinization and the Nature of Comparison. *Annual Review of Sociology* 27:47–76.

Heimer, Carol A., and Lisa R. Staffen. 1998. *For the Sake of the Children: The Social Organization of Responsibility in the Hospital and the Home.* Chicago: University of Chicago Press.

Heimer, Carol A., and Mitchell L. Stevens. 1997. Caring for the Organization: Social Workers as Front-Line Risk Managers in Neonatal Intensive Care Units. *Work and Occupations* 24:133–63.

Honig, Bonnie. 1991. Declarations of Independence: Arendt and Derrida on the

Problem of Founding a Republic. *American Political Science Review* 85(1): 97–113.

James, William. 1984. *Psychology: Briefer Course.* Cambridge: Harvard University Press.

Kahneman, Daniel, Paul Slovic, and Amos Tversky, eds. 1982. *Judgment under Uncertainty: Heuristics and Biases.* Cambridge: Cambridge University Press.

LaRossa, Ralph, and Maureen Mulligan LaRossa. 1981. *Transition to Parenthood.* Beverly Hills, CA: Sage.

Latané, Bibb, and John M. Darley. 1970. *The Unresponsive Bystander.* New York: Meredith.

Layne, Linda L. 1996. "How's the Baby Doing?" Struggling with Narratives of Progress in a Neonatal Intensive Care Unit. *Medical Anthropology Quarterly* 10(4): 624–56.

———. 2000. Baby Things as Fetishes? Memorial Goods, Simulacra, and the "Realness" Problem of Pregnancy Losses. In *Ideologies and Technologies of Motherhood*, ed. Helena Ragone and France Winddance Twine, 111–38. New York: Routledge.

Leidner, Robin L. 1993. *Fast Food, Fast Talk.* Berkeley and Los Angeles: University of California Press.

Meyer, John W., and Brian Rowan. 1977. Institutionalized Organizations: Formal Structure as Myth and Ceremony. *American Journal of Sociology* 83(2): 340–63.

Mynatt, Clifford, and Steven. J. Sherman. 1975. Responsibility Attribution in Groups and Individuals: A Direct Test of the Diffusion of Responsibility Hypothesis. *Journal of Personality and Social Psychology* 32:1111–18.

Pollock, Linda A. 1983. *Forgotten Children: Parent-Child Relations from 1500 to 1900.* Cambridge: Cambridge University Press.

Powell, Walter W., and Paul J. DiMaggio, eds. 1991. *The New Institutionalism in Organizational Analysis.* Chicago: University of Chicago Press.

Rossi, Alice S., and Peter H. Rossi. 1990. *Of Human Bonding.* New York: Aldine.

Roth, Julius A. 1972. Some Contingencies of the Moral Evaluation and Control of Clientele: The Case of the Hospital Emergency Service. *American Journal of Sociology* 77(5): 839–56.

Rutkowski, Greg. K., Charles. L. Gruder, and Daniel Romer. 1983. Group Cohesion, Social Norms, and Bystander Intervention. *Journal of Personality and Social Psychology* 44:545–52.

Schneider, Joseph W., and Peter Conrad. 1983. *Having Epilepsy.* Philadelphia: Temple University Press.

Scott, W. Richard. 1995. *Institutions and Organizations.* Beverly Hills, CA: Sage.

Sewell, William H., Jr. 1992. A Theory of Structure: Duality, Agency, and Transformation. *American Journal of Sociology* 98(1): 1–29.

Skolnick, Arlene. 1975. The Limits of Childhood: Conceptions of Child Development and Social Context. *Law and Contemporary Problems* 39(3): 38–77.

Smith, Dorothy. 1984. Textually Mediated Social Organization. *International Social Science Journal* 36(1): 59–75.

Star, Susan Leigh. 1985. Scientific Work and Uncertainty. *Social Studies of Science* 15:391–427.

Stevens, Mitchell L. 2001. *Kingdom of Children: Culture and Controversy in the Home Schooling Movement.* Princeton, NJ: Princeton University Press.

Sudnow, David. 1965. Normal Crimes: Sociological Features of the Penal Code in a Public Defender Office. *Social Problems* 12(3): 255–76.

Swidler, Ann. 1986. Culture in Action: Symbols and Strategies. *American Sociological Review* 51(2): 273–86.

Timmermans, Stefan, and Marc Berg. 1997. Standardization in Action: Achieving Local Universality through Medical Protocols. *Social Studies of Science* 27(2): 273–306.

Vaughan, Diane. 1996. *The Challenger Launch Decision.* Chicago: University of Chicago Press.

Wildavsky, Aaron. 1987. Choosing Preferences by Constructing Institutions: A Cultural Theory of Preference Formation. *American Political Science Review* 81(1): 3–21.

Wilson, Ann L. 1983. *Footsteps.* Philadelphia: Wyeth Laboratories.

Zajonc, Robert B. 1980. Feeling and Thinking: Preferences Need No Inferences. *American Psychologist* 35(2): 151–75.

Zelizer, Viviana A. Rotman. 1985. *Pricing the Priceless Child.* New York: Basic Books.

———. 1989. The Social Meaning of Money: "Special Monies." *American Journal of Sociology* 95(2): 342–77.

Zucker, Lynne G. 1983. Organizations as Institutions. In *Research in the Sociology of Organizations,* ed. Samuel B. Bacharach, 1–47. Greenwich, CT: JAI Press.

4

Documents of Documents

Scientists' Names and Scientific Claims

Mario Biagioli

THIS CHAPTER IS ABOUT the name of the scientist, how it functions, and the kinds of relationships it documents. When we think about documents in science, what comes to mind most naturally is scientific evidence: measurements, diagrams, photographs, statistics, inscriptions of particles' trajectories, fossils, specimens, and so on. A scientist's name printed at the beginning of an article does not stand out as an obvious document, but may be taken to be part of the post facto packaging of a claim, of what happens when a claim is written up, made public, and credited. Names may seem to belong to an article's prefatory matter, the part of the text one glances at on the way to its real content.

I argue, instead, that authors' names are crucial documents of the workings of the economy of science, of the process through which scientific documents are constituted. Names work as the hinge between two apparently distinct moments of scientific production: the development and the publication of a claim. Such a demarcation plays a constitutive role in the economy of science as it strives to separate "natural" scientific facts from the "social" actors who produce them, but is also fraught with unavoidable tensions. By following the scientists' names around we can trace some of these tensions while also mapping the ways in which different communities connected to science (scientists, administrators, policymakers, and science studies practitioners) attach different documentary value to these names.

What counts as a document or evidence to a scientist is quite different from the range of materials that science studies practitioners look at to understand how science works. In its attempt to map out the processes through which scientific authority is constructed, science studies considers a far broader spectrum of documents than the evidence scientists present in their publication to buttress their claims.[1] Teasing out the many components of their "authority," their genealogies, and how they are brought and held together in specific contexts has directed the field toward increasingly detailed analyses of scientific practices and their documentary traces—documents that may have looked like trivia to previous generations of historians and especially philosophers of science who based their work on the analysis of printed sources only. The documentary trend associated with sociocultural analyses of scientific practices has expanded the range of relevant documents not only to manuscript drafts of printed texts, but everything from laboratory notebooks, instruments, correspondence, gifts and exchanges, patent applications, illustrations, accounting documents, citation patterns, literary, artistic, and filmic representations of science, oral histories, institutional ecologies, water-cooler gossip, architectural layouts of laboratories and departments, and a slew of other objects and texts.[2]

It is, then, surprising to see that such an empirical focus on the construction of scientific authority seems to have left scientific authorship by the wayside.[3] Scientists' names have not been ignored by science studies, but have been usually treated within macroanalyses of citation patterns (which tend to treat names as "units" to be counted, not as documents to be opened up), or as traces of struggles for scientific authority.[4] Most science studies practitioners (and, I believe, quite a few scientists) would say that the presence of a name on the byline of a science article should not be taken at face value as a document of the agency behind the production of that text. Rather, the presence of a name, or its position in relation to other names, could be the result of negotiations, tactical decisions, or even usurpations. But while such a perspective has added complexity to our understanding of how credit and agency may or may not be attached to names, it has also upheld the apparently natural connection between agency and authorial names while acknowledging that social negotiations or power play may modify, amplify, or distort such a connection in specific contexts. Even those who have proposed epistemological models in which nonhuman actants, instruments, or cyborgs share agential roles with social actors have not expanded their critiques of human agency to include what may be its very epitome: authorship.[5]

In sum, while science studies has moved in different directions toward questioning traditional notions of agency and individual creativity that had helped construe scientific authorship as an unproblematic concept, in the end it has stopped short of opening up the authorship "black box." That is, the field has not asked the fundamental question of how and why the name of the scientist has become the fundamental unit in the "metrology" of both professional credit and epistemological responsibility of academic science. This essay looks at the space between the scientific text and the scientist's name to understand the unstable relations that link and constructs them as two different kinds of documents: one of nature, the other of human agency.

....

Scientists' Mundane Philosophy of Their Names

Authors' names are of a peculiar kind, and not only in science. At first they seem to have a simple relation to the work, like cause to effect or, as it is often said, like father to son.[6] But with a little more work one can see that the kinship relation moves in other directions too: personal names (even some that do not refer to actual people) become authors' names by being linked to works they are deemed to (but may not) have produced. The kinship between authors and works is a tricky two-way street, if indeed "street" is the appropriate model.

Legal and literary studies have analyzed the inherent instability of authorship—an instability that affects the relationship between the authors' name and the work, but also extends to the categories of "author" and "work" themselves (e.g., Foucault 1977, 113–38; Coombe 1998; Rose 1993; Hesse 1991, 1789–1810; Woodmansee and Jaszi 1994; Gaines 1991; Boyle 1996). Many of the tensions surrounding the name of the author take different shapes in relation to the specific kinds of work and the economies in which they circulate. For instance, the scientist's name functions very differently from the name of the literary author or the patent holder. This follows from the way "work" is specifically defined in academic science, and from the kinds of functions (credit and responsibility) that are attached to the author's name within that economy. As I will discuss in a moment, an academic scientist is not an author who can hold intellectual property rights on his or her claims, nor one who receives credit by producing artifacts (novels, music, paintings, and so forth). The author function in science is related to intellectual property law, but that relation is one of complementarity, not analogy.

It is not completely clear why a scientific text would need to have an author, as one could argue that the epistemological status of a scientific text ought to be grounded in nature, not in an author's name. However, far from fading in importance or dwindling in number, more and more names are being attached to scientific articles, and their placement order in the byline has become an increasingly complex and contentious issue (e.g., Fye 1990, 317–25; Huth 1990; Strub and Black 1976; Regalado 1995, 25). Furthermore, the recent development of large-scale multiauthorship has added a new important twist (perhaps much more than a twist) to the function of the scientist's name. These days, especially in biomedicine and particle physics, it is not uncommon to find articles with hundreds of authors name listed on them, papers whose authors' byline may take up as much space as the technical part of the text (fig. 4.1). Because of the sheer amount of work entailed by "big science" projects and the corresponding need to bring together different skills within one research team, multiauthorship has become a fact of scientific life.

Quantitative change has triggered a qualitative change that, in turn, has pushed the scientific author-function into unmapped territories. In the last ten years or so, hundreds of articles, editorials, and empirical studies published in scientific journals have tackled the thorny problem of redefining authorship in the context of large-scale collaborations.[7] Much of this literature reflects widespread concerns about the definition of authorial responsibility (not just authorship credit). The embarrassment produced by a series of well-advertised cases of scientific fraud, the extensive finger-pointing and self-exculpations among the coauthors of these publications, and the politicians' growing interest in regulating science have driven the scientists' analyses of authorship as much as their concerns about the distribution of credit in collaborative scenarios (Relman 1983; Engler et al. 1987; Stewart and Feder 1987; Braunwald 1987; Institute of Medicine, Committee on the Responsible Conduct of Research 1989).[8]

The new contexts produced by multiauthorship, I believe, escape much of the traditional theoretical discourse about authorship—a discourse that, despite its analytical power, has been typically constrained by the figure of the single author and the conceptual scenarios it makes thinkable.[9] Current discussions about definitions of authorship developed among scientists, science administrators, editors, and funding agencies do acknowledge the remarkable instability of authorship, but have had little or no use for the tools developed by critical legal scholars or literary critics.[10] This reflects the specificity of the problems connected to scientific authorship as well as the very different division of labor between users and critics of authorship that we find in science and literature or legal studies. While authorship studies outside of science have been mostly the domain of theorists and critics (not authors or consumers), the discourse about scientific authorship has been developed by its very users and producers. The scientists' discourse about authorial names is in and of itself a document of differences between disciplinary economies.

The indigenous discourse about authorship in science was set in motion by practical, rather than theoretical questions. Most of the time, scientists use "authorship" in a very specific, documentary sense: the physical presence of one's name in the author's byline. But as the range of questions spiraled quickly in all directions, the discourse about whose name should or should not appear on a byline has become necessarily more comprehensive and theoretical. Scientists and their administrators started out by confronting issues such as these: How are institutional evaluators and funding agencies supposed to assess the credit to be attached to each name listed in the byline? How is that credit to be weighed according to these names' placement and modalities of order? How does the name of the journal in which an article is published affect the credit to be bestowed on the name of the author? How can readers be sure that those long strings of names are neither too inclusive nor too exclusive? Are senior practitioners given authorship without having done the work, and are junior researchers unjustly denied it? And, if a paper is deemed fraudulent, on whose name should that responsibility fall?

These questions extended seamlessly to other aspects of the system of scientific authorship.[11] For instance, given the specific economy of scientific publications (an economy where the role of the market is deemed to be replaced by that of peer evaluation) should referees and editors share in the author function? Should the referees' names be withheld or published? And what about the names of the so-called ghost writers, professionals who, while not scientists themselves, may take over the writing, that is, the very emblem of traditional authorship? Furthermore, does peer review certify the truth of an article? If not, what can peer review do, and how does it really work?[12] And how is the status of a work modified by the fact that it may have been funded by the private sector? How is the function of the author's name modified by appearing together with another name, that of a pharmaceutical company that sponsored the research?[13]

As the scientists and their administrators try to deal with these issues in a pragmatic, managerial way, it has become increasingly evident that we are no longer just talking about the name of the author (or of several authors), but about many different names (of journals, institutions, editors,

Measurement of the Lepton Charge Asymmetry in W-Boson Decays Produced in $p\bar{p}$ Collisions

F. Abe,[17] H. Akimoto,[39] A. Akopian,[31] M. G. Albrow,[7] A. Amadon,[5] S. R. Amendolia,[27] D. Amidei,[20] J. Antos,[33] S. Aota,[37] G. Apollinari,[31] T. Arisawa,[39] T. Asakawa,[37] W. Ashmanskas,[18] M. Atac,[7] P. Azzi-Bacchetta,[25] N. Bacchetta,[25] S. Bagdasarov,[31] M. W. Bailey,[22] P. de Barbaro,[30] A. Barbaro-Galtieri,[18] V. E. Barnes,[29] B. A. Barnett,[15] M. Barone,[9] G. Bauer,[19] T. Baumann,[11] F. Bedeschi,[27] S. Behrends,[3] S. Belforte,[27] G. Bellettini,[27] J. Bellinger,[40] D. Benjamin,[35] J. Bensinger,[3] A. Beretvas,[7] J. P. Berge,[7] J. Berryhill,[5] S. Bertolucci,[9] S. Bettelli,[27] B. Bevensee,[26] A. Bhatti,[31] K. Biery,[7] C. Bigongiari,[27] M. Binkley,[7] D. Bisello,[25] R. E. Blair,[1] C. Blocker,[3] S. Blusk,[30] A. Bodek,[30] W. Bokhari,[26] G. Bolla,[29] Y. Bonushkin,[4] D. Bortoletto,[29] J. Boudreau,[28] L. Breccia,[2] C. Bromberg,[21] N. Bruner,[22] R. Brunetti,[2] E. Buckley-Geer,[7] H. S. Budd,[30] K. Burkett,[20] G. Busetto,[25] A. Byon-Wagner,[7] K. L. Byrum,[1] M. Campbell,[20] A. Caner,[27] W. Carithers,[18] D. Carlsmith,[40] J. Cassada,[30] A. Castro,[25] D. Cauz,[36] A. Cerri,[27] P. S. Chang,[33] P. T. Chang,[33] H. Y. Chao,[33] J. Chapman,[20] M.-T. Cheng,[33] M. Chertok,[34] G. Chiarelli,[27] C. N. Chiou,[33] F. Chlebana,[7] L. Christofek,[13] M. L. Chu,[33] S. Cihangir,[7] A. G. Clark,[10] M. Cobal,[27] E. Cocca,[27] M. Contreras,[5] J. Conway,[32] J. Cooper,[7] M. Cordelli,[9] D. Costanzo,[27] C. Couyoumtzelis,[10] D. Cronin-Hennessy,[6] R. Culbertson,[5] D. Dagenhart,[38] T. Daniels,[19] F. DeJongh,[7] S. Dell'Agnello,[9] M. Dell'Orso,[27] R. Demina,[7] L. Demortier,[31] M. Deninno,[2] P. F. Derwent,[7] T. Devlin,[32] J. R. Dittmann,[6] S. Donati,[27] J. Done,[34] T. Dorigo,[25] N. Eddy,[20] K. Einsweiler,[18] J. E. Elias,[7] R. Ely,[18] E. Engels, Jr.,[28] W. Erdmann,[7] D. Errede,[13] S. Errede,[13] Q. Fan,[30] R. G. Feild,[41] Z. Feng,[15] C. Ferretti,[27] I. Fiori,[2] B. Flaugher,[7] G. W. Foster,[7] M. Franklin,[11] J. Freeman,[7] J. Friedman,[19] H. Frisch,[5] Y. Fukui,[17] S. Gadomski,[14] S. Galeotti,[27] M. Gallinaro,[26] O. Ganel,[35] M. Garcia-Sciveres,[18] A. F. Garfinkel,[29] C. Gay,[41] S. Geer,[7] D. W. Gerdes,[15] P. Giannetti,[27] N. Giokaris,[31] P. Giromini,[9] G. Giusti,[27] M. Gold,[22] A. Gordon,[11] A. T. Goshaw,[6] Y. Gotra,[28] K. Goulianos,[31] H. Grassmann,[36] L. Groer,[32] C. Grosso-Pilcher,[5] G. Guillian,[20] J. Guimaraes da Costa,[15] R. Guo,[33] C. Haber,[18] E. Hafen,[19] S. R. Hahn,[7] R. Hamilton,[11] T. Handa,[12] R. Handler,[40] F. Happacher,[9] K. Hara,[37] A. D. Hardman,[29] R. M. Harris,[7] F. Hartmann,[16] J. Hauser,[4] E. Hayashi,[37] J. Heinrich,[26] W. Hao,[35] B. Hinrichsen,[14] K. D. Hoffman,[29] M. Hohlmann,[5] C. Holck,[26] R. Hollebeek,[26] L. Holloway,[13] Z. Huang,[20] B. T. Huffman,[28] R. Hughes,[23] J. Huston,[21] J. Huth,[11] H. Ikeda,[37] M. Incagli,[27] J. Incandela,[7] G. Introzzi,[27] J. Iwai,[39] Y. Iwata,[12] E. James,[20] H. Jensen,[7] U. Joshi,[7] E. Kajfasz,[25] H. Kambara,[10] T. Kamon,[34] T. Kaneko,[37] K. Karr,[38] H. Kasha,[41] Y. Kato,[24] T. A. Keaffaber,[29] K. Kelley,[19] R. D. Kennedy,[7] R. Kephart,[7] D. Kestenbaum,[11] D. Khazins,[6] T. Kikuchi,[37] B. J. Kim,[27] H. S. Kim,[14] S. H. Kim,[37] Y. K. Kim,[18] L. Kirsch,[3] S. Klimenko,[8] D. Knoblauch,[16] P. Koehn,[23] A. Köngeter,[16] K. Kondo,[37] J. Konigsberg,[8] K. Kordas,[14] A. Korytov,[8] E. Kovacs,[1] W. Kowald,[6] J. Kroll,[26] M. Kruse,[30] S. E. Kuhlmann,[1] E. Kuns,[32] K. Kurino,[12] T. Kuwabara,[37] A. T. Laasanen,[29] S. Lami,[27] S. Lammel,[7] J. I. Lamoureux,[3] M. Lancaster,[18] M. Lanzoni,[27] G. Latino,[27] T. LeCompte,[1] S. Leone,[27] J. D. Lewis,[7] P. Limon,[7] M. Lindgren,[4] T. M. Liss,[13] J. B. Liu,[30] Y. C. Liu,[33] N. Lockyer,[26] O. Long,[26] C. Loomis,[32] M. Loreti,[25] D. Lucchesi,[27] P. Lukens,[7] S. Lusin,[40] J. Lys,[18] K. Maeshima,[7] P. Maksimovic,[19] M. Mangano,[27] M. Mariotti,[25] J. P. Marriner,[7] A. Martin,[41] J. A. J. Matthews,[22] P. Mazzanti,[2] P. McIntyre,[34] P. Melese,[31] M. Menguzzato,[25] A. Menzione,[27] E. Meschi,[27] S. Metzler,[26] C. Miao,[20] T. Miao,[7] G. Michail,[11] R. Miller,[21] H. Minato,[37] S. Miscetti,[9] M. Mishina,[17] S. Miyashita,[37] N. Moggi,[27] E. Moore,[22] Y. Morita,[17] A. Mukherjee,[7] T. Muller,[16] P. Murat,[27] S. Murgia,[21] H. Nakada,[37] I. Nakano,[12] C. Nelson,[7] D. Neuberger,[16] C. Newman-Holmes,[7] C.-Y. P. Ngan,[19] L. Nodulman,[1] A. Nomerotski,[8] S. H. Oh,[6] T. Ohmoto,[12] T. Ohsugi,[12] R. Oishi,[37] M. Okabe,[37] T. Okusawa,[24] J. Olsen,[40] C. Pagliarone,[27] R. Paoletti,[27] V. Papadimitriou,[35] S. P. Pappas,[41] N. Parashar,[27] A. Parri,[9] J. Patrick,[7] G. Pauletta,[36] M. Paulini,[18] A. Perazzo,[27] L. Pescara,[25] M. D. Peters,[18] T. J. Phillips,[6] G. Piacentino,[27] M. Pillai,[30] K. T. Pitts,[7] R. Plunkett,[7] A. Pompos,[29] L. Pondrom,[40] J. Proudfoot,[1] F. Ptohos,[11] G. Punzi,[27] K. Ragan,[14] D. Reher,[18] M. Reischl,[16] A. Ribon,[25] F. Rimondi,[2] L. Ristori,[27] W. J. Robertson,[6] T. Rodrigo,[27] S. Rolli,[38] L. Rosenson,[19] R. Roser,[13] T. Saab,[14] W. K. Sakumoto,[30] D. Saltzberg,[4] A. Sansoni,[9] L. Santi,[36] H. Sato,[37] P. Schlabach,[7] E. E. Schmidt,[7] M. P. Schmidt,[41] A. Scott,[4] A. Scribano,[27] S. Segler,[7] S. Seidel,[22] Y. Seiya,[37] F. Semeria,[2] T. Shah,[19] M. D. Shapiro,[18] N. M. Shaw,[29] P. F. Shepard,[28] T. Shibayama,[37] M. Shimojima,[37] M. Shochet,[5] J. Siegrist,[18] A. Sill,[35] P. Sinervo,[14] P. Singh,[13] K. Sliwa,[38] C. Smith,[15] F. D. Snider,[15] J. Spalding,[7] T. Speer,[10] P. Sphicas,[19] F. Spinella,[27] M. Spiropulu,[11] L. Spiegel,[7] L. Stanco,[25] J. Steele,[40] A. Stefanini,[27] R. Ströhmer,[7,*] J. Strologas,[13] J. Strumia,[10] D. Stuart,[7] K. Sumorok,[19] J. Suzuki,[37] T. Takahashi,[24] T. Takano,[24] R. Takashima,[12] K. Takikawa,[37] M. Tanaka,[37] B. Tannenbaum,[22] F. Tartarelli,[27] W. Taylor,[14] M. Tecchio,[20] P. K. Teng,[33] Y. Teramoto,[24] K. Terashi,[37] S. Tether,[19] D. Theriot,[7] T. L. Thomas,[22] R. Thurman-Keup,[1] M. Timko,[38] P. Tipton,[30] A. Titov,[31] S. Tkaczyk,[7] D. Toback,[5] K. Tollefson,[19] A. Tollestrup,[7] H. Toyoda,[24]

0031-9007/98/81(26)/5754(6)$15.00   © 1998 The American Physical Society

4.1. Physical Review Letters, vol. 81 n. 26 p. 5754

W. Trischuk,[14] J. F. de Troconiz,[11] S. Truitt,[20] J. Tseng,[19] N. Turini,[27] T. Uchida,[37] F. Ukegawa,[26] J. Valls,[32] S. C. van den Brink,[28] S. Vejcik III,[20] G. Velev,[27] R. Vidal,[7] R. Vilar,[7,*] D. Vucinic,[19] R. G. Wagner,[1] R. L. Wagner,[7] J. Wahl,[5] N. B. Wallace,[27] A. M. Walsh,[32] C. Wang,[6] C. H. Wang,[33] M. J. Wang,[33] A. Warburton,[14] T. Watanabe,[37] T. Watts,[32] R. Webb,[34] C. Wei,[6] H. Wenzel,[16] W. C. Wester III,[7] A. B. Wicklund,[1] E. Wicklund,[7] R. Wilkinson,[26] H. H. Williams,[26] P. Wilson,[5] B. L. Winer,[23] D. Winn,[20] D. Wolinski,[20] J. Wolinski,[21] S. Worm,[22] X. Wu,[10] J. Wyss,[27] A. Yagil,[7] W. Yao,[18] K. Yasuoka,[37] G. P. Yeh,[7] P. Yeh,[33] J. Yoh,[7] C. Yosef,[21] T. Yoshida,[24] I. Yu,[7] A. Zanetti,[36] F. Zetti,[27] and S. Zucchelli[2]

(CDF Collaboration)

[1]Argonne National Laboratory, Argonne, Illinois 60439
[2]Istituto Nazionale di Fisica Nucleare, University of Bologna, I-40127 Bologna, Italy
[3]Brandeis University, Waltham, Massachusetts 02254
[4]University of California at Los Angeles, Los Angeles, California 90024
[5]University of Chicago, Chicago, Illinois 60637
[6]Duke University, Durham, North Carolina 27708
[7]Fermi National Accelerator Laboratory, Batavia, Illinois 60510
[8]University of Florida, Gainesville, Florida 32611
[9]Laboratori Nazionali di Frascati, Istituto Nazionale di Fisica Nucleare, I-00044 Frascati, Italy
[10]University of Geneva, CH-1211, Geneva 4, Switzerland
[11]Harvard University, Cambridge, Massachusetts 02138
[12]Hiroshima University, Higashi-Hiroshima 724, Japan
[13]University of Illinois, Urbana, Illinois 61801
[14]Institute of Particle Physics, McGill University, Montreal, Canada H3A 2T8
and University of Toronto, Toronto, Canada M5S 1A7
[15]The Johns Hopkins University, Baltimore, Maryland 21218
[16]Institut für Experimentelle Kernphysik, Universität Karlsruhe, 76128 Karlsruhe, Germany
[17]National Laboratory for High Energy Physics (KEK), Tsukuba, Ibaraki 305, Japan
[18]Ernest Orlando Lawrence Berkeley National Laboratory, Berkeley, California 94720
[19]Massachusetts Institute of Technology, Cambridge, Massachusetts 02139
[20]University of Michigan, Ann Arbor, Michigan 48109
[21]Michigan State University, East Lansing, Michigan 48824
[22]University of New Mexico, Albuquerque, New Mexico 87131
[23]The Ohio State University, Columbus, Ohio 43210
[24]Osaka City University, Osaka 588, Japan
[25]Università di Padova, Istituto Nazionale di Fisica Nucleare, Sezione di Padova, I-35131 Padova, Italy
[26]University of Pennsylvania, Philadelphia, Pennsylvania 19104
[27]Istituto Nazionale di Fisica Nucleare, University and Scuola Normale Superiore of Pisa, I-56100 Pisa, Italy
[28]University of Pittsburgh, Pittsburgh, Pennsylvania 15260
[29]Purdue University, West Lafayette, Indiana 47907
[30]University of Rochester, Rochester, New York 14627
[31]Rockefeller University, New York, New York 10021
[32]Rutgers University, Piscataway, New Jersey 08855
[33]Academia Sinica, Taipei, Taiwan 11530, Republic of China
[34]Texas A&M University, College Station, Texas 77843
[35]Texas Tech University, Lubbock, Texas 79409
[36]Istituto Nazionale di Fisica Nucleare, University of Trieste, Udine, Italy
[37]University of Tsukuba, Tsukuba, Ibaraki 315, Japan
[38]Tufts University, Medford, Massachusetts 02155
[39]Waseda University, Tokyo 169, Japan
[40]University of Wisconsin, Madison, Wisconsin 53706
[41]Yale University, New Haven, Connecticut 06520

(Received 2 September 1998)

We describe a measurement of the charge asymmetry of leptons from W-boson decays in the rapidity range $0 < |y_l| < 2.5$ using $W \rightarrow e\nu, \mu\nu$ events from 110 ± 7 pb^{-1} of data collected by the CDF detector during 1992–1995. The asymmetry data constrain the ratio of d and u quark momentum distributions in the proton over the x range of 0.006 to 0.34 at $Q^2 \approx M_W^2$. The asymmetry predictions that use parton distribution functions obtained from previously published CDF data in the central rapidity region ($0.0 < |y_l| < 1.1$) do not agree with the new data in the large rapidity region ($|y_l| > 1.1$). [S0031-9007(98)08026-0]

PACS numbers: 13.85.Qk, 13.38.Be, 14.70.Fm

referees, "ghost writers," private-sector sponsors, and public funding agencies) and their complex relations. The multitude of these relations indicates that a scientific publication is not so much a "work," that is, a well-demarcated object produced by one author. Rather it is something whose boundaries are harder to define, something that, while attached to the name of an author, was constituted through the work and resources of many other actors (who, nevertheless, may not be called authors). In sum, the authorial names on an article's byline begin to appear more as the "packaging" of this product, and less as its sole, necessary "causes."

Observers familiar with literary and legal analyses of the author function would notice that the scientists seem to have gone a long way toward deconstructing scientific authorship while still using it almost as a term under erasure. In literature, the mapping out of the many actors behind a text (the papermaker, the font-cutter, the typesetter, the printer, the editor, the publisher, and other works that may have inspired the author) is a move historically associated with critiques of intellectual property rights (Woodmansee 1994). The author is often presented as little more than a convenient legal device developed to rationalize yet another version of the fencing of the commons, this time into privately held intellectual property rights. The mapping of the collective nature of cultural production is seen to expose the problematic logic of intellectual property, and to support arguments for the curtailing of the legal and financial privileges attached to the name of the author as the sole holder of intellectual property rights. In science, instead, we find that the names of the other actors behind the publication of an article are all acknowledged as part of a constructive process (though the modalities of that acknowledgment might be quite complex). In sum, the discourses on the author function in literature and in science are not substantially different in terms of content, but while the former appears to belong to the genre of critique, the latter seems much closer to that of management.

....

Names and Their Geography

These differences can be traced to the different professional ethos of those who produce these discourses, but there are underlying logical distinctions as well. The peculiarity of scientific authorship is that, provided the many actors of the economy of scientific production and publication are attributed an appropriate place, their presence does not weaken, but rather strengthens the role of the author. Instead, in literature (or other fields operating within intellectual property law) the name of the author functions by casting a caesura between the "work" and the "rest"—the public domain whose role must be minimized as much as possible so as to enhance the creative contribution of the author.[14] This caesura is crucial (if problematic) because it is through this that an author's work can be constituted as property and thus generate rewards through its sale or licensing. On the contrary, in science the "rest" is the author's ally, not a nemesis. By not acknowledging other scientists' work in footnotes, or by denying the role of editors and peer reviewers, authors would damage (not increase) the value of their work.[15] This is because a scientific publication does not bring rewards by being sold as property, but by being accepted as true. And the "truth effect" is best achieved by listing all actors and resources as distinctly as possible so as to transform them into many "testimonials." In sum, academic science does not construe the function of the author's name through a dichotomy between the holder of intellectual property rights and the public domain, but breaks up and rearranges such a dichotomy into a series of demarcations between different names. Many of them are people's proper names; others are names of instruments, reagents, institutions, and journals. But all of them are acknowledged while being put in different places and assigned different functions. The scientific author cannot exist as a point of production but only as a distinct link in a network that is extended chronologically and spatially.[16] Its function is maximized by making that link as distinct as possible, while making the chain as long as possible. In this sense, the scientific author is always a coauthor, even when a single name appears in an article's byline.

The extended figuration of scientific agency is clearly inscribed in its publications. If we look at a scientific article as a whole (not only at the "main" body of the text) we see that several of the extended actors' names (sponsors, home institutions, acknowledgees, and the authors of other publications the work draws from) do appear on the same paper, but in different locations, usually printed in different fonts (the acknowledgments section, the footnotes, conflict-of-interest statements, the authors' addresses, and so on). Other actors (editors, reviewers, administrators, policymakers, for example) may not be mentioned in the scientific article itself, but are not erased either. They are simply discussed in other kinds of texts that may still be published in that same scientific journal (though often in other issues) and cast in other genres (the first page, the editorial, the letter to the editor, policy discussions, invited commentaries, or, say, a special issue on peer review). These background actors—the "circumference of authorship," as an editor has aptly put it—are not usually linked explicitly to any of the specific articles published in the journal. But any member of the scientific community who reads these journals on a routine basis (the way a nonscientist would read a daily paper) understands that his or her work counts as a "work" precisely by being constituted within this complex economy of names.[17]

Novels do not carry all this information between their covers, and for good reasons. Their value as commodities (or perhaps even their author's intellectual property rights) would only be damaged by a documentation of the borrowings and collective contributions that went into their production. Usually novels do not even have an acknowledgments page. If they do, it is not about their borrowings from the public domain, but rather about close kin who have more or less suffered the neglect imposed by the allegedly necessary creative isolation of the author—an isolation that is reiterated even when framed within a thankful gesture.[18]

The different function of the name of the author in science and literature is also inscribed in the material appearance of the work. Literary works tend to have covers, but scientific articles do not. A novel is materially contained by two covers (usually decorated to stress the message that "this is a cover"), with the author's name conspicuously printed on one of them. There is a material and functional symbiosis between the name and the covers in that, together, they circumscribe the novel as a singular object and isolate it (materially as well as symbolically) from other literature and, more broadly, from all that stuff called the public domain. Scientific articles, instead, appear in a much less demarcating material packaging. The author's name still separates one article from another, but its demarcating function is much less stark (either because it may appear with a hundred others, or because the reader's eye might focus more on the descriptive title than on the author's name). Furthermore, an article's pagination (uninterrupted by covers) casts it not as an isolated object, but as one product of a discipline (whose news, politics, and debates are clearly laid out in other sections of the journal).

As a genre, the scientific journal (especially the major ones like *Science* or *Nature* that have a weekly schedule) is perhaps closer to a newspaper than to a novel. A newspaper article is separated from other articles reporting other events (though several of them may appear on a same page), and yet they are all framed as the "news of the day" or, as the *New York Times* says, "All the news that's fit to print." The function of the novels' covers is taken up by the daily demarcation of one newspaper issue from the next.

The calendar, not the authorial name, circumscribes the text. These different "cover functions" flag what is in between the two covers in dramatically different ways: in one case we are told we are reading a product of individual creation; in the other we have reports of facts and events. In a sense, the author authors a novel, but the day authors the news.[19] The scientific journal is a hybrid of these two genres. Like the newspaper, the scientific journal casts itself as a weekly slice of science, yet it does not present its articles as reports of events that have just "happened." They did happen, but they happened because they were produced, and produced through a lot of labor and resources. The material appearance of the article inscribes this hybridity. Like a news article (and unlike a novel) a scientific article is part of a larger printed product, but unlike a news report it comes with an apparatus (the long authors' byline, the footnotes, the description of the apparatus and methodology, the acknowledgments, and so on) indicating that it is not just a report of the news of the day, but a product of science.

As a corollary to the discussion of the scientists' own discourse about the function of the authorial name, the notion of scientific authorship as a figuration helps explain why scientists seem able to criticize a crucial category of their economy while holding on to it, if only temporarily. No one talks about the "death of the author" in science, and no one argues that authorship is not their problem and that only "critics" should bother with it. The casting of authorship as a wide (if high-maintenance) figuration seems to allow the scientists to treat it the way they would treat a problematic but wide-ranging scientific theory—a theory that leaks in many spots and yet holds the picture together and therefore should not be dropped unless something better comes along. Paradoxically, the spreading of the instabilities of names in science seems to stabilize their role while making its problems all the more visible. The problems of scientific authorship are seen as anomalies (that is, challenges), not death knells.

....

From Names to Addresses

The image of the coin appears in some of the scientists' analyses of authorship. We are told that, like a coin, authorship has two inseparable sides: credit and responsibility (Rennie and Flanagin 1994, 469–71). Such an emphasis on the inseparability of credit and responsibility hinged on the author's name may come as a surprise, as the issue of responsibility is marginal in authorship studies outside of science—studies that focus almost exclusively on the name as a function of authority, or on the rights of the author.[20] One could say that the emphasis on the nexus between author-ship and responsibility in science is a direct result of the recent visibility of scientific fraud, but the logic and modalities of that nexus predate them. To understand that logic we need to take a roundabout path and look in some detail at how authors' names work as both designators and descriptors.

In "What is an Author?" Foucault argues that the name of the author works like a proper name, but not completely so. Following Searle, he points out that proper names perform more than an indicative function (like, say, a finger pointed at someone). Proper names are not just indicative but also descriptive, as we always attach some additional information to a proper name in order to link it to a specific person (like "Annelise Riles is the person who has edited this volume"). Often the name of the author works like a proper name (as when we say that Aristotle is the author of the *Posterior Analytics*), but it can also function as a label that does not refer to any specific person and yet constitutes a certain body of texts as a unified whole (as in the case of Hermes Trismegistus, the "author" of the Hermetic corpus). Far from being arbitrary, the distribution of these different functions of the author's name reflects the different ways in which regimes of fields and disciplines operate:

> To learn that Pierre Dupont does not have blue eyes, does not live in Paris, and is not a doctor does not invalidate the fact that the name, Pierre Dupont, continues to refer to the same person; there has been no modification of the designation that links the name to the person. . . . The disclosure that Shakespeare was not born in the house that tourists now visit would not modify the functioning of the author's name, but, if it were proved that he had not written the sonnets that we attribute to him, this would constitute a significant change and affect the manner in which the authors' name functions. Moreover, if we establish that Shakespeare wrote Bacon's *Organon* . . . we would have introduced a third type of alteration which completely modifies the function of the author's name. [Moreover], it is altogether different to maintain that Pierre Dupont does not exist and that Homer or Hermes Trismegistus have never existed. While the first negation merely implies that there is no one by the name of Pierre Dupont, the second indicates that several individuals have been referred to by one name or that the real author possessed none of the traits traditionally associated with Homer or Hermes. Neither is it the same thing to say that Jacques Durand, not

Pierre Dupont, is the real name of X and that Stendhal's name was Henri Beyle. (Foucault 1977, 122)

He continues by linking the role of the author's name to the construction of what we called a "work":

> [The author's name] is functional in that it serves as a means of classification. A name can group together a number of texts and thus differentiate them from others. A name also establishes different forms of relationships among texts. Neither Hermes nor Hippocrates existed in the sense that we can say Balzac existed, but the fact that a number of texts were attached to a single name implies that relationships of homogeneity, filiation, reciprocal explanation, authentification, or of common utilization were established among them. . . . We can conclude that, unlike a proper name, which moves from the interior of a discourse to the real person outside who produced it, the name of the author remains at the contours of texts—separating one from the other. . . . The name of an author is a variable that accompanies only certain texts to the exclusion of others: a private letter may have a signatory, but it does not have an author; a contract can have an underwriter, but not an author; and, similarly, an anonymous poster attached to a wall may have a writer, but he cannot be an author. (124)

Foucault then focuses on the function of the author's name in modern scientific texts, and on how that function differs from that of the author in both modern literature and ancient scientific texts. He places the emergence of the modern regime of scientific authorship somewhere in the seventeenth century, around the time of the development of so-called scientific method. In his view, scientific method took over some of the certifying features of the author and reframed the role of his name:

> Texts that we now call "scientific" . . . were only considered truthful during the Middle Ages if the name of the author was indicated. Statements on the order of "Hippocrates said . . ." or "Pliny tells us that . . ." were not merely formulas for an argument based on authority; they marked a proven discourse. In the seventeenth and eighteenth centuries, a totally new conception was developed when scientific texts were accepted on their own merits and positioned within an anonymous and coherent conceptual system of established truths and methods of verification. Authentification no longer required reference to the author who had produced them; the role of the author disappeared as an

index of truthfulness and, where it remained as an inventor's name, it was merely to denote a specific theorem or proposition, a strange effect, a property, a body, a group of elements, or pathological syndrome. At the same time, however, "literary" discourse was acceptable only if it carried an author's name; every text of poetry or fiction was obliged to state its author and the date, place, and circumstance of its writing. The value and meaning attributed to the text depended on this information. (126)

More recent historical scholarship and the current discussions around definitions of scientific authorship have questioned several of Foucault's empirical assertions, though they have not undermined his claim that scientists' names do not function like those of Shakespeare, Pliny, or Hermes Trismegistus.[21] That claim too, however, needs some substantial reframing. In love with his notion of episteme, Foucault was carried away by his belief that the scientific method (the apparent embodiment of science's rules of discursive formation) had supplanted the name of the author as the entity demarcating scientific texts from other kinds of works. Instead, the name of the scientist has always remained crucial. While it no longer needs to be an especially authoritative name like Pliny or Hippocrates (as Foucault had pointed out), it still has to be the name of a specific person, a person with a valid address. The author's name may have become "banal" in modern science, but its role is more crucial then ever.

Foucault focused on the epistemological and authoritative dimensions of scientific texts but missed the fact that responsibility is a constitutive element of the scientific author-function. Curiously, responsibility played a major role in other aspects of his discussion of authorship, as when he claimed, correctly, that before the author had emerged as a category within the intellectual property system, it was construed by the state as the person legally responsible for the content of a text.[22] Books could not be published without the name of the author, of the printer, and the printer's address because the police needed to know on what door to knock if that book was deemed subversive.

Similarly, in today's science, the name is the point around which credit accrues, but it is also the name of the person who is responsible for the content of that publication. Unlike modern literary authors (but like renaissance translators of the Bible) the scientific author needs to have a real name (not a pseudonym), and a real address to be included in the article itself (something we do not see in literary publications). Like Foucault's "Pierre

Dupont," scientific authors can live wherever they please, have blue or brown eyes, be famous or not, belong to whatever nationality, race, religion they happen to belong to. At the same time, the scientist's name has a strong (if remarkably narrow) descriptive function in that it must refer to a *physically traceable body*. To perform its function, the scientific author does not need to be an Author (that is, an auratic entity) but does need to be a point on a geographical map. Similarly, the voice of a scientific text may be most impersonal, but it works only by being directly traceable to a person's name (as opposed to a literary text where the voice of the narrator may sound most personal but is usually uttered by a fictitious character that may bear little or no resemblance to the author of the work). In sum, the name of the scientific author does not need to refer to a special person, but to a specific one. His or her name needs to be as specific as the claims the author produces.

To put it differently, the scientific author is not the creator of a certain text, but functions more like one of the "initial conditions" of a study or an experiment—conditions that may (or may not) be crucial to a given result but need to be specified nevertheless. As a thought experiment, try to think of the author's name and address as the settings of a detector, as the dilution of a certain reagent, as the brand and model of an instrument. This analogy is certainly problematic as one could say that the scientist's identity should have nothing to do with the epistemological status of a scientific claim. And yet, the analogy between the scientist's name and experimental conditions is useful in pointing out that the name must be part of a series of very mundane specificities that, in and of themselves, do not constitute a certain claim as true and yet cast it as a candidate for a true or false statement within the discursive regime of science.

It is precisely because of this string of specificities that a scientific claim can be made "universal" and apparently author-independent (in the same way a "fact" comes to be seen as independent from the instrument that "detected" it only after that instrument is deemed to have been "black-boxed," that is, after it has become epistemologically "banal"). Modern science would see an author's name like "Hermes Trismegistus" as illegitimate because, while high-sounding, it lacks specificity.

....

The Peculiar Economy of Scientists' Names

The unique relationship between scientists' names and the claims attached to them may be better understood by looking at the specific logic of the scientific economy of authorship and how it differs from that of intellectual property law and, more generally, from liberal economy.

In liberal economy, the objects of intellectual property are artifacts, not nature (see Biagioli 1999). One becomes an author by creating something new, something that is not to be found in the public domain. Copyright is about "original expression," not content or truth. If you paint a landscape, you may claim intellectual property (a form of private property) on the painting (the expression), but not on the landscape itself (the content). Scientists, therefore, cannot copyright the content of their claims. Facts (like the landscape that provides the subject of a painting) cannot be copyrighted because they are not the result of the author's original expression, but belong to the public domain. Also, saying that scientists are authors because their papers reflect personal creativity and original expression (the kind of claim one has to make to obtain copyright) would actually disqualify them as scientists because it would place their work in the domain of artifacts and fictions, not truth. Therefore, while researchers (or journals) can copyright scientific publications (i.e., the "form" they have used to express the "facts") and gain some protection against piracy, their rights in these texts do not and cannot translate into scientific credit. In sum, copyright can make scientists authors, but not scientific authors.

Like copyright, patents too reward novelty as they cover "novel and nonobvious" claims. But, unlike copyrights, such claims need to be useful to be patentable. Scientists, then, can become "authors" as patent-holders, but cannot patent theories or discoveries per se (either because they are "useless" by virtue of not having practical applications yet, or because they are about something that belongs to the public domain) (Phillips and Firth 1995, 39–42). While it is increasingly common for scientists (mostly geneticists) to patent what would appear to be natural objects, they make these objects patentable by extracting them from their original state of nature and by packaging them within processes (often diagnostic tests) that are deemed useful or potentially useful.[23] Scientists can patent useful processes stemming from their research, but academic scientific authorship is defined in terms of the truth of scientific claims, not of their possible usefulness in the market. In sum, according to the categories and tools of intellectual property, a scientist qua academic scientist is, literally, a nonauthor.

Moreover, intellectual property is deemed to result from taking as little as possible from the public domain and transforming it into some kind of "original expression." But a scientist is not represented as someone who transforms reality or produces "original expressions" out of thin air, but as a researcher who, with much work, "detects" something specific within nature—the domain of public and "brute" facts. Then, for that finding to be recognized as true, the scientist has to put it back in the public domain (here construed as the public sphere, which includes, but is not limited to, the community of scientists). Although this is a loop that begins and ends in some version of the public domain, fundamental changes take place along the way. The starting point is generic nature, but the result is a specific item of true knowledge about nature. While the production of value in liberal economy involves a movement between two complementary categories (from generic public domain to specific private property), in science the movement is within the same category (the public domain), and it goes from unspecified to specified truth claims.

Both cases involve a transformation from something unspecific to something specific. But if in the case of intellectual property such transition can be legally tracked (as it moves across two different categories), the case of scientific credit is much trickier because the movement from nature and the public domain to a specific true claim about nature does not cross any recognizable legal threshold. As a result, it cannot be legally tracked or quantified monetarily. The unique role of the author's name in science stems precisely from these difficulties. The name becomes the only device left to mark the production of a scientific claim out of nature. It also becomes the only possible tool for marking scientific credit.

The pinning of the epistemological responsibility for a claim on the author's name follows from a similar logic. If a true claim about nature were like an artifact, a novel expression, or a piece of literary fiction, responsibility could be negotiated legally. In market environments, an author's responsibility is usually construed as financial liability. Also, the legally responsible author may not be the actual producer of those claims, but the individual or corporation that paid the producers for their labor or rights in those claims. But this cannot apply to true claims about nature because they are in the public domain—a category complementary to that of property and, therefore, to monetary liability. As a result, the responsibility for scientific claims is made to fall on the scientist who produced them simply because his or her name is the only hook on which the movement from unspecified to specified truth can be pinned.

While intellectual property works through three related but distinct devices (the object of intellectual property rights, the name of the holder of such rights, and their monetary value), science has only the name to work with. The author's name marks the object, designates the person who has produced (and is responsible for) that object, and embodies the credit for its production. This last statement may sound paradoxical, and it probably is. What I am trying to convey through the awkward notion of embodiment is that the name of the scientist becomes something other than the point around which scientific credit accrues. Such a picture would assume there was one thing called "credit" and another called "owner of that credit." But because in science there is neither an owner, nor a property, nor a unit of measurement for such a property, everything (whatever that "everything" is) gets folded into the name (and onto the body attached to that name).

In science, credit is attached exclusively to the author's name, construed as symbolic and nonmonetary, and assigned through peer recognition (reputation, prizes, tenure, membership in societies, and so on) (Bourdieu 1975). Some have argued that science works like a peculiar gift economy (Hagstrom 1982). Furthermore, credit accrues on a scientist's name during his or her career, but each "unit" of credit results from the scientist's ability to produce new claims, that is, to be recognized as the first to have made that specific claim. There is no Coca-Cola and Pepsi-Cola in science. The first "cola" takes all. Credit in science does not come from market shares, but from first discovery (Merton 1973, 294–95, 323).

The use of eponymy in science reflects such a name economy. Discoveries, laws, and theories are sometimes attached to a scientist's name (for example, Boyle's law, Golgi's apparatus, Fermat's theorem, Feynman's diagrams). But these associations indicate neither actual property (as in "this house belongs to Robert Boyle"), nor certify the "authenticity" of a product (like trademarks attached to sneakers or designer clothing). Rather, eponymy works as a form of symbolic capital (because monetary capital or material property cannot translate into scientific authorship). Eponymy usually comes into play only after the scientist's death, strengthening its role as a "monument" rather an acknowledgment of property.[24]

But while one can map in some detail the logic of scientific authorship, the quantification of scientific credit remains elusive.[25] This has to do with two related issues. The first is that scientific credit is defined not as the outcome of an algorithmic procedure but of peer judgment.[26] A claim's empirical basis may be tied to standardized techniques of observation and data analysis, but the relevance of such a claim and the credit its producer should receive remains a matter of expert judgment. The second issue is that this community of peers (while distributing various kinds of rewards and awards) does not operate in an economy regulated by units of measurement of value (such as money in a capitalistic economy). For lack of a better analogy, I would say that science's predicament resembles art connoisseurship without an art market. While in art the critics or the connoisseurs express qualitative judgments that are then variously translated into the artwork's monetary price, in science the expert judgment and the currency through which value is expressed are both qualitative. This makes sense if we realize that, unlike objects traded in a public market (a context in which producers are by and large distinct from evaluators and buyers), academic science is done, evaluated, and "consumed" by the same people.

The lack of standardized protocols and units for the quantification of scientific credit is simultaneously a curse and a blessing. It makes promotion cases and other kinds of professional evaluation difficult, and casts an aura of arbitrariness about them.[27] At the same time, it also helps to construe scientific credit as "pure" (not something like a currency among others), thus reinforcing the perception of science as dealing with truth. However, while everyone agrees that not all articles have the same value (and actually only a minority of all published scientific articles are ever cited), there is also a widespread awareness that, in practice, the number of one's publications is a reliable index of one's chances of succeeding in science's extremely competitive marketplace (Hamilton 1990, 1332; Rennie and Flanagin 1994, 469; Angell 1986; Culliton 1988; Maddox 1988). There is, in practice, a gap between the qualitative logic of scientific reward and its de facto everyday quantification.

These two apparently incommensurable positions are, in my view, necessarily linked. The routine complaints about the fact that promotions should be judged on the quality rather than quantity of publications indicates that scientific credit, precisely because it is defined as unquantifiable, often ends up being quantified, by default, in the most crude manner: by adding up the articles bearing the author's name. While the judgment-based logic of scientific reward and value is predicated on the assumption that the evaluators' time is a limitless resource, in practice time is anything but limitless (and most, if not all, decisions about scientific value are made in contexts structured by severe time constraints). Perhaps one could see this aporia as the mirror image of what happens in liberal economy, that is, in an exchange system whose logic is buttressed by the assumption that information about value and price is free and equally available to all players when instead liberal economy works (and can only work) through the selective, limited availability of that information (Boyle 1996, 40–41).

There are other interesting differences between liberal and scientific economies and the ways they shape the function of the author's name. When we buy a novel we do not expect to receive the producer's address. We simply take the risk of paying twenty dollars for what could turn out to be a disappointing read. Neither the author nor the publisher guarantee that we will be satisfied. We do not buy truth but only the possibility of intellectual pleasure, and the cash transaction between us and the bookseller is the beginning and end of the story. Alternatively, when we buy a product based on its performance, we expect it to work according to its specifications, and we may decide to hold on to the receipt in case something goes wrong. And if something does go wrong, we start our chain of grievances from the store who sold us the product and find our way up to the original producer only if we need (and have the time) to do so.

In science, instead, the name and address of the author is all a reader gets. The store owner, the wholesaler, the distributor, the importer, and all the other intermediate actors in a chain of commercial transactions are not entities that have an analog in science. While the production of a claim is indeed lengthy and involves many people and institutions, all these steps are represented as irrelevant to the epistemological value of that claim—a value that rests solely on the published author and his or her name. And such a value is of a peculiar kind anyway. A scientist who reads another scientist's work does not do so by buying it, either because journal subscriptions are usually provided by institutions, or because the scientific author does not receive royalties for the published research. (If this does not apply to textbooks, it is because they are not seen as presenting new research claims and fall, therefore, in the category of commercial books.)

Furthermore, upon reading a scientific article, a scientist may make professional decisions, such as investing time and money in a related line of research. These decisions are based on a claim the scientist has not purchased and therefore cannot "return" in case the claim turns out to be "defective." Again, the author's name is the only entry point for a grievance process (though it is not clear what shape a grievance can take beyond the production of damaging critiques of the original author's reliability and competence). Also, while in science the "producer" may lose symbolic capital as a result of such complaints, the "consumer" gets little or no reparation. In this sense the scientific consumer is in a position similar to a customer who has bought a bad novel that can't be returned (though, in science, that text would have cost the consumer nothing).

....

Too Many Names, Too Few Names

The scientist's name looks plain and unproblematic, and it is precisely because of its apparent naturalness that it can cover up the inherent opacity of its functions—functions it can perform only by leaving them shrouded in an aura of tacitness and unspecificity. Because the peculiar logic of scientific credit and responsibility prevents the construction of scientific authors either as holders of intellectual property rights or as workers paid for their work, it is hard, perhaps impossible, to find appropriate legal or economic categories to manage the function of the name. Scientific authorship, then, is a vast "underground economy" regulated by practices that are inherently administrative and private because they cannot be explicitly articulated in legal or economic terms. Not only do different institutions, disciplines, and journals have different authorship policies, but it is not even clear who should have the authority to legislate on these matters. Legally speaking, authorship definitions seem, at most, private contracts between scientists and journals, scientists and their institutions, or scientists and the colleagues who make up their research project. I believe that if these arrangements seem to survive (with some difficulty), it is because there is no body of legal doctrine that would challenge their arbitrariness. At the same time, such an absence is not an accident but the very result of the peculiarity of the scientific economy. In a sense, scientific authorship is a paralegal discourse predicated on the absence (perhaps the impossibility) of a Law.

Until the emergence of large-scale multiauthorship, science administrators and editors were able to treat scientific authorship as something similar to its literary cousin (or, more specifically, to the literary author before the development of intellectual property law). After all, a scientist is a person who had the idea, did the work, wrote the paper, and took credit and responsibility for it. Despite all the differences between credit and responsibility in science and literature, the individuality of the scientific author seemed to provide an envelope to contain its hard-to-define functions.

Multiauthorship has unhinged this unstable but plausible-looking conceptualization, and has produced opposite reactions among science administrators and practicing scientists. Science administrators have tried to hold on to traditional notions of individual authorship and to treat multiauthorship as an aggregate of individual authors. For instance, until recently the

ICMJE (International Committee of Medical Journal Editors), an influential body representing hundreds of anglophone biomedical journals, has required that each name listed in an article's byline (no matter how long that byline might be) must refer to a person who is fully responsible for the entire article (not just for the task he or she may have performed).[28]

This position emerged also as a response to the finger-pointing that tends to develop among coauthors accused of having published fraudulent claims. In some of these cases, senior authors listed in the byline have argued that they were either unaware that their name had been added to the author list (a sort of inverse plagiarism aimed at increasing the publication chances of the article), or that, although they did participate in the research, they had nothing to do with the fraudulent aspects of the publication (Relman 1983; Engler et al. 1987). While these claims were found ad hoc and self-serving in some instances, they did match the investigators' ·findings in others.

Additionally, the ICMJE has been concerned with the potential inflation of authorship credit due to multiauthorship. For instance, how can one be sure that all these names refer to people whose diverse skills were actually necessary for and contributed to such a large project? The ICMJE's overall response has been to put forward stringent definitions of authorship in an attempt to control the scale of multiauthorship, rein in inflation, and facilitate the enforcement of authorial responsibility. Rather than developing a radical redefinition of authorship in the light of conditions of production brought about by large-scale collaboration, the ICMJE has gone back to, and reinforced, the figure of the individual author—the only figure it saw fit to sustain the credit-responsibility nexus. Accordingly, what qualifies a person for authorship are intellectual contributions, not other forms of labor that are deemed nonintellectual:

> Authorship credit should be based only on substantial contributions to (1) conception and design, or analysis and interpretation of data; (2) drafting the article or revising it critically for important intellectual content; and on (3) final approval of the version to be published. Conditions 1, 2, and 3 must be all met.
>
> Participation solely in the acquisition of funding or the collection of data does not justify authorship. General supervision of the research group is also not sufficient for authorship. (ICMJE 1997, 928)

Like the so-called romantic author, the scientific author is separated from and placed above those "workers" who contributed to the production of that text but did not contribute to its "uniqueness," to the specificity of its claims and its epistemological status.

The "workers," of course, have objected to this definition. Many scientists feel that they cannot be responsible for those aspects of a project that fall outside of their work and expertise, and have argued that a narrow definition of authorship is unfair to many scientific workers who, while not engaged in the conceptualization and writing of a certain publication, still made such work possible. If these contributors do not receive authorship credit, they would receive almost no credit at all. Being thanked in the acknowledgment section is not something one can put on one's vita. In sum, the "workers" of large-scale biomedicine tend to think of authorship in corporate terms, that is, as stocks in a company that carry credit and responsibility in proportion to their share of the total value of the enterprise. To them, their names are, literally, their stocks.

But while one can empathize with the "workers" (as I tend to do), their position is fraught with as many tensions as that of ICMJE. Their perspective would require a means to demarcate and quantify their contributions and responsibilities that, as I have tried to show, flies in the face of the current logic of the economy of science and of authorial names. In some ways, they are trying to apply the categories of liberal economy to something that, instead, is complementary to it.

It is easy to slip into familiar social imagery and picture the tensions between scientists and the ICMJE as those between workers and their bosses (as I have just done here). But that misses the nature of the economy of scientific names, as well as the relationship between editors and scientists. Scientific authorship would then appear to be something like wages or, perhaps, stock options. But authorship is not something editors alone can "give" to scientists in exchange for their work, and it is not that editors become "poorer" by giving them authorship. Similarly, while one can conceive of "authorship inflation" in qualitative terms, it is not at all clear how one could measure it.

Scientific authorship makes for a very unusual pie because cutting it in thin slices does not necessarily reduce the value of each slice. As surprising as this might sound, it is not unlike what we find in copyright law, where all "authors of a joint work are co-owners of copyright in the work," which means that "each joint owner of a work may exercise all the rights of a copyright owner with respect to that work" (Halpern, Nard, and Port 1999, 55). Of course, an author of a joint work cannot simply sell it and take off with the bundle. Authors are legally accountable to the other joint authors, that is, they may have to share the profits with them and may not sell or license the work in a way that would violate the rights of the other joint authors (as by giving out an exclusive license to a third party) (55). But what is interesting here is that even copyright law, despite the range of legal categories it can draw upon, is unable to divide up the authorship pie. All it can do is to make each joint author responsible for splitting the income deriving from the uses of the pie (though even then the modalities of that split remain a matter of negotiation).

Things are much more complicated in the case of scientific multiau-thorship because the value of a scientific work is not expressible in a stan-dardized unit of measurement. While the joint author of a copyrighted work can at least use money as a unit of measurement in negotiating the distribution of income generated by that work, scientists and their admin-istrators do not have that option (at least not within current definitions of scientific credit). As a result, scientific authorship is not a zero sum game. Adding a name to the byline does not reduce the value of the other authors' contributions by any tangible amount because it is not clear what the over-all value of that text (or of its parts) might be.[29] In the end, scientific authorship seems to work like a hologram in which each fragment "con-tains" the whole.[30] However it is not that each name "contains" full authorship in a determinable, positive sense. It works that way, but only as a negative, default effect. In science, coauthors may become de facto full authors because it is not clear how one could deny them that status given the chain of indeterminacies surrounding the function of the scientist's name and the value of a scientific work.

In sum, both the ICMJE and the "workers" are walking on logical quicksand as they try to legitimate their views on the role of the name—views that, nevertheless, are not unreasonable in and of themselves.

....

Conclusions

I do not see this situation as a recipe for chaos or paralysis, but only for the proliferation of new arrangements of the function of the name—arrange-ments that, sooner or later, will clash with some aspect of the current logic of the economy of science. New interesting proposals are being floated and tried out. Some of them may lead to more radical redefinitions of credit and responsibility and their nexus (Davidoff 2000; Rennie, Yank, and Emanuel 1997; Rennie and Yank 1999; Smith 1997; Horton 1997; Horton and Smith 1996; Godlee 1996; Leash 1997). Or perhaps the dramatic development of patenting activities by geneticists (academic and not) may not be an isolated trend, but may be marking the beginning of more sweeping changes of the economy of science (including academic science) in the direction of intellectual property law.

Whether scientific claims will continue to circulate mostly in the public domain (as public documents) or will be carved away more frequently as private property (covered by patents or copyrights), it appears that the name of the scientist is not going to lose its central role in the economy of science (though the logic, relations, and objects of that economy may change substantially in the near future). But, independently from what the future may bring, I hope to have shown that the mundane problems surrounding the role of the scientist's name point quite directly to more general, theoretical tensions (perhaps aporias) stemming from the current conceptualization of scientific authorship and the contradictory notions of human agency it is asked to juggle.

....

NOTES

Debbora Battaglia, Pierre Bourdieu, Sande Cohen, Yves Gingras, Annelise Riles, Marilyn Strathern, and Rochelle Dreyfuss (and the students in her seminar at NYU School of Law) provided important comments and criticism on previous versions of this essay. I wish there was a way to credit them without making them coauthors of my mistakes. Written in 2000, this essay reflects the state of the debate at that time.

1. It would be impossible to discuss the many positions, approaches, and methodologies through which science studies has dealt with the construction of scientific authority without writing a very long review of the field. However, several key examples of this literature can be found in Biagioli 1999, while critical synopses of the main research questions in the field can be found in Jasanoff et al. 1995.

2. The trend toward the analysis of an increasingly broad range of mundane documents of the construction of science, however, has not gone unchecked. It also hit some serious snags when confronted with the issue of tacit knowledge, skill, and other forms of bodily knowledge—limits that have brought into question the epistemological status that science studies had conferred to the notion of "practice" (Turner 1994). Turner is a critic of science studies' conceptualization of the causal role of tacit knowledge and skill, but his work provides a good survey of the key literature and of the debate.

3. Biagioli and Galison (2002) attempt to initiate a discussion about the disciplinary and historical specificity of the author function in science.

4. Many examples of the first approach can be found in the journal *Scientometrics*. The second kind of analysis is much more diversified across periods and disciplines and hard to map in a footnote, but some examples are plagiarism and various accusations of appropriation that often emerge within priority disputes; the

erasure of women's authorship (or women's use of pseudonyms) in the early modern period; the erasure or limited acknowledgment of technicians' work (from the early modern to the present); the use of collective names in early modern academies, contemporary "big science" (e.g., ATLAS Collaboration, CDF Collaboration, etc.) or in collective authorship experiments like the Bourbaki group in mathematics; the "Mathew Effect" studied by Robert Merton (i.e., the inordinate accumulation of scientific credit on the names of famous scientists, though they may have not been the authors of that work, e.g., Boyle's Law, actually discovered by Robert Hooke); the many disputes about the ordering and contents of author bylines in multiauthored publications (discussed later in this essay); the construction and crediting of mythological authors such as Hermes Trismegistus; the use of anonymity or pseudonymity as a protective shield, especially in the early modern period; and the so-called reverse plagiarism, that is, the publication of one's work under the name of another scientist.

5. Examples of these directions are Haraway 1992, Latour 1999, and Pickering 1999.

6. This topos emerged in the very early debates about copyright in eighteenth-century England (Rose 1993, 38).

7. My own bibliography on this topic (available upon request) contains about eight hundred items. A selected and updated bibliography on scientific authorship in biomedicine (and a discussion forum) can be found at www.councilscienceeditors.org/services.

8. One of the most visible and more studied instances is the so-called Baltimore case (see Kevles 1998).

9. There are exceptions. Art historians have dealt with the complicated figure of the author in early modern artists' workshops (Alpers 1988). The trend can be traced to contemporary forms of artistic collaboration (Afterimage 1999) and to the development of the artist's studio into a space in which social relations of production are not unlike those of the factory or the laboratory (Jones 1996). The other exception is anthropology, where authorship of artifacts within non-Western cultures tends to be treated as a cultural or collective (rather than individual) category.

10. I have not found one reference to Foucault, Barthes, Benjamin, or other analysts of the author function in the scientific literature about authorship.

11. Davidoff gives a very recent synopsis of the state of the debate on authorship in biomedicine (and its boundaries) (2000, 111–19).

12. Until recently, the actual workings of peer review in science had received scant attention; a surprising pattern given the fundamental role everyone attributes it. Daryl E. Chubin and Edward J. Hachett (1990) is the most notable exception. Since this chapter was written in 2000 a number of publications have substantially corrected the literature gap.

13. Even conflicts of interest, in fact, can be seen as an authorship problem, that is, as a lack of transparency about the author's ties to "background authors."

14. The tensions between privately held intellectual property rights and the public domain have been discussed elsewhere (e.g., Woodmansee 1984, 425–45; Boyle 1996; Litman 1990).

15. Greg Myers (1995) provides an analysis of the diametrically opposed ways in which scientific articles and patents buttress their claims.

16. Here I draw from the so-called actor-network theory (see Callon and Latour 1981).

17. The remark by Richard Horton, editor of *Lancet*, was made at the Council of Biology Editors' retreat on authorship, Montreal, May 1999.

18. Academic publications in the social sciences and humanities occupy the middle ground between literature and the sciences. There we do find extensive acknowledgment sections thanking colleagues, librarians, archivists, research assistants, editors, informants, etc. In this case, the author function is still very close to the individual figure of the literary author, while the acknowledgment page points to the fact that, in practice, the "figuration" of the author is already expanding, though not as widely as in the sciences. One could also think of the "writing culture" debate in ethnography as being about more than the construction of ethnographic authority, but also the very author function of the ethnographer vis-à-vis that of the informant.

19. By "day," of course, I mean the social day, that is, what people (not only nature) have done in that slice of time.

20. Besides Foucault, the other scholars who have looked into the connection between authorship and responsibility are those who have studied the early modern period, when the state control of the press was a crucial factor in framing the author function. The other (partial) exception can be found in modern and contemporary debates about pornography and so-called obscene art. But even here the focus is more on the definition of "pornography" or the "obscene" rather than on the detailed articulation of the author's responsibilities.

21. An interesting reassessment of Foucault's views on the author function can be found in Roger Chartier's *The Order of Books* (1994, 25–59).

22. "It is important to notice, as well, that its [the work's] status as property is historically secondary to the penal code controlling its appropriation. Speeches and books were assigned real authors, other than mythical or important religious figures, only when the author became subject to punishment and to the extent that this discourse was considered transgressive" (Chartier 1994, 124).

23. Eliot Marshall provides a review of recent trends (1997a, 1997b). Dorothy Nelkin gives an earlier overview on these issues (1984).

24. There are exceptions. Feynman's diagrams, for instance, were given that name during his life (Kaiser 2000).

25. As Drummond Rennie, deputy editor of *JAMA*, candidly puts it: "The coin of publication has 2 sides: credit and accountability. On the credit side, no one has the least idea what the coin is worth, or who should be awarded the coins, or how the coins should be lined up for inspection" (Rennie, Yank, and Emanuel 1997, 580).

26. Figures from citation indexes may be used as "supplements" in the evaluation of an article's impact, but do not exhaust that process.

27. Although here I am dealing with the evaluation of scientific publications, many of these issues surface also in the assessment of "scholarship" in the humanities and social sciences.

28. "All persons designated as authors should qualify for authorship. Each author should have participated sufficiently in the work to take public responsibility for the content" (ICMJE 1997, 928).

29. "[T]he expansion in numbers of authors per article has tended to dilute accountability, while scarcely seeming to diminish credit" (Rennie, Yank, and Emanuel 1997, 580). While the scarce diminution of credit is cast as a pathology by Rennie et al., I believe that what they have correctly observed is a structural (not abnormal) feature of scientific authorship.

30. Other factors may contribute to this. Readers or evaluators experience a scientific publication as a whole, not an assemblage of authorial contributions. That has much to do with the way an article is written and printed. The names of the authors are presented at the beginning, but their specific contributions are not flagged within the technical narrative. The "voice" of that narrative is a unified one, no matter how many people may be behind it. Therefore, the readers' perception of a work as an entity casts its authors as the producers of a whole. Consequently, more names on a byline does not mean more "owners" of identifiable and quantifiable shares of the work, but more authors of the same whole.

....

REFERENCES

Afterimage. 1999. *Afterimage* 27(3).

Alpers, Svetlana. 1988. *Rembrandt's Enterprise*. Chicago: University of Chicago Press.

Angell, Marcia. 1986. Publish or Perish: A Proposal. *Annals of Internal Medicine* 104:261–62.

Biagioli, Mario. 2002. From Book Censorship to Academic Peer Review. *Emergences* 12:11–45.

———, ed. 1999. *The Science Studies Reader*. New York: Routledge.

Biagioli, Mario, and Peter Galison, eds. 2002. *Scientific Authorship: Credit and Intellectual Property in Science*. New York: Routledge.

Bourdieu, Pierre. 1975. The Specificity of the Scientific Field and the Social Conditions of the Progress of Reason. *Social Science Information* 14(6): 19–47.

Boyle, James. 1996. *Shamans, Software, and Spleens*. Cambridge: Harvard University Press.

Braunwald, Eugene. 1987. On Analyzing Scientific Fraud. *Nature* 325(6101): 215–16.

British Medical Journal. 1994. President of Royal College Resigns. *British Medical Journal* 309:1530.

Callon, Michel, and Bruno Latour. 1981. Unscrewing the Big Leviathans: How Do Actors Macrostructure Reality? In *Advances in Social Theory and Methodology: Toward an Integration of Micro and Macro Sociologies*, ed. Karin Knorr-Cetina and Aron Cicourel, 277–303. London: Routledge.

Chartier, Roger. 1994. *The Order of Books*. Stanford, CA: Stanford University Press.

Chubin, Daryl E., and Edward J. Hachett. 1990. *Peerless Science*. Albany: SUNY Press.

Coombe, Rosemary J. 1998. *The Cultural Life of Intellectual Properties: Authorship, Appropriation, and the Law*. Durham, NC: Duke University Press.

Culliton, Barbara J. 1988. Harvard Tackles the Rush to Publication. *Science* 241(4865): 525.

Davidoff, Frank. 2000. Who's the Author? Problems with Biomedical Authorship, and Some Possible Solutions. *Science Editor* 23(4): 111–19.

Editorial. 1993. Are Academic Institutions Corrupt? *Lancet* 342(8867): 315–16.

Engler, Robert L., James W. Covell, Paul J. Friedman, Philip S. Kitcher, and Richard M. Peters. 1987. Misrepresentation and Responsibility in Medical Research. *New England Journal of Medicine* 317(22): 1383–89.

Foucault, Michel. 1977. What is an Author? In *Language, Counter-Memory, Practice*, ed. Donald Bouchard, Ithaca, NY: Cornell University Press.

Fye, W. Bruce. 1990. Medical Authorship: Traditions, Trends, and Tribulations. *Annals of Internal Medicine* 113(4): 317–25.

Gaines, Jane. 1991. *Contested Culture: The Image, the Voice, and the Law*. Chapel Hill: University of North Carolina Press.

Godlee, Fiona. 1996. Definition of "Authorship" May be Changed. *British Medical Journal* 312: 1501–2.

Hagstrom, Warren O. 1982. Gift Giving as an Organizing Principle in Science. In *Science in Context: Readings in the Sociology of Science*, ed. Barry Barnes and David Edge, Cambridge: MIT Press.

Halpern, Sheldon W., Craig A. Nard, and Kenneth L. Port. 1999. *Fundamentals of United States Intellectual Property Law: Copyright, Patent, and Trademark*. The Hague: Kluwer Law International.

Hamilton, David P. 1990. Publishing by—and for?—the Numbers. *Science* 250(4986): 1331–32

Haraway, Donna. 1992. The Promises of Monsters: A Regenerative Politics for Inappropriate/d Others. In *Cultural Studies*, ed. Lawrence Grossberg, Cary Nelson, and Paula A. Treichler, 295–337. New York: Routledge.

Hesse, Carla A. 1991. *Publishing and Cultural Politics in Revolutionary Paris, 1789–1810*. Berkeley and Los Angeles: University of California Press.

Horton, Richard. 1997. The Signature of Responsibility. *Lancet* 350(9070): 5–6.

Horton, Richard, and Richard Smith. 1996. Time to Redefine Authorship. *British Medical Journal* 312:723.

Huth, Edward J. 1990. Editors and the Problems of Authorship: Rulemakers or Gatekeepers? In *Ethics and Policy in Scientific Publication*, ed. John C. Bailar, Marcia Angell, S. Boots, E. Myers, N. Palmer, M. Shipley, and P. Woolf, 175–80. Bethesda, MD: Council of Biology Editors.

Institute of Medicine, Committee on the Responsible Conduct of Research. 1989. *The Responsible Conduct of Research in the Health Sciences*. Washington, DC: National Academy of Science Press.

International Committee of Medical Journal Editors (ICMJE).1997. Uniform Requirements for Manuscripts Submitted to Biomedical Journals. *Journal of the American Medical Association* 277:928.

———. 2003. Uniform Requirements for Manuscript Submitted to Biomedical Journals. www.icmje.org. Accessed on 24 August 2004.

Jasanoff, Sheila, Gerald E. Markle, James C. Petersen, and Trevor Pinch, eds. 1995. *Handbook of Science and Technology Studies.* Thousand Oaks, CA: Sage.

Jones, Caroline. 1996. *Machine in the Studio.* Chicago: University of Chicago Press.

Kaiser, David. 2000. Stick-Figure Realism: Conventions, Reification, and the Persistence of Feynman Diagrams: 1948–1964. *Representations* 70:49–86.

Kevles, Daniel J. 1998. *The Baltimore Case.* New York: Norton.

Latour, Bruno. 1999. *Pandora's Hope: Essays on the Reality of Science Studies.* Cambridge: Harvard University Press.

Leash, Evangeline. 1997. Is It Time for a New Approach to Authorship? *Journal of Dental Research* 76:724–27.

Litman, Jessica. 1990. The Public Domain. *Emory Law Journal* 39:965–99.

Maddox, John. 1988. Why the Pressure to Publish? *Nature* 333:493.

Marshall, Eliot. 1997a. Companies Rush to Patent DNA. *Science* 275(5301): 780–81

———. 1997b. Gene Fragments Patentable, Official Says. *Science* 275(5303): 1055.

Merton, Robert K. 1973. Priorities in Scientific Discovery. In *The Sociology of Science: Theoretical and Empirical Investigations,* ed. Norman W. Storer, 286–324. Chicago: University of Chicago Press.

Myers, Greg. 1995. From Discovery to Invention: The Writing and Rewriting of Two Patents. *Social Studies of Science* 25(1): 57–105.

Nelkin, Dorothy. 1984. *Science as Intellectual Property: Who Controls Research?* New York: Macmillan.

Phillips, Jeremy, and Alison Firth, eds. 1995. *Introduction to Intellectual Property Law,* 3rd ed. London: Butterworths.

Pickering, Andrew. 1999. The Mangle of Practice: Agency and Emergence in the Sociology of Science. In *The Science Studies Reader,* ed. Mario Biagioli, 372–93. New York: Routledge.

Regalado, Antonio. 1995. Multiauthor Papers on the Rise. *Science* 268(5207): 25.

Relman, Arnold S. 1983. Lessons from the Darsee Affair. *New England Journal of Medicine* 308(23): 1415–17.

Rennie, Drummond, and Annette Flanagin. 1994. Authorship! Authorship! Guests, Ghosts, Grafters, and the Two-Sided Coin. *Journal of the American Medical Association* 271: 469–71.

Rennie, Drummond, and Veronica Yank. 1999. Disclosure of Researcher Contributions: A Study of Original Research Articles in *The Lancet. Annals of Internal Medicine* 130(8): 661–70.

Rennie, Drummond, Veronica Yank, and Linda Emanuel. 1997. When Authorship Fails: A Proposal to Make Contributors Accountable. *Journal of the American Medical Association* 278:579–85.

Rose, Mark. 1993. Authors and Owners: *The Invention of Copyright.* Cambridge: Harvard University Press.

Smith, Richard. 1997. Authorship: Time for a Paradigm Shift? The Authorship System is Broken and May Need a Radical Solution. *British Medical Journal* 314:992.

Stewart, Walter W., and Ned Feder. 1987. The Integrity of Scientific Literature. *Nature* 325:207–14.

Strub, Richard L., and F. William Black. 1976. Multiple Authorship. *Lancet* 2(7994): 1090–91.

Turner, Stephen. 1994. *The Social Theory of Practices.* Chicago: University of Chicago Press.

Woodmansee, Martha. 1984. The Genius and the Copyright: Economic and Legal Conditions of the Emergence of the "Author." *Eighteenth-Century Studies* 17(4): 425–48.

———. 1994. On the Author Effect: Recovering Collectivity. In *The Construction of Authorship: Textual Appropriation in Law and Literature,* ed. Martha Woodmansee and Peter Jaszi, 16–28. Durham, NC: Duke University Press.

Woodmansee, Martha, and Peter Jaszi, eds. 1994. *The Construction of Authorship: Textual Appropriation in Law and Literature.* Durham, NC: Duke University Press.

5   Documents Unfolding

Adam Reed

I WANT TO START with a found object of fieldwork—the warrant cover or intake record from the maximum-security jail in Papua New Guinea where I conducted my research (1994–95). This artifact of prison bureaucracy exists as a copy, reproduced in printed form on one side of single sheets of paper. It is kept, with other papers—classification reports, parole forms, transfer memos, punishment records, drafted appeals, and letters to prison authorities by kin, in the individual files of prisoners. As well as being an ordinary object of prison life, the warrant cover is also an artifact of modern knowledge practice, a conventional kind of document technology in the world. But the familiarity of its design—in some ways too obvious and mundane a piece of technology—makes it difficult to assess. In this essay, I want to examine what prisoners and warders make of objects like the warrant cover in order to draw out which actions we might properly attribute to documents of this kind.

Of course, there is already a familiar way of assessing the technology of documents; in particular those produced in disciplined institutions such as prisons. They can be analyzed for their normative dimensions. Foucault (1977) has directed our attention to the discursive power of these artifacts; documents should not simply be viewed as tools, but also as texts, responsible for producing or objectifying the subjects that use them. As we look at the warrant cover, we might attend to the duplicated format of the document and the way it acts as a basis for comparison and hierarchical measurement between prisoners. Criteria such as "name," "language," "religion," "education," "sex," "age," "height," "normal occupation," and "village" allow for uniform types of differences to be expressed and assessed, creating an archive of individual case histories. This work of

158

classification takes place over time; certain categories of the document anticipate future events—the escape, transfer, or release of the prisoner. Further, links might be drawn between the technology of the document and the regimes of observation or surveillance that make this documentation possible. From this perspective, the intake records of a prison make a certain kind of political subject (and a certain kind of inquiry) visible and hegemonic.

But at the jail in Papua New Guinea where I conducted research the normative status of the warrant cover is complicated by the fact that prisoners also produce a document, one that is intended to reproduce the design of the intake record. Each inmate creates what he calls an "autograph"—a single sheet of paper whose uniform set of criteria are handwritten on one side.

The autograph is presented as a record of the individual's life in prison and as a souvenir of that experience after his release. Its format, which is consistently duplicated by prisoners, includes some of the same criteria displayed on the warrant cover, asking for the respondent's "name," "age," "village," and "jail sentence." It also sets questions on the deprivations of jail life—criteria such as "favourite food," "girls," "best friends," and "loved ones" draw attention to what is missing, on the bonds made in jail—on "wantok" (language group mates), "gang," and "comrades," and on plans for what happens after discharge—"ambition" and "revenge." Although the formats of criteria differ, the autograph and the warrant cover are examples of the same kind of document technology, one that clearly impresses prisoners.

From the perspective of Foucault and those who assess the normative dimensions of documents, the emergence of an artifact like an autograph can be read in two ways. The fact that prisoners not only forcibly submit to the action of the warrant cover, but also copy that design and voluntarily submit to the action of the autograph, can be taken as evidence of the hegemony of document technology and of the political subject it describes. Through the autograph prisoners are reproducing the objectified subject of the warrant cover. Alternatively, the manufacture of the autograph can be read as an act of resistance; prisoners may be mimicking the form of the official intake record in order to subvert it (cf. González Echevarria 1998).[1] Criteria on the autograph such as "hates," "worst moment," "happiest moment," and "revenge" would appear to support this reading. The autograph may be said to make visible an alternative political subject, one that challenges the disciplined subject of the warrant cover. In either reading,

WARRANT COVER

.... CORRECTIONAL INSTITUTION

MEDICAL EXAMINATION ON ADMITTANCE.

....

....

....

....

....

MEDICAL EXAMINATION ON RELEASE.

....

....

....

....

....

DETAINEE PROPERTY:

Amount in cash K ....

Receipt No. ....

....

....

....

....

....

....

REMARKS:

Height: ....

Build: ....

Marks: ....

Register No.: ....

Date Admitted: ....

Name: ....

Language: ....

Religion: ....

Education: ....

Sex: ....

Age: ....

Marital Status: ....

Village: ....

Town: ....

Province: ....

Normal Occupation: ....

Employment: ....

+ + Money

+ + Cash

+ + Subsistence

+ + Unemployed

+ + Unfit

+ + Not Stated

Name of Next of Kin: ....

Address: ....

5.1. Warrant cover

CRIMINAL HISTORY: ....

Previous Convictions: YES/NO   ....

(If 'Yes' how many times) ....

Previous Detention: YES/NO   SENTENCE:

(If 'Yes' how many times) ....   Offence: ....

                                               Date of sentence commence: ....

REMAND: Offence committed with others: YES/NO

Date due for court: ....   DDR Without Remission: ....

                                               Amount of Remission: ....

I certify that I have received ALL my property and   DDR With Remission: ....

Claim form for my money.   Escape: ....

....   Recapture: ....

          Signature of Detainee

....   TRANSFERS:

          Witness   From: .... To.........................

                                               From: .... To: ....

....

          Signature of OIC

AUTOGRAPH

Name: ....   Nickname: ....

Date of birth: ....   Age: ....

Village: ....   Town residence: ....

Favourite food: ....   Favourite drink: ....

Most love: ....   Most fear: ....

Comrades: ....   Best friends: ....

My wantok: ....

Would like to see: ....   Would like to meet: ....

Hates: ....

Worst moment: ....   Happiest moment: ....

Jail: ....   Jailed for: ....   Jail sentence: ....

Admired person: ....   Admired gang: ....

Street: ....

Gang: ....

Girls I like: ....

Ambition: ....

Revenge: ....

5.2. Autograph

emphasis is placed on the strategic status of the document; the autograph, like the warrant cover, is understood as an instrument of political control.

But in this essay I want to do something different; like the other contributors to this volume I am concerned to explore the nonstrategic status of these documents. The strength of Foucault's argument has led us to know them in a highly specific way; they appear mundanely strategic in nature. In her introduction, Riles invites the reader to show a less assured interest in documents—a sense of appreciation that does not necessarily claim to transform or complete its subject. This reading (more akin to listening) should include paying attention to the aesthetic dimensions of the document, its status as artifact and the actions of its design (commentators have tended to look behind or beyond the design to find the object's significance). Yet my essay is not simply concerned to re-situate or recover the status of a familiar object. Documents like the warrant cover or autograph are important because they are good to think with. This essay tries to demonstrate one way in which documentary practice may become an orienting analytical procedure.

....

Form Filling

The prisoners I worked with at Bomana jail just outside Port Moresby (there are on average seven hundred male inmates, a mixture of convict and remand prisoners), the capital city in Papua New Guinea, distinguish their state of incarceration by reference to what they are missing (Reed 1999, 2003). They complain at their inability to meet obligations to kin and friends outside the jail, at the everyday consumer goods and foodstuffs they can no longer enjoy. In this climate, documents stand out by their positive presence, as an object provided, rather than taken away, in the moment of being detained. Upon arrival at Bomana, warders escort new convicts and remand inmates to the reception offices, there to be interrogated or interviewed and led through the process of registration. This often involves the use of abusive language and beatings, applied by reception clerks to those prisoners they regard as recalcitrant or disrespectful. While warders employ force to extract answers to the questions on the warrant cover, inmates do their best to conceal or disguise their own biographies. The violence and energy of this transaction seems to imply that a form of personal freedom is at stake. Prisoners are certainly concerned to resist interrogation and avoid revealing compromising details about themselves. However, the nature of this encounter left me puzzled, for when I later inspected the warrant covers they seemed poor conveyors of information. The consistency of criteria on the printed form is not matched by consistent responses. Warders fill out the warrant covers in what seem haphazard, incomplete ways. Varying sections of the document are left blank, with no obvious scheme to the choice of which criteria are answered. Despite this, warders and prisoners ascribe power and agency to these documentary forms. The half-filled-out warrant cover is not discarded, but instead remains an object of great impression.

My confusion is in a sense an old problem; Garfinkel (1967) discusses another example of what appears careless form-filling. During an investigation of the intake application forms and case folder files of a Californian psychiatric outpatients clinic, he became frustrated by the relative lack of comparable information provided (187). Garfinkel found that his initial intention, to survey the records for the selection criteria by which patients are admitted, was not sustainable. While the clinical files consistently recorded the age and sex of a patient, other inquiries, such as those into occupational history or ethnic background, were irregularly filled out. Like the half-completed warrant covers at Bomana, these documents appear useless instruments of information or political control. Their strategic value, as a classificatory survey (according to Foucault the basis for surveillance and comparison in a disciplined institution), is highly questionable. But rather than dismissing these clinical files as of no significance, Garfinkel became interested in the phenomenon of "bad records," something he found to be a surprisingly frequent and uniform feature of institutional life. Indeed, he suggests that there might be organizationally sound reasons for not filling out forms in the manner expected by an outside investigator. What seemed like inefficiency might in fact make sense when reconsidered as part of the purpose and routine of clinical practice (192). To him, the least interesting aspect of these files was the fact that they appeared poorly kept.

Garfinkel puts forward several reasons for the state of clinical files. He notes that the value of added information may not equal the costs of its labor. Filling out all the criteria on a document is a time-consuming affair, one that may not be justified when balanced against other clinical priorities. Thus, those sections in a form that demand longer attention are more likely to be left uncompleted. He states that documentary self-reporting is never valued as highly as other forms of clinical expertise and therefore fails to attract the same levels of attention (194). Garfinkel observes that another reason may be the distance that exists between the nature of the questionnaire criteria and the practice they aim to describe (195). Clinical staff may find some file sections irrelevant and so leave them empty, or they may distort their answers in order to accommodate what they take to be the correct response. Garfinkel states that the fixed terms of document criteria can never meet the variable nature of actual events; small alterations in clinical procedures can render sections of the file obsolete (196–97). The document is in constant negotiation with itself—sections of it are not necessarily answered at once, but rather over time and in a manner that sometimes places them in opposition or allows for repetition (204–5). Garfinkel argues that documents such as clinical files might be viewed as reconstructable accounts of patient-staff transactions (197). Rather than considering the half-filled report as something that staff have managed to get away with, he recommends acknowledging the phenomenon as evidence of the procedures and consequences of clinical activities (198). So the occasional and variable nature of response to document criteria might be compared to a form of verbal utterance addressed to an unknown audience who already know the parameters of conversation (200–201). Garfinkel suggests that staff, in filling out the clinical file, assume that any future reader understands the order of interaction that is the basis of reportage.

Among warders at Bomana jail the requirement to fill out documents is often met with ambivalence. They regard the activity as energy sapping and boring, and try to avoid the task if they can (the management of warders is weak). Indeed, prisoners complain that the low numbers of inmates gaining parole is a direct consequence of their indifference—the reluctance of staff to invest their time in completing a five-page assessment form. Similarly, drives to reclassify prisoners and introduce new documents usually fail; warders give up the task as soon as the supervisory officer has left them. However, the apparently slapdash manner of their form filling does not always conform to the logic of time saved. The criteria omitted on warrant covers are harder to predict; it is quite as common to see categories such as "age," "name," or "sex" left blank as it is to see those that demand longer responses. It is true that certain sections of the warrant cover now appear redundant (the "medical examination on admittance" section is usually left unanswered because there is rarely a doctor or paramedic on hand), but warders never express their frustrations with form filling in terms of worries about the distorting effect of fixed criteria. There is no discussion of a reality that precedes recording or great fears expressed about what is left out of the format. Finally, the warrant cover may be an

WARRANT COVER

Bomana........ CORRECTIONAL INSTITUTION

MEDICAL EXAMINATION ON ADMITTANCE.

Register No.: ....

....

Date Admitted: *29/11/1990*....................

....

Name: *Jada Heni*...........................

....

Language: ....

....

Religion: ....

....

Education: *grade 3*................................

MEDICAL EXAMINATION ON RELEASE.

Sex: ....

....

Age: *26*..

....

Marital Status: *married*.........................

....

....

Village: *Ndranou*....................................

....

Town: *Lorengau*.....................................

DETAINEE PROPERTY:

Province: *Manus*......................................

Amount in cash K *10.68*

Normal Occupation: ....

Receipt No. *1 long jeans, 5 underpants, 1 shirt,*

Employment: ....

1 shoes & socks, 1 tee-shirt, 1 cap, 1 lawyer

receipt for K250..

+ + Money

....

+ + Cash

....

+ + Subsistence

....

+ + Unemployed

....

+ + Unfit

REMARKS:

+ + Not Stated

Height: *172 cm*..

5.3. Warrant cover

Build: 65 kg..

Marks: *tattoo on forehead & right shoulder*..

CRIMINAL HISTORY:

Previous Convictions: YES/NO

(If 'Yes' how many times) ....

Previous Detention: YES/NO

(If 'Yes' how many times) ....

REMAND:

Date due for court: *29/11/90*.................................

I certify that I have received ALL my property and

Claim form for my money.

....

Signature of Detainee

.............*cpl. Ned Kopi*...................................

Witness [ACO clerk]

....

Signature of OIC

Name of Next of Kin: *Mr Bernard Heni*...

Address: *Kerevat agricultural college*

Rabaul...

....

SENTENCE:

Offence: *wilful murder*........................

Date of sentence commence: *15/2/1991*........

Offence committed with others: YES/ -

DDR Without Remission: *24/11/2006*........

Amount of Remission: *5 years, 3 months*..

DDR With Remission: *24/8/2001*...............

Escape: ....

Recapture: ....

TRANSFERS:

From: *Kavieng*....... To: *Bomana*...

From: *13/10/91*...... To: ....

artifact of the transaction that takes place between warders and prisoners during registration, but I do not believe that this exchange determines the value placed on document technology. The warrant cover is left half-completed not because warders and prisoners anticipate the context for what is filled in or left blank, but because their attention is focused on the action or capacity of design, the analytical practice the document appears to already contain.

Typically, the act of form filling is presented as a discretionary move on the part of the respondent. Someone chooses or is forced by another to answer the criteria set by the questionnaire. That individual imposes himself on the document, stamps his mark on the record in a distinctive way. Yet for prisoners and warders at Bomana the moment of form filling seems anticipated in the constitution of the document's design, which suggests both a complete and unfinished state. The pattern of criteria and response spaces is constant and self-contained, but at the same time open to an infinite number of interventions. Each act of form filling concludes the document in a different way, replicating the format while extending its consequences. The respondent seems to add depth or concrete detail to the design's abstract level of inquiry, or seen the other way around, the design makes individual response conform to an abstract pattern. Indeed, prisoners and warders feel themselves to be passive actors, unable to pre-empt or go beyond format coordinates. There is an air of inevitability to the answers they provide, since every response calls up the same pattern. In this regard it matters little which sections of the document are filled in or left blank. Prisoners and warders know that in a sense their answer is already there, forecast in the design of warrant cover and autograph.

This perception, that agency lies not with them but with the document technology, is a very different kind of analytical procedure. Here every event is presaged as pattern. Innovation is replication, just another variation of the same design. There can be no position outside, before, or after the document. Pickering (1997) provides a parallel insight from the knowledge domain of science. He asserts that while scientists assign a level of agency to machines, they do not recognize the same force in the concepts of their discipline (40). The scientist, in this relationship, presents himself or herself as the only purposeful, goal-oriented actor. But Pickering states that this denies the trained, repetitive, and routinized forms of intellectual behavior that are easily distinguishable in their methods. He locates three analytical moves in conceptual practice: what he calls "bridging," an exploratory connection that posits possible new fields of inquiry; "transcription," the extension of established procedures to that field; and "filling," completing the field without obvious guidance from previous models (42). The first and last moves appear free and voluntary, but the middle one is not. With transcription it is the concept, not the scientist, who has agency. Concepts coerce reactions, producing unthinking, automatic patterns of thought. So the scientist knows that the criterion 3 + 4 warrants the response 7, or that the algebraic equation $a(b + c) =$ should be followed by the answer $ab + ac$ (Pickering 1997, 41). In this situation the scientist is passive. Pickering notes the "dance of agency" (42), which necessarily entangles free and forced responses. He argues that analytical moves such as bridging, which appear discretionary in nature, may in fact only exist to invoke the noncontingent move that follows them. In form filling it is even harder to locate a free response. Prisoners and warders at Bomana view the act as coerced from the start.

To demonstrate the power of form filling, as an analytical step, it will be useful to describe a parallel kind of move within prison culture. I provide the example of dream interpretation among prisoners. Dreams, like documents, are a positive feature of life at Bomana. Indeed, inmates claim that the state of incarceration actively promotes dreaming episodes (since there is little organized work or leisure activity in the jail, individuals spend most of their time locked in their cells, dozing and sharing dream experiences). Prisoners believe that these dreams are received rather than composed by the individual mind; exterior agents, such as kin and friends outside the jail, spirits or God, cause them. Like respondents to the warrant cover and autograph, the dreamer seems to lack agency. He is believed to be inside his dream, part of its design.

Prisoners claim that these dreams have a predictive quality; they are said to "bear fruit" *(karim kaikai)* or anticipate the form of upcoming events.[2] When an inmate wakes from dreaming, he usually relates the experience to his cellmates. Together they sit down in a circle and discuss it, attempting to "turn the dream" *(tainim driman)* and make a forecast of what kind of event it anticipates. Here is one example of a reported dream that received much discussion.

A man rolls a plasticine block into the shape of a rope. He looks up and sees a cassowary bird standing next to him. When he returns to his task, he discovers that the rope has become a snake, with a black skin and white belly. Surprised and afraid, the man jumps up and looks away. From behind he hears a sound like crunching paper and, daring to turn around, discovers the snake, now again a plasticine rope, strangling the neck of the bird. The cassowary cries out in anger, and the man fears that he might be attacked. But instead the bird drops excrement on the rope and succeeds in breaking it apart. The cassowary runs around with the remains of the coil still hanging from it like a necktie. The man feels sorry for the cassowary and offers to remove the last bits of the rope. But the bird rejects the offer, and they go their separate ways. When the man reaches his house he discovers the cassowary already asleep inside. He is angry and demands to know where he will rest. But the bird ignores him and goes back to sleep.

The prisoner, a remand inmate, who experienced this dream came to the following conclusion about it. He told me that the cassowary (a tall forest bird) seemed like himself, and the rope like the evidence mounted against him in his upcoming court case. By transforming the rope into a snake, the dream perhaps indicated the strength of sorcery behind those witnesses who accused him. However, the fact that the cassowary breaks its bonds would seem to suggest that the presiding judge will not have enough evidence to convict him. All his speculations were premised on the notion of a dreaming technology. Like the act of form filling, for prisoners the interpretation of these dreams involves responding to a format or pattern of criteria. Whatever the event believed to be anticipated, it must be seen to conform to that design. As analytical moves, dream interpretation and form filling both reproduce by replication. What remains constant is form (cf. Bateson 1973), filled in differently but duplicated again and again.

Just as the sections of a warrant cover can be answered in many ways and filled in over time, so prisoners at Bomana hold that a dream has many sides. There is no definitive interpretation (a dream may anticipate more than one event, and inmates expect to have to readjust their forecasts). Some months after his dreaming experience, the remand inmate had his trial and as a consequence extended his first interpretation. While the judge did decide that there was not enough evidence to continue the prosecution, he did not release him. Instead the judge sent him back to Bomana to await a final ruling from a higher court. Though disappointed by this delay, the remand inmate expressed no surprise. He examined his dream again and explained that his failure to gain discharge was predicted by the image of the cassowary asleep in a house. His dreaming, like the warrant cover or autograph, seemed able to accommodate, maybe even coerce, any outcome. As technologies that are received rather than used, documents and dreams are taken to extend prisoners and draw actions from them.

....

Abbreviation

While anthropologists have paid little attention to the aesthetic dimensions of documents, there does exist a long tradition of concern for the form and perceived efficacy of indigenous art and design. Attempts to provide semantic analyses have been criticized for failing to recognize the priority often given to the object's plastic qualities. Gow (1990, 93), for instance, who works among the Piro people of Peru, notes the failure of those analyses to understand the elaborate painted, woven, and engraved patterns that are central features of local artwork. The Piro are not concerned with the representational significance of these designs, but rather with the manner in which they are adapted to differing surfaces (94). The source of aesthetic pleasure, Gow argues, lies in the pattern's successful integration to that medium. Munn (1973, 166), in her study of the Walbiri of Aboriginal Australia, highlights graphic designs that act as formula for referencing an indefinite range of items. Thus, a circle may describe a camp, a topographical feature, the path an individual takes across the landscape, a species, or the outlines of a specific ancestor. At the same time the sand drawing or body painting is also a nonrepresentational pattern, one that has the potential to absorb anything (173). These designs, Walbiri claim, are received from the ancestors and ascribed with their generative strength and efficacy (55). They have a power to direct action and ensure future survival.

Riles (1998, 2000) salvages from such accounts an emphasis on form in order to help describe the documentary practice of her own subjects—the agents of nongovernmental organizations in Fiji and of nations sitting at global United Nations conferences. She is interested in the mundane designs—networks, rectangles, matrices, brackets, and facts, which seem to become the focus of aesthetic attention. Indeed, Riles reports that agents treat and negotiate the language of documents without regard for meaning or representational load. Instead the intention is to produce an object that meets strict criteria for correct form; success in negotiation being measured by the replication of specific format across drafted papers. In this process, she observes, the document swings between its status as concrete object and as abstract nonrepresentational pattern. What disappears from these agents' view is the document's value as text.

A look at analyses of artwork in Papua New Guinea might further
extend these insights, and in particular offer commentary on the documentary practice of prisoners and warders at Bomana. Losche (1995) has
recently returned to the problems of aesthetic judgment first highlighted
by Forge (1970, 289), when he noted the ambiguity of signification displayed in the design elements used by the Abelam people of Papua New
Guinea. Forge was referring to a series of simple motifs—horizontal and
vertical lines, zigzags, triangles, ovals, spirals, and star shapes—that feature
on the front of ceremonial houses, as well as on carvings, bark paintings,
and headdresses worn during rites of initiation. Each design would spark
wildly varying interpretations, so that, for instance, one person might perceive the spiral motif as a fern frond, while someone else saw it as a leg of
pork or swirl of water. In response to this apparent semantic confusion,
Forge concluded that the Abelam did not seek meaning from their artwork, but rather affect. Those young men who were exposed to these
motifs during initiation ceremonies were taught to recognize the power of
design to act upon the beholder. This idea, that art is important to peoples
in Papua New Guinea because of its perceived productivity and not its
signification, has influenced many who came after Forge (cf. Strathern and
Strathern 1971; O'Hanlon 1989; Gell 1992). But Losche takes his suggestion forward for the Abelam themselves. She argues that these motifs are
actually viewed not as static images, but as kinds of movement or process
(1995, 53). Thus the spiral shape, whether imagined as fern frond, swirl of
water, or leg of pork, denotes the generative act of unfurling or opening
from the inside out. She claims that the Abelam appreciate the spiral for its
power to continually give forth from within itself and reveal previously
hidden multiplicity (55). Here the design is a form of self-generating
action, and it is this capacity that I wish to emphasize.

The act of form filling has already been noted for its qualities of replication and self-extension. Both warrant cover and autograph are held by
prisoners to contain infinite numbers of possible responses. The pattern of
criteria appears to pull these answers out of itself, to unfold them in the
moment of filling out the document. Like the spiral shape described by
Losche, this action is part of the document's design, a movement that prisoners at Bomana recognize and feel led by. The transfers of format and criteria from the surface of the warrant cover to that of the autograph testifies
to the perceived importance of that capacity. Prisoners are hoping to redi-
rect its self-generating power, to let the design draw from them other sets
of responses and answers.

AUTOGRAPH

Name: *John*................................

Nickname: *Jay Olando*......................

Date of birth: 3/4/75...........................

Age: 20...

Village: *Baruni, National Capital District*

Town residence: *desert land Branvilla*

Favourite food: *rice & tinned fish*..........

Favourite drink: *cool water*.................

Most love: *mother & father*..................

Most fear: *Father in heaven*..............

Comrades: *Desert, Joker, 007*...............

Best friends: ....

My wantok: *Pune, Sere, Sibona, Toru*...

Would like to see: *grave of friend in Hula*

Would like to meet: *family in village*...

Hates: *cops, arseholes, mother*

fuckers..

Worst moment: *hiding talent in jail*.....

Happiest moment: *leaving this second*

Hell on earth

Jail: *Bomana*.........

Jailed for: *manslaughter*

Jail sentence: *six solid years*.....

Admired person: ....

Admired gang: *Kouvera*......................

Street: *Wall Street & Ghost Town*..

Gang: *Junior Jawas of Toks*..

Girls I like: *simple village girls, my mother*...

Ambition: *base guitarist*..

Revenge: *witnesses in court, bastards*...

5.4. Autograph

At the heart of this transfer lies an appreciation for the abbreviated form of prison documents. The compactness of the warrant cover's format is held to be the basis of its self-generating power. Like the simple design elements of the Abelam, this pattern of abrupt criteria—"name," "language," "religion," "education," "village," "occupation," "name of next of kin," and so on—reduces the movement of inquiry to a single printed sheet. As a consequence, prisoners have a sense of the format as a motif pregnant with its own hidden possibilities, just waiting to be opened up. The criteria of the autograph—"nickname," "favourite food," "girls I like," "gang," "worst moment," and so on—achieve the same sense of contracted energy, so that the answers solicited appear to burst from the formatted page. This impression leads prisoners to compare the autograph to the graphic design of tattoos, which are also drawn in Bomana and cover the bodies of most inmates. Known as the "hand marks of jail" *(hanmak blong haus kalabus)*, tattoos have motifs that resist signification (prisoners either refuse to identify the design as a sign or they offer competing interpretations of it). Like the autograph, they are held to act as a "memory" *(memori)*—marks copied on the skin in order to affect people in the future (when prisoners are released, those outside the jail will see their tattoos and be moved to ask them about life in Bomana). Both kinds of document (autograph and tattoo) are valued for the stories they will recall; together they condense multiplicity to its tightest form, reduced to the limits of the design and thus allowing for exhilarating moments of release.

Prisoners borrow this document technology when naming gangs (which are another positive presence in jail). They tend to favor titles that take an abbreviated form, especially those that use acronyms or cryptic wordplay. Thus the gang name 585 can be turned upside down and converted from numbers to letters in order to reveal the designation GBG, whose initials stand for the two main language groups from which members come (Goilala Boys Garaina). The name contracts and disguises; like the format of the warrant cover or autograph, it is capable of unfurling itself and revealing interior extensions. Acronyms are popular gang names because they are seen to allow an infinite number of possible releases. The name KGK, for instance, first uncovered the language groups of Kerema, Goilala, and Kairuku. Later on, when prisoners from Hagen joined the gang, they also revealed the word "boy" *(kange)* in the language of these new members. Gang names therefore seem to draw the same action as documents.

The perceived capacity of abbreviated form to unfold itself and give forth multiplicity runs counter to other, less favorable assessments of its power. Thus Garfinkel (1967, 196) dismisses it as a distorting agency, narrowing the freedom of response by presenting fixed alternative answers. Benjamin (1993, 92) goes further and associates the drive to abbreviate with what he disdainfully labels the modern appetite for "information." For him, this negative intervention is responsible for condensing happenings into digestible and verifiable facts and thus contributing to the demise of storytelling (88). Media such as documents are said to be concerned with describing the "essence" of events (91), culling attributes such as digression and nondeliberate acts of remembrance (Benjamin's information age is one that is thin and contracted to the point of lifeless statements of fact). He claims that the introduction of document technologies, such as abbreviation, reduces the collective store of memory and imagination. Yet for both prisoners and warders at Bomana abbreviation expands, rather than narrows, their field of expression. The compact format of the warrant cover and autograph (like tattoos and gang names) is precisely what allows them (and others) to remember and spark digression. It disguises infinite responses and allows multiple memories to be held in reduced form. For them, the abbreviated criteria of these documents are dense with possibilities, weighed down not by information, but by the potential of its own self-generating fashion.

....

Conclusion

At Bomana, prisoners identify what they regard as the principal qualities of the warrant cover and autograph. They highlight the self-expanding power of document criteria and the potential contained by the move to abbreviate. Their attention is upon the actions these documents draw out (such as the act of form filling). The design of the warrant cover or autograph is a technology that extends them, without necessarily making prisoners the subjects of political control (as a basis of classification and hierarchical measurement between prisoners the half-completed warrant cover is practically useless). If that document technology can be seen to borrow some of its analytical moves from the tradition of dream technology, then the reverse may also be true. The action that prisoners first ascribe to documents may also come to be read in the action ascribed to dreams, tattoos, and gang names. Perhaps document technology does colonize prison culture, but it is not mundanely strategic in nature. The warrant cover and autograph are not tools to be exploited by competing agencies (inmate and prison authority), nor are they simply objects for conveying normative value. Instead, they are appreciated as actors, whose pattern or movement is capable of presaging the events of incarceration.

....

Acknowledgments

I wish to thank the prisoners and warders of Bomana jail in Papua New Guinea. For their comments and constructive criticism, I am grateful to Tony Crook, Hiro Miyazaki, Marilyn Strathern, and the other authors of this collection. In particular, I am indebted to Annelise Riles, for inviting me to contribute and attend the workshops that led up to this collection, but also for her general encouragement and intellectual example. The fieldwork upon which this paper is based was made possible by a grant from the Cambridge Commonwealth Trust.

....

NOTES

1. González Echevarria (1998, 8) suggests one way of understanding the narrative of Latin American fiction. Rather than the more conventional appeal to literary precursors, he aims to demonstrate how the novel is circumscribed by the presence of hegemonic documents. Breaks or discontinuities in the dominant text of these societies determine shifts in the form of narrative (the picaresque novel emerges as a simulation of the notarial rhetoric of legal submissions, nineteenth-century novels mimic the form of the scientific report or travel journal, and twentieth-century literature borrows its form from the documents of anthropology). But he argues that fiction does more than obey the constraints imposed by contemporary documents; Latin American novels copy the form of these records in order to subvert them.

2. Anthropologists of Papua New Guinean societies report that people regularly connect events to their dreaming. Gillison (1993, 199) states that among the Gimi of the Eastern Highlands the first sweet potato is believed to have been seen in a dream. Indeed, the Gimi say that women must dream a child before conceiving it (209), and that future marriage partners should first view each other in dreams (233). People often regard dreams as the source of myth and ritual, as the basis for new forms of knowing (cf. Stephen 1979, 14).

....

REFERENCES

Bateson, Gregory. 1973. *Steps to an Ecology of Mind: Collected Essays in Anthropology, Psychiatry, Evolution, and Epistemology.* London: Granada.
Benjamin, Walter. 1992. *Illuminations.* Ed. Hannah Arendt. Trans. Harry Zohn. London: Fontana Press.

Forge, Anthony. 1970. Learning to See in New Guinea. In *Socialization: The Approach from Social Anthropology*, ed. P. Mayer, 269–93. New York: Tavistock.

Foucault, Michel. 1977. *Discipline and Punish: The Birth of the Prison*. Trans. Alan Sheridan. London: Penguin.

Garfinkel, Harold. 1967. *Studies in Ethnomethodology*. Englewood Cliffs, NJ: Prentice-Hall.

Gell, Alfred. 1992. The Technology of Enchantment and the Enchantment of Technology. In *Anthropology, Art, and Aesthetics*, ed. Jeremy Coote and Anthony Shelton, 40–63. Oxford: Clarendon Press.

Gillison, Gillian. 1993. *Between Culture and Fantasy: A New Guinea Highlands Mythology*. Chicago: University of Chicago Press.

González Echevarria, Roberto. 1998. *Myth and Archive: A Theory of Latin American Narrative*. Durham, NC: Duke University Press.

Gow, Peter. 1990. Could Sangama Read? The Origin of Writing among the Piro of Eastern Peru. *History and Anthropology* 5:87–103.

Losche, Diane. 1995. The Sepik Gaze: Iconographic Interpretation of Abelam Form. *Social Analysis* 38:47–60.

Munn, Nancy. 1973. *Walbiri Iconography: Graphic Representation and Cultural Symbolism in a Central Australian Society*. Ithaca, NY: Cornell University Press.

O'Hanlon, Michael. 1989. *Reading the Skin: Adornment, Display, and Society among the Wahgi*. London: British Museum Publications.

Pickering, Andrew. 1997. Concepts and the Mangle of Practice: Constructing Quaternions. In *Mathematics, Science, and Postclassical Theory*, ed. Barbara Herrnstein Smith and Arkady Plotnitsky, 40–82, 90–94. Durham, NC: Duke University Press.

Reed, Adam. 1999. Anticipating Individuals: Modes of Vision and Their Social Consequence in a Papua New Guinean Prison. *Journal of the Royal Anthropological Institute* 5(1): 43–56.

———. 2003. *Papua New Guinea's Last Place: Experiences of Constraint in a Postcolonial Prison*. Oxford: Berghahn Press.

Riles, Annelise. 1998. Infinity within the Brackets. *American Ethnologist* 25(3): 378–98.

———. 2000. *The Network Inside Out*. Ann Arbor: University of Michigan Press.

Stephen, Michele. 1979. Dreams of Change: The Innovative Role of Altered States of Consciousness in Traditional Melanesian Religion. *Oceania* 50:3–22.

Strathern, Andrew, and Marilyn Strathern. 1971. *Self-Decoration in Mount Hagen*. London: Duckworth.

Part 3   **Collaboration and**

Response

Bullet-Proofing

A Tale from the United Kingdom

··

Marilyn Strathern

> The existence of a mission statement is tantamount to an admission by the university that it is *missionless:* as a general idea, the university is without mission.
>
> —Barnett 2000, 94

HOW MIGHT ONE CRITIQUE good practice? *Good practice* carries the double resonance of ethical behavior and effective action. Simultaneously a standard of measurement and a target to which to work, it is thought to bring its own reward: organizations will be more effective in their performance if they are at once explicit about their goals and honest about their own behavior. Explicitness is often achieved through documentation, and it is a form of documentary good practice that is the subject of this chapter. But why should one wish to mount such a critique? To answer this I divide the chapter through three rather different registers.

The first section opens with a complaint about the formatting of university mission statements, with an example from the United Kingdom as illustration.[1] The second and longest section pursues issues prompted by this genre of documents, starting with a phenomenon that appears to have a remote connection but with each case moving closer to explicitness. Showing the manner in which these cases may be grasped as analogies is the subject of the final section, which returns to some of the points made by Annelise Riles in her introduction to the volume. In particular it suggests that the anger evident behind the complaint is anger at obtuseness, that is, at a failure to make use of knowledge. It raises questions about the implicit realism at work here.

....

Formatting of University Mission Statements

"To participate actively at national and international levels"; "to respond to the needs of the community"; "to provide [services] of the highest quality"; "to attract outstanding [personnel] from all backgrounds . . ." Do you recognize these phrases? Probably you recognize them as the kind of aims one might find in an institution's mission statement. But do you *understand* them? Do they make sense? Superficially, of course, they could not be more obvious. But perhaps we ought *not* to understand them.

These are "detailed aims" laid out by an educational institution, and the public participation is in matters of policy affecting higher education, the needs of the community refer to continuing education, the service is that of "education" itself, and it is outstanding students whom the institution hopes to attract. The institution in question, which has been taking in students since about A.D. 1209 and was already a corporation by 1225, also has a long-term strategy that heads this list: "to foster and develop academic excellence across a wide range of subjects and at all levels of study, to enhance its position as one of the world's leading universities, and to continue to play the wider intellectual and cultural role which has characterized its activities for centuries." I am quoting from the University of Cambridge's mission statement, specifically as it appeared in their Strategic Plan for 1995–96 to 1999–2000 (reprinted in the university's official organ, the *Cambridge University Reporter*, 14 August 1996). Having responded to the Higher Education Funding Council of England's (HEFCE) requests for such documents each year since 1993, the 1996 version is referred to as a new and updated plan.

It is the first time that bullet points appeared in this otherwise sober news sheet; little else had changed in its 126 years. Their precursors had been there in previous issues, but set out as though a sequence were intended: points were labeled (a) to (f).[2] But in 1996 this hint of sequence is abandoned, and the discrete points are rendered visually by bullets. The statements signaled by bullet points are marshaled under two rubrics, one the "long term strategy" of the university, and the other its collegiate character.[3] The previous year's counterpart to what is now called "long term strategy" had been a simple reference to the "main purpose" of the university. The 1996 version also dropped the university's implicit observation on HEFCE's flexible management practices (cf. Martin 1992)—it had been in the habit of spelling out the dates of request and deadline for the updated strategic plan. The no-time-to-do-it-in demand had become an annual and thus foreseeable matter. Insofar as these aims and objectives were being produced in response to such requests there seems nothing remarkable about them. And nothing remarkable, it would seem, about a gradual evolution of language.

Yet what are bullet points? Can one understand them? Silly questions, since they are not themselves for "understanding" in the way that one might, say, absorb the notion of a sequence from (a) to (f). On the contrary they simply highlight the individual impact that each statement or "point" is supposed to make by itself. These are not being related or enumerated: it is just that there are several of them, and each needs highlighting. The bullets are after all visual markers. So what about the brief statements highlighted in this way? In fact I left one out. Repeating the phraseology of the point bulleted as providing education of the highest quality, which is then specified as producing graduates of the caliber sought by industry, the professions, public service, and the academic world (in that order), appears: "to encourage and pursue research of the highest quality across the full range of subjects studied in the University, and [new since 1996] to develop new areas of research and teaching in response to the advance of knowledge and scholarship." Do you understand what *this* means?

Some of its intentions at least are transparent. In response to HEFCE, and behind HEFCE's government interest in policy-driven work, this document (the strategic plan) also emphasizes the autonomous value of knowledge and scholarship. While these concerns could have been taken for granted in higher education, the university's reference to a full range of subjects is there no doubt to remind the government of its identity as a "university," should there be any move to discriminate against particular disciplines. But its principal message is nonsense. What could it mean not to pursue research of the highest quality? Might other institutions pursue research of high, but not the highest quality? Impossible: the highest quality of any institution's research will be *its* "highest." Is one being asked to supply the implicit comparative? Is the meaning that in relation to a universe of universities there could be some institutions with higher qualities than others and one or some with "the highest," depending on mode of ranking? Yet mission statements are supposed to be free-standing self-descriptions. On the other hand, if all can reach the highest, then the universe is presumably wider—nonuniversity institutions doing similar things perhaps but not getting there. Here the contradiction is that the categorical difference means that these others could never in fact aim for the *same* "highest."

Or should one simply accept as a fact that the idea of pursuing research of the highest quality does not make propositional sense? Perhaps those who put the statement together—intelligent, educated persons—never meant it to make sense. They would say it is "just" a matter of rhetoric or style. Diverse phrases would seem to fall into the same category. For example: "to respond to the needs of the community." Whose needs? What community? Why does the university produce education for students but continuing education for the community? "The needs of the community" seems to work as a preformed package, a shorthand, a bundled together set of images, of the kind that abounds in certain political and international languages.[4] It does not have to be spelled out each time. The phrase "highest quality" has something of the same effect. By simply pointing to the fact that it is going to encourage an activity of "the highest quality" the university somehow suggests that it must be a high-quality outfit already.

But these *are* all absurd questions. We all know that the text is not there to be analyzed and scrutinized in this way. Yet if these are absurd questions, then there is a serious one to be asked: what is an institution of higher education doing producing what is (in the sense of being unanalyzable) nonsense? In raising this final question, we might start seeing the document rather than the text. I begin with unraveling some of the hidden metaphors: what exactly is being aimed at what?

....

Deflecting Bullets

John and Jean Comaroff (1992) open their book on ethnography and the historical imagination with the sad little newspaper story of Naparama and his army in 1990 fighting in Mozambique. Several thousand men and boys with spears are protected by nothing more than marks on their chests, which are claimed to be the scars of "vaccinations" against bullets. The story is sad for the social anthropologist, since the Comaroffs see it as evidence of anthropology's failure to dislodge the stereotype of the primitive. The *Chicago Tribune*'s report is all about the superstitious beliefs that predominate in Mozambique, evoking straw huts and magic amulets by contrast with the technology of modern warfare.[5] It is not sad for Naparama's army, however. On the contrary, the victims of superstition included heavily armed rebels and government troops who alike fled from the bullet-proof soldiers (authors' phrase) in awe. Western analysts, the newspaper report said, can only scratch their heads in amazement (Comaroff and Comaroff 1992, 3). One suspects that Naparama's soldiers are probably somewhat in awe of themselves too.

Now it is as a tactic that finds favor on both sides that strategic plans are put forward to HEFCE by universities: they are part of the general installation of "good practices" by which these institutions will show they can govern themselves and thus ward off too much government from the center. This tactic is at the same time encouraged by central government, which regards its own mission as enabling, at least insofar as government itself uses the very idea of government interference as a threat to institutions to get their houses in order.[6] Mission statements are part of the universities' bullet-proofing. And like Naparama's army with their marks on their chests, the aims set down so awkwardly in these mission statements are meant to point to genuinely superior qualities within. They are protective aversion tactics.

The match is not equal. HEFCE can ask what it wants, and at short notice (keep-them-on-their-toes management); it has sanctions at its back (controls the university's funding), and it is heavily armed with a language of accountability. By language I do not just mean concepts and terms; I mean also instruments, since accountability these days depends on information technology (unthinkable to submit a strategic plan that is handwritten or manually typed).

The Naparama men and boys were not shooting bullets back at the soldiers they confronted; they were instead *deflecting* the soldiers' aim. It was the power to stop the enemy from using their guns that they displayed on their chests. In other words, some of their own strength they took from their opponents—the greater the enemy power, the greater their own. Did the "vaccinations" on the chest imply that these people had already been shot?[7] That would seem to have been part of Naparama's claim—he was said to have been resurrected from the dead, and his living soldiers to bear, not wounds, but the very marks of bullets from the guns previously aimed at them. Now we do not know the exact logic here, but we might surmise that these troops are invincible because they have already absorbed the missile that will protect them from further ones. So although the bullets they expect will come from "outside" themselves, their power is to show that they can take them "within" and demonstrate that they have not been harmed. It is as enchanted men, one might say, that they set themselves apart from their opponents. Indeed, an observer might even add that what would defeat Naparama's army would be shooting back—adopting the weapons of the other side—for their untrained soldiers would not stand a chance. Their only strength is incommensurability.

Universities are deflecting what they see as possibly punitive measures (get into order or be put into order). They attempt a small and important defense of invincibility in their own terms, as when they appeal to knowledge and scholarship, and in the case of Cambridge a spirited defense of the collegiate system. But, with much less courage than these Mozambique soldiers, they also try to use the weapons that are aimed at them. They not only answer back in the language of assessment-accountability, they may well adopt it for their own internal regimes. So they go on regarding as powerful the actual weapons of the other side since these weapons must be sustained as equally powerful for use themselves. It is a poor strategy of deflection. It means that they cannot really acquire any immunity to them.

Reflecting the Aim

In using some of the weapons of the other side, universities are doing more than trying to deflect punitive measures. They are also trying, with greater or lesser consciousness about it, to *reflect* other aspects of themselves and their "opponents." That reflection is accorded power of its own. I take this as my second position.

Consider certain fear-inducing shields that Gell (1998) discusses from Papua New Guinea.[8] Traditionally wooden, nowadays also metal (O'Hanlon 1995), and in many cases nearly man-size, these especially strengthened outer skins are painted with designs said to demoralize the enemy. The shield's surface deflects the enemy's arrows or bullets; but it is also marked to reflect the strength of the warrior[9] carrying it. The designs portray the fierceness of the man concealed behind. In other words there is a strength behind the strength. Strength is protected in being concealed—the enemy is not fully aware of just how strong the defender is. Concealed strength is implied in the 1996 text that follows the Cambridge "mission statement" with "aims and objectives." "The aims and objectives of the University have now to be constrained by the severely adverse financial settlement in respect of the Funding Council grant for 1996–97 . . . [but: we have hidden strengths] every effort will be made to ensure" that quality will be maintained (*The Reporter*, 14 August 1996). Such a response only makes sense of course if there is an agreement on both sides about the aims.

At this point the analogy with combat gets rather strained. There are not really two "sides." The universities' case introduces a whole other set of issues that follow from the fact that what might look like weapons pointed at them by HEFCE are embraced as their own aims, all part of the institutionalization of best practice. It is not just a matter of warding off more punitive measures (though that too) but of seeking approval. Universities want, by and large, to be told they have got it right, and that they have accurately reflected HEFCE's concerns in that sense. It is not only themselves that they are reflecting, then, but in the documents they produce they hope to be reflecting back to them the will of their opponents. So in what sense is HEFCE an opponent?

While the combat analogy has nearly outrun its usefulness, let me keep with it a moment longer. For those Papua New Guinea shields point in a further direction. Look more closely at how they are supposed to motivate people. There is more to reflection than the simple idea that the shields held in front of the body reflect the body behind or aggrandize it for effect. What is painted on those shields is how that body is supposed to look from the vantage point of the opponents. It is meant to be a body capable of terrifying them, and in thus eliciting the opponents' own terror also depicts it. Submitting to their fascination, the opponents are obliged to share in the emotions that these designs objectify. Yet this is no straightforward mirror. Gell (1998, 31) argues that these shields function as "false mirrors": they seem to show the victim (the opponent, enemy) his own terror when in fact it is someone else's. For it is the warriors holding the shields as they face the enemy who are first of all terrified—they are terrified *of themselves*, of their own power.[10] The point is that this terror is guaranteed—it has already happened. If the shield bearers are already terrified by the power they can produce, then the shields should indeed terrify the enemy by persuading him that these artifacts are exactly capable of what they show.

This double reflexive is to be observed in myriad ethnographic contexts, Gell adds. He cites Benjamin: it "constitutes the very secret of mimesis; that is, to perceive (to internalise) is to imitate and thus we become (and produce) what we perceive" (1998, 31). Emotions are produced by the objects or events persons produce, and people can be in awe of their own products. Here I take my cue from Gell's (1992) earlier paper on the technology of enchantment—the ability to enthrall others—that so often derives from the enchantment of technology. He refers, for example, to a world where spells and other magical actions accompany the manufacturing process. People are taken aback by the magical skill that produces the technology in the first place, and that apprehension of skill is part of the magic it in turn conveys. But there are processual effects other than magic. Efficacy may also be conveyed through the "halo-effect" of technical virtuosity (Gell 1992, 46–47).

Sheer technical skill holds a prime place in the current awe that Euro-Americans have of technology. This is nowhere more true than in information and communications technology. They are amazed by the skills it appears to elicit from them. And these skills are brought into being through interactive programs held to be the very acme of new educational techniques. One becomes clever by interacting with a clever machine. For the clever machine helps people communicate through having them communicate with it. Communication, not terror or magic, is the crucial effect. It is shown, so to speak, to particular effect when it is deliberate "communications" as such that are being produced. Not surprisingly, then, these skills are brought visibly into play in documents such as the mission statement. At any rate, if you can get your machine to do bullet points for you, that is a small reminder of the myriad marvels the word processor opens up: the mission statement with its bullet points is the institution holding up to itself its amazement at what it might be capable of. If the institution thereby becomes in awe of what it can produce, what it can bring out from itself, the contemporary spin on such "educative" processes is that this awe is indeed very largely awe of technique, at how it is done. The new accountabilities use a false mirror device. For they require that on the shield be painted not just a depiction of ourselves produced in order to impress others but *a picture that shows how impressed we are with ourselves.*

This brings me to my third vehicle for asking about aims. It drops the notion of there being opponents, and develops a model of confrontation between parties with convergent as well as divergent interests. It requires broadening the context in which mission statement documents appear.

Auditing Aims

Bullet points are often used in order to make an institution's aims and objectives crystal clear, and the resultant mission statement joins myriad documents that fuel practices of public accountability. The connection can be quite explicit. Thus the assessors' handbook that accompanied the first national British exercise in Teaching Quality Assessment emphatically stated that assessors were not being asked to judge the validity of subject aims and objectives, what constitutes proper training in a discipline, say, but to judge how far they could be met by the institution's aims and objectives. Obviously these have to be spelled out in the first place.

One umbrella colloquialism for the expanding practices of accountability in Britain is "audit." It belongs to a global pond where institutions and organizations jostle for recognition in an information and communication technologies soup of logos and websites. So routine as to be unnoticed, it is through the way they describe themselves that organizations demand attention—coerced into giving such descriptions, they also force their descriptions of themselves on others. *But in either case they have to persuade others that it is "themselves" they are describing.* They have to create the conditions of trust under which their representations will hold conviction. Submitting to good practice would seem to do some of this validating work. It has thus become "good practice" simply to be able to describe one's mission through stating aims and objectives and the procedures to achieve them. Organizations have learned how to describe themselves. And good practice concerns the comportment of this much-described self in (as we shall see) a thoroughly reflexive manner.[11]

I take "audit" as a particular example of the way in which the more general ethics of good practice get implemented. Scrutiny of higher education in Britain is managed through the Quality Assurance Agency, whose remit includes rationalizing the four yearly national Research Assessment Exercises (RAEs) and the rolling Teaching Quality Assessment program.[12] Linked on the one hand to public funding and thus to the financing of whole universities, and on the other to the individual performance of academics, that is, the productivity of researchers and teachers, the unit of accountability is the individual department (cost center). Departmental performance is scored and ranked. The whole process is meant to be at once enabling (of institutional improvement) and evaluative (making value for money [public funds] evident). It also gives policymakers criteria on which to base selectivity, for example, in funding (Bekhradnia 1999). Key to the exercises is the way in which departments are invited to describe their accomplishments, in a variety of formats but often with appeal to the institution's mission statement. To the extent that their claims about performance are auditable, regardless of outcome, auditors can credit an organization with having given a demonstrable account of "itself." Most academics, however, would declare that the categories into which they are forced to render their account of themselves is no such thing. Typically they complain of the complexity that is lost along the way. This banal sense of confrontation holds a modicum of interest.

Consider Power's amplification of audit. It is a set of practices, he says, that links diverse fields of activity, provides people with the tools to make sense of what they do, responds to changing environmental conditions, supplies its own rationale, regenerates itself in the face of apparent failure, and above all "actively constructs the contexts in which it operates" (Power 1994, 8). Audit defines its own context insofar as it creates organizations responsive to the auditing process. Although Power does not put it like this, one could add that as part of its ongoing *self*-definition, as an enabling mechanism, audit creates perturbations on the boundaries of organizations—it activates them by making them perform in public, and then absorbs new details of performance to enhance its own changing definitions of good practice.[13] Thus early attempts at quantitative research assessment through number of publications gave way before the academics' criticism that the RAE should be attending to quality, criticism it incorporated without a murmur into subsequent exercises.[14] Perturbations lead to perpetual restructuring, and to the ever-changing "measurements" that audits produce in order to turn data into assessable units that the auditees will accept.[15]

Suppose indeed one understood audit as a system that defined its own boundaries, constituting everything beyond itself as its environment. A system can be described as coupled to its environment through perturbations, disturbances that require it to make sense of an external and indeterminate world through its (miniaturizing) representations of it. Information is not transferred between system and environment; rather the system creates a distinction between the "information" it can use internal to itself and unusable "data" beyond.[16] This description I have lifted almost verbatim from an explication of Niklas Luhmann's writings.[17] Written on the eve of the audit explosion, his essays (1990) on self-reference are uncanny in the circumstances. He anticipates—with almost predictive force—the conditions under which practices of good practice might start taking off as a self-organizing system.

For Luhmann, systems are axiomatically self-referential; each can only realize itself. They are also self-changing—constant selection and dissolution of elements is a condition of their continuing reproduction. Events cannot be saved; a system is inherently restless (1990, 9).[18] An organization concerned about its identity is constantly communicating information particular to itself: if it does not, then it has ceased to exist.[19] What gives systems in general their self-organizing properties is their capacity to define their own boundaries. A boundary is created when a system simplifies or streamlines ("rationalizes") phenomena otherwise perceived to lie outside it. Reduction of external complexity, the indeterminacy of what lies beyond the system, may increase the system's internal complexity where not everything within is yet under control. The more the system can take on, the more powerful its interactions with its environment. However, environment and system are not symmetrical, do not "meet."

Self-referential systems are able to "observe" their own operations, and will insert descriptions of themselves into themselves (Luhmann 1990, 184). Now this formal theoretical proposition (which specifies the properties by which one may recognize "a system") turns up in another location altogether: in the hands of social planners and theorists, it appears as a literal aim or objective. Thus we may understand modern societies as developing various *theories about social process* as "instruments of self-observation within different functional sectors" (1990, 185).[20] Theorizing about education or law, say, has been concerned with the reflexive foundations of these functional components (finding educational principles on which, for example, to base educational institutions).

With audit, literalization is taken one step further. Added to what a system is doing in its own communications is an invitation for metacommunication for—literally—a "self-description." But this is not reflexivity for its own sake. Reflexivity under the prospect of audit sustains a judgmental and thus an ethical self (Hoskin 1995). We can see audit as a social system with its own self-organizing properties, regenerating itself through the auditable accounts it elicits. For it inspects the auditees' *own* auditing methods; auditees are thus turned into ethical self-auditors—typically they do their own audit on themselves before the experts come in.

Rendering practices explicit becomes part of audit's internal complexity, and points to its boundary condition, a key means by which audit systems reduce and absorb outside complexities into themselves. But audit constitutes its environment in a rather special way: it fishes in a pond potentially full of organizations—such as institutions of higher education or health service trusts—perceived as *other systems* each required to be explicit about its own organization.[21] Yet this is no reciprocal relationship; the systems do not "meet." When a university department (cost center) becomes subject to audit, the interactions all seem to work in audit's way. If environmental perturbations facilitate the continuation of the self-organizing process (the words are Nowotny's) through allowing a system to restructure itself, it is as though audit deliberately caused perturbations in order to enable the restructuring of these "other systems." It thus presents to organizations, as we may imagine university departments, an environment with the constant capacity for perturbation, in a state of perpetual demand, and it is the relationship of demand that from the organization's point of view defines the boundary between itself and its auditors. I said that a frequent complaint made of audit is that it fails to comprehend the "complexity" of the organizations it monitors. Of course: as a system itself, audit's complexity lies in its own internal mechanisms of conduct. These it "improves" by sucking complexity out of the external organizations into itself. The notion that measurements can always be improved contributes to the restlessness of the audit system. It is in retrospect that we can see that the whole audit apparatus in Britain amounts to a self-organizing "system" that can take on any other.

The apparent simplification of knowledge that occurs in translations between domains of expertise, then, is not simply because an expert language has to be made easy for the layperson, the general public as (say) represented by the government, to understand. There is a systemic effect here. In Luhmann's view, reduction through translation is the identifying property of a "system." Given that a system is identified by the fact that it cannot take on the complexity of other systems, in converting or translating outside data into meaningful information for itself, it is also identified by the limits of its own self-modeling of the world. I would repeat that it translates data into information; it does not transform one kind of information into another. In short, the model of self-organizing systems helps sharpen the usual accounts social scientists give of actors moving between (potentially symmetrical) contexts. It also reminds us of a type of system that is neither open nor closed (e.g., Luhmann 1990, 229) but, to the contrary, is constantly evolving and changing the conditions for its own complexity.

Now what makes audit virtuous is its power to purify the principles of (good) organization as such. Audit does not just produce auditees and auditors; it is an organization that produces trust in organization(s). Its own self becomes recognizable in the efforts others make to come up to standard. Auditing practices make sense of an organization, then, by requiring that it "perform" *being* an organization. Audit practices are archetypes: as instruments of purification, their own smooth running is not up for scrutiny. The practitioners (auditors) are ethical arbiters with guidelines to implement rather than social observers with a job of analysis to do. Audit keeps its own virtue through its own self-description as (the phrase is mine) an enabling technology.

In writing about the knowledge-making role of the U.S. National Science Foundation in assessing applications for funding, Donald Brenneis (1997) points out the extent to which its bureaucratic practices depend on the intermittent but consequential input from outside scholars: we have met the bureaucrats, he says, and they are us.[22] But what "us"? The peer review that goes on outside feeds into a different formation within the NSF, where panelists from diverse disciplines instead find themselves peers of one another.[23] They have to create their own self-referential arena. It would seem that an academic cannot "meet" a bureaucrat—the relationship between our different selves is not a face-to-face one. What we take as information will not be the same. For instance, it is impossible—absurd—to contemplate carrying implicit knowledge across this boundary.

If that is the case, then there is a serious question about exactly what "selves" are involved in documents of self-description when the mission statement is archetype. Munro (1999) points to a mystification in the very demand for self-description. Taking issue with Power's (1994, 36–37) comment that "audit becomes a formal 'loop' by which the system observes itself," he suggests (personal communication) that rather what is at issue is the extent to which one system is mediated by others. A university that failed to declare access as one of its goals, for instance, would be out of the race. Systems interacting with one another are as cumbersome as this third context has been, perhaps because they impinge on one another not as parties to a conversation but in the nonmutual, nonsymmetrical manner that defines any one system's response as a response not to entities similar to itself but to entities that from its point of view form its environment.

Aiming at Format

The fourth conjunction brings us back to the mission statement as document, in this case embedded in other kinds of documents with which it shares features of format. Consider the following description of a set of historical documents. The documents had a standardized structure, dictating a given progression from preamble to mission statement to global framework. This simple structure was, however, the sum total of any analytical framing. One could negotiate paragraphs in virtually any order, and indeed the compilers would skip from one to another without any apparent loss of continuity or cohesion. The logic that linked the paragraphs was like the logic that linked huge quantities of documents themselves to one another—the collection and collation of a potentially infinite number of concrete and distinct entities (words, paragraphs, the minutes of meetings). Stylistic conventions ensured that the documents replicated one another in organizational logic, language, formatting, typeface, and layout. Although there could be changes from one document to the next, the emphasis was not on innovative details, but on the success of the replication of a given pattern from one artifact to the next.

This is taken, in places verbatim, from Annelise Riles's (1998; this volume) account of the 1995 preparations for the Pacific Platform of Action, documents to be fed into the United Nations Fourth World Conference on Women in Beijing. It was one of many regional efforts at the intergovernmental level.[24] Form was central—and much attention was devoted to the aesthetic quality of the documents. The aim was to produce a good specimen of a particular genre.

Each document came into existence within a whole population of documents. Some were coeval, produced by drafting bodies similar to the present one; others were documents to which this was contributing or from which it had derived. In the case of the Beijing meeting, conferences at national regional and global levels replicated the myriad levels of consultation and drafting that had gone on earlier within each country. Indeed, part of Riles's own argument concerns the "infinity" of consultation as well as sheer effort at drafting that the documents contain. She analyzes the procedures of the Pacific Island drafters through concepts of pattern and layering, observations prompted by the manner in which Fijians collect vast numbers of mats to pile up and distribute on ceremonial occasions. The collation of these mats had one crucial characteristic: they were nontransformative. Mats were piled in such a way that their fringes were exposed, and this produced a distinctive pattern so that the arrangements had a visual coherence; when the mats were distributed, however, each was taken away as a concrete and distinct entity. The pattern was neither retained nor elaborated upon. "When one took the [pile] apart one had both nothing (an absence of form) and a collection of concrete things, but not one form emerging out of another" (1998, 385).

This material is of twofold interest. First, it draws attention to the fact that a university's mission statement is not just responding to the demands of a particular governmental organ in a particular country (the UK's Higher Education Funding Council of England and its associated bodies). And it is not just laying out the academic purpose in nonacademic language in order to do so. Rather, we are dealing with utterances of a specific kind, even though they are as ubiquitous as the market, namely a turn-of-the-century international language of good governance. Reaching well beyond national audit practices, then, is a wider cultural environment to which the university's mission statement also responds, and which creates a specific kind of institutional "self" for it. This makes it mystifying to think parochially—as though English universities were just responding to HEFCE, say, or the particularities of British audit culture.

The language of the university mission statement is *not* an academic language made simple. The document incorporates textual practices that might look familiar to an academic—writing, quotations, paragraphs—but in truth it belongs to a world of its own. This means in turn that the universities are not necessarily deflecting or reflecting in the way they might think they are; they are not just reacting to national needs or making themselves intelligible to the general public. They are participating in a global communications network of document production whose underlying cultural tenets remain largely unexamined. What is unexamined, among other things, is their relationship to the texts that academics do produce for themselves. Side by side with academic communications, the international language of mission statements exists as another "system" of communications altogether. When it translates academic language into "information" for itself, it thereby treats academic textual practices as no more than unformed environmental data.

This brings me to the second interest in such material. Bullet points, like paragraphs in the Platform for Action document, are nontransformative. You cannot do intellectual operations on them. They allow no growth. "As in the mats, then, the skill of the exercise [compiling documents], lay in the detail . . . and in the patience this extremely labor-intensive task demanded, not in the invention of new designs or in the transformation of one form into another" (Riles 1998, 386). Riles comments that after hours of work at one set of meetings on issues to do with violence against women, by the close of the conference "this subject had not evolved, expanded, come into focus or been [otherwise] transformed" (1998, 387). Her emphasis on the nontransformative nature of this language holds a serious message for academic practice.

The documents these conferences produced cannot be "read" as scholarly publications are read. There is no argument to critique since there is no argumentative structure underlying the sequence of paragraphs. There is no analysis or interpretation to be done beyond analysis of the politics of compilation. There is no denouement, no unfolding, no discovery to be made, nothing that emerges from the "texts" as whole entities or from any kind of journey through them. Indeed one might add that not only is there no narrative and no plot, there is no record of the process of compilation, no internal monitoring of discourse, no authorial self-scrutiny, but then there is also no social observation, no science, and in that sense no facts.[25] There are, in short, no internal relations to be followed through. There certainly is implicit knowledge of the immense labor, and negotiating skill, that lies behind the formulation of every sentence. But apart from that, all we have in these documents is the this-that oscillation of whether this is included or that is omitted. In short, you cannot do intellectual operations on them. They allow no growth. They create no knowledge.

The language of bullet points is no harmless nonsense;[26] this kind of language is actively *opposed* to the task of education if education is a matter of providing the tools by which people find things out for themselves, and is opposed to research if this is taken to rest on knowledge, and to scholarship for that matter as a critical enterprise. The enemy within: the textual form in which statements are made about the very issues of education and research undermine the textual means by which such aims are accomplished in real life.[27]

To the Point

What is an institution of *higher education* doing in producing unanalyzable nonsense? A body such as Cambridge University is not producing unanalyzable nonsense of its own volition. It is doing so in response to demands, directly from HEFCE, and indirectly from widely distributed cultural expectations, whether from national practices of accountability or the language of international conventions. There are dangers here. Following Munro (1999), I want to suggest that among them is the nonmutuality of excessive responsiveness. A human virtue, and one that social anthropologists among others have long commented upon, namely the ability to see things from the vantage points of others, appears here in an ugly form. It is time, fifth then, for something a bit more hard hitting, and I focus on the fatal flaw in responsiveness.

> *Exploitation.* Bullet-proofing and false mirrors evoked persons in confrontation with one another as a way of responding to one another's aims. If I personified them as combatants, this was meant to convey the nonmutuality of their engagement: one side was always trying to co-opt the other's power. In the case of human combatants, then,

reflection and deflection may have nothing to do with augmenting the relationship between the parties and everything to do with aggrandizing oneself at another's expense. Self-referential systems and the reflexivity of audit, on the other hand, evoke abstract entities, systems, examples of the reifications upon which institutional documents thrive. Again these entities try to absorb one another in nonmutual confrontation. Audit exploits people's interests in their own identity (describing "themselves") by demanding that the selves be made visible and then making sure that what can be made visible depends on the technology available to see it with.[28] Not everything will count as a self-description. In both cases, what is being pressed into service for one party at the expense of another is a fundamental social capacity: responsiveness to others.

Cost. Needham[29] wonders if we should not invent the "dreyfus." The dreyfus could be an international unit of injustice that would enable us to measure (how many millidreyfus) the numbers of hours spent responding to audit requirements against the degree of injustice that not doing so would incur. His context is recruitment protocols, and the casualty he points to is trust. Accountability regimes imply a negation of trust. Trust in turn relies on implicit knowledge about the conditions under which actions are appropriate, the values that inform (say) the making of appointments. Implicit knowledge may be problematic enough, notoriously so in this area, but audit does not solve it. The problem is not that audit makes the implicit explicit, but that it is a false presentation of visibility, a false mirror indeed: with audit in place, no one need *look for* the implicit values.

Loss. What may be lost along the way, which McIntyre notes in relation to scientific debate, is a certain ideal or ethic of communication. This is the "ethic of honest public and personal communication and openness of discussion . . . which includes the ability to get up in a large scientific conference and say of your favourite theory, 'I got it wrong'" (1998, 45). Peer review for the purposes of quality assessment, by publication for example, simply erodes that ethic.[30]

Moving goalposts. The expectation is that both sides are out to get whatever advantage they can from learning about the other, and not just about the performances and protocols, but about their future aims, and somehow be there one jump ahead. This also enrolls (manipulates) a specific social capacity (e.g., Goody 1995), interest in anticipating how people are going to behave. That kind of anticipation may be projected onto the instruments of audit itself—how the measurements are going to be applied in the future brings with it the idea that one should work at how to anticipate one's response to them.

Cheating. Anticipation, as in the University of Cambridge's double intention to provide education and to pursue research "of the highest quality," offers a version of Goodhart's law (Hoskin 1996).[31] Goodhart's law was derived from observations on protocols for monetary control ("as soon as . . . an asset is publicly defined as money in order to enable monetary control, it will cease to be used as money and replaced by substitutes which will enable evasion of that control" [Hoskin 1996, 279–80]). In formulaic terms, when a measure becomes a target, it ceases to be a good measure. An example, brought home by the experience of Cambridge University Press,[32] is the distortion of the book-publishing market in response to the use of publications as a measure of academic excellence in the RAE. Measure collapses into target, and the conventional distance that measurements are supposed to provide shrinks.

Subversion. Overresponsiveness subordinates content to form. Bullet points and mission statements are antimeaning. They appear to be text (form), but they are not to be analyzed (content). Anthropologists are aware of the class of utterance that Malinowski long ago dubbed as phatic communion, utterances for the sake of talking rather than conveying information: no one would object in principle to the sociability, or otherwise, such utterances engender. But being built into professional practice is another matter; they give cause for objection to these diverse kinds of meaninglessnesses.

Attack. Perhaps those points on the mission statement were never really bullet points after all—perhaps they are the bull's-eye, the center of the dartboard, the targets on the firing range. One aims or shoots *at* them. Perhaps as academics and scholars, we now know why we should take out an injunction against bullet points and mission statements. One should *not* (try to) understand them. For to even think we were doing that would put us in a position of bad faith with ourselves—those selves, that is, who do produce texts in order to create knowledge through the "understanding" they demand.

....

Conclusion

The situations detailed in the five preceding sections could be thought of as bullet points themselves, parodied in the final one, insofar as the cumulative progression is largely a stylistic matter: they could have been given in any order, are of wildly divergent status (a metaphor, a position, a context, a conjunction, a set of admonitions), and there is neither rhyme nor reason to the number five. But they are not "real" bullet points. Each contains discursive prose and requires some sustained attention. I now want to suggest where realism lies.

Emotional tenor offers a clue. Sarcasm (at the university by contrast with Naparama's army) is followed by irony (the out-mirroring mirrors) and exaggeration or pompousness (taking systems seriously), and then just before the closing parody, by explication (explaining why meaninglessness matters). The account is prefaced, the reader will recall, by the scarcely concealed anger of the academic's complaint. Part of the problem is how to complain, how to criticize good practice and still appear moral, credible, and public spirited, and thus offer a critique that is edifying. The procedure that then followed was to point to certain underlying truths, most explicit in the final example with its open reference to human proclivities that are being apparently perverted or undermined. The truths in all these situations are offered not as realisms but as realities, that is, not as indices of a real world outside these various devices but as political and social realities made evident through these devices. The devices consist of bringing in forms of knowledge otherwise overlooked.

Thus the case of Naparama's men is there to point up the *real* lack of courage on the part of the universities being pushed around by politically motivated demands for accountability—however foolhardy being courageous would turn out to be. The Papua New Guinea shields point to people who *really* know how to put reflexivity into action, and whose intellectual convolutions are quite unsurpassed. Luhmann introduces what looks like a *real* context for understanding the behaviors of systems and thus what one can expect of audit regimes, a serious attempt at illuminating the loss of complexity that academics complain about. The Fijian mats move the reader closer toward interrogating the unanalyzable nature of these kinds of documents, a *real* criticism of what is wrong with them. And the parody at the end includes a scatter of none other than *real* aims or objectives! The latter are presented negatively, as aims and objectives seemingly abandoned by these reductive formats. (The aims include engaging people's sense of identity, the promotion of trust among colleagues, an ethic of open communication, learning from experience, having a system of independent standards, paying attention to the content and meaning of what we do, understanding knowledge as the transformation of one set of meanings into another.)

My five situations are contrived as analogies, then, for different aspects of the problem identified earlier. Each such aspect can be understood as a reality of a kind for which analogies can be sought from outside. But the device they draw on, making (other) knowledges useful, is also of course right inside, at the root of the initial protest: we ought to be making knowledge useful. I underline the convergence through the particular anthropological method of drawing in a range of comparative materials, some of them on the face of it quite strange to the problem. The message is that these materials would have no value if no one took the trouble to go into the details, to explicate, to pay attention to content, to find meaning in them. This in turn scarcely conceals a further "reality": certain types of academic practice, based on argumentative practices, analytical model-building, fact-finding, deductive procedures, and a heavy investment in interpretation and understanding appear to be ones that the writer *assumes* she shares with her readers.[33] Without that assumption the sarcasm, irony, exaggeration, explication, and parody would have little effect. So do they fail, now, with the writer having revealed this assumption?

I am attracted to the idea also prevalent in the academy that bullet points may have their uses in all kinds of nonacademic contexts, that they focus the mind, that they go over well in lectures, that they have their own kind of creativeness and that all that is wrong with them is that they are mundane, or in the words of one colleague, just boring.[34] But this is irrelevant in respect of the kind of knowledge I have wished to turn them into, and use in response to a question. My question is stated at the beginning: how to critique good practice. For that, the present version of this chapter had to be preceded by a *real* version, written in good faith, which flowed with the anger of criticism.[35] What I have learned in the process, or made known again, is that in a world of supercomplexity (the term is Barnett's [2000]), where criticism is speedily gobbled up as part of reflexivity, to answer the question in the coinage of critique would only result in bigger and better Good Practice.

A social scientist might wish, rather, to seek how best to describe. And to only do that (see introduction) out of what is to hand. Here I have drawn on a series of emotional reactions triggered by an everyday formatting convention. It elicits a mundane kind of complaint and equally banal remedy: restore meaning! If one already knows it is absurd to search for meaning "in" anything, least of all mission statements, to find oneself yearning after the possibility is to offer a sardonic comment on the lengths to which one can be pushed. In that we may begin to see the effects of certain documentary practices, such as these statements, at the particular moment when they abut others, such as the papers and chapters of discursive argumentation.

NOTES

The ethnographic present is 1998. I am in debt to participants in the session Conditions of Work and Conditions of Thought, and the associated workshop Auditing Anthropology: The New Accountabilities held at the fifth European Association of Social Anthropologists conference, Frankfurt, September 1998. My thanks to Karen Sykes for earlier comments on ethics, to Tony Becher on auditing in higher education, and to Jeremy Mynott for insisting that there are some serious issues here. Rolland Munro and Michael McIntyre both offered illuminating comments, as did Paul Cartledge, and have allowed me to quote them.

Parts of the chapter were delivered to the American Anthropological Association meetings in November 1998 in Philadelphia, in a session organized by Peter Pels and Annelise Riles and titled "Ethics and Other Technologies of Self." To my profit, the "real" version was read to the Department of Social Anthropology at Queen's University, Belfast, in May 2000.

1. I am grateful to Caroline Bledsoe for pointing out the fact that many universities in the United States would be writing such documents for their individual boards of trustees. In the United Kingdom the mission statement is required by the state funding body (Higher Education Funding Council of England and related regional bodies).

2. One of them, *(e)* "to maintain the position of Cambridge as one of the world's leading universities," had been pushed to the forefront of the mission statement in 1996. Note that I have used documents from my own university to illustrate some points here, but they are only illustrative. The principal virtue of mission statements is that they enable an institution to "protect" from mindless standardization certain unique arrangements by drawing attention to them (if that is protection); Cambridge examples are the tripos system, supervision arrangements, and relations with colleges.

3. Both rubrics had been followed by the same number of points, so there were two series (a) to (f).

4. Of course there is a history of slogans and mottos that can travel long distances bundled together (Latour's mutable mobiles). "To produce research of the highest quality" is rather like "to serve the king" or "universal human rights" (see Riles 1998).

5. "In the battle-ravaged regions of northern Mozambique, in remote straw hut villages where the modern world has scarcely penetrated, supernatural spirits and magic potions are suddenly winning a civil war that machine guns, mortars and grenades could not" (*Chicago Tribune*, quoted by Comaroff and Comaroff 1992, 3).

6. A British development of the last twenty years; on the way in which under successive recent governments the "social state" has given way to the "enabling state," see Rose 1992, 1993, 1999; anthropological observations on this development can be found in Wright 1994.

7. I do not know what weight the term *vaccination* carries; the Comaroffs do not dwell further on the story in this context (their main concern is with the nature of the media portrayal).

8. Initially Asmat, West Irian and later the Trobriands, Papua New Guinea.

9. Warrior rather than soldier because these are ad hoc fighting forces rather than armies.

10. I may be extrapolating beyond the original here. Gell observes that the designs on the shields are composed in a mood of terror, and adds: "The tiger which is about to pounce and devour its victim looks, above all, terrified—of itself as it were—and the same is true of warriors bearing down with grimaces of fear and rage" (1998, 31; emphasis omitted).

11. Power would claim that accountability practices have become central to the reinvention of government, indeed that in Britain they have reached an extreme form: "Audit is an emerging principle of social organization [that] . . . constitutes a major shift of power: [in this case] from the public to the professional, and from teachers, engineers and managers to overseers" (1994, 47). The audit process reproduces organizational behavior as cultural performance (Munro 1999): participants construct their cultural performances in ways that make themselves visible to one another, including visible (to overseers) "as" managers "in" control.

12. See the contributions to Velody 1999; for anthropological commentary, Davis 1999; Shore and Roberts 1995; Shore and Wright 1999, who also offer criticism of the place of "reflexivity"; Strathern 2000.

13. This is one way of reading the increasing professionalism of CVs, application forms, and the like, and not least the TQA (teaching quality assessment) move away from a three-tier evaluation system (unsatisfactory, satisfactory, and excellent) into a point-based matrix (allowing multiple scoring).

14. Being responsive to criticism is good practice on the part of neoliberal governments (cf. Weir 1996).

15. Cf. Harper 1998 for examples of negotiation between auditors and auditees of financial accounts in order to reach a computation that both sides agree is fair.

16. Hence the boundary conditions of information overload. "We have access to everything and control of nothing, unable to properly sift and filter the avalanche of information that pours down on us. It's not information at all, but a hailstorm of data" (*Guardian*, 5 November 1996; emphasis removed).

17. From Nowotny's chapter (1990), in a volume on self-organization in science, on self-organization as applied to social systems by Luhmann (1990).

18. Memory and writing preserve, Luhmann says (1990, 9), not the events but their structure-generating properties: they are turned into elements of communication.

19. Indeed it is only as networks of communication that social organizations can be considered as self-organizing systems at all. In this, they are at once analogous to and different from living systems or psychic systems. A social system communicates not with its environment but about its environment within itself, already self-referentially defined as apart from it; "the interface can become an instrument of reflexivity for the system itself, thereby increasing its internal complexity" (Nowotny 1990, 230). Social systems do not of course have the consciousness of human agents to be observers: "self-observation," Luhmann remarks, occurs through people's communications with one another.

20. This belongs to a wider argument: basing its sense of purpose aims and objectives on the function of different aspects of social process, modern society has

become increasingly differentiated into different systems (legal, educational, and so forth)—each such system in turn becoming self-generative.

21. Almost as though in response to Law's (1994, 22) complaint about Foucault's discourses: we do not "learn much about how they might interact together when they are performed or embodied."

22. And see Strathern 1997 on the relationship between audit and university examination systems.

23. As he remarks, the highly collaborative nature of panel work makes disagreement difficult. There are not just gatekeepers: Brenneis's paper is about the imaginative work that panelists do in making new knowledge.

24. The principal task of the Beijing Conference was to ratify a document called "The Global Platform for Action." The Pacific Platform for Action, a text of some twenty pages, was produced by the South Pacific Commission in 1994. The Cambridge University mission statement is part of a strategic plan put together through elaborate consultation exercises from departments to faculties to councils of the schools.

25. Though of course these could no doubt be found in ample measure in adjunct feeder documents. I note that most of the points here are made at various places during the course of Riles's 1998 article.

26. Mercifully, likely to be restricted to portions of the total document only: certainly parts of the Cambridge document also contain coherent discursive prose.

27. Jeremy Mynott (personal communication) refers to the debasement of language. He takes as an example the inanities often promulgated under the rubric of "Aims and Objectives" when, as he says, objectives do in fact matter.

28. This can reach absurd proportions through the gigantism of enabling information and communications technology. McIntyre (personal communication) coins the phrase "self-audit catastrophe" to describe the spiraling need to keep check on the procedures by which one keeps checks; the self-observing self (cf. Hoskin 1995)—and its institutional counterparts—is infinitely capable of further self-splitting and self-observation.

29. The late Roger Needham, former pro-vice-chancellor of the University and director of Microsoft Research Ltd., Cambridge; I draw with his permission from remarks titled "Equal Opportunities, Promotions and the Like" (unpublished ms.).

30. In the view of this natural scientist (professor of atmospheric dynamics, Cambridge), it is the ethic that gives scientists credibility in one another's eyes, bound up in turn with an aim he calls "the scientific ideal," namely, the ideal of producing reliable knowledge despite variability and lapses in human behavior. The audit that discourages the ethic is also likely to encourage the lapses (concealing errors, etc.). The casualties in other disciplines may be different. But a general casualty is certainly the old scholarly understanding that one did not publish until one had something both worth saying and well worked out enough to say it properly.

31. Now beginning to acquire, after Hoskin, a small history of its own; see Strathern 1997; McIntyre 1998, n.d.

32. My thanks to Jeremy Mynott, chief executive, Cambridge University Press (personal communication and Mynott 1999).

33. I am very grateful to members of the Department of Social Anthropology at Queen's University, Belfast, for driving this and other points home to me.

34. This last observation I owe to Huon Wardle, Queen's University, Belfast (see note 33).

35. Anyone who would like a copy is welcome to apply to me at the Department of Social Anthropology, Free School Lane, Cambridge CB2 3RF, UK. It was composed beforehand, without the present version in mind; the latter I owe to the editor, with many thanks.

....

REFERENCES

Barnett, Ronald. 2000. *Realizing the University in an Age of Supercomplexity.* Buckingham: Society for Research into Higher Education and Open University Press.

Bekhradnia, Bahram. 1999. The Research Assessment Exercise and Its Intellectual Consequences. *History of the Human Sciences* 12(4): 113–16.

Brenneis, Donald. 1997. New Lexicon, Old Language: Negotiating the "Global" at the National Science Foundation. In *Critical Anthropology Now: Unexpected Contexts, Shifting Constituencies, Changing Agendas,* ed. George E. Marcus, 123–46. Santa Fe, NM: SAR Press.

Comaroff, John, and Jean Comaroff. 1992. *Ethnography and the Historical Imagination.* Boulder, CO: Westview Press.

Davis, John. 1999. Administering Creativity. *Anthropology Today* 15(2): 4–9.

Gell, Alfred. 1992. The Technology of Enchantment and the Enchantment of Technology. In *Anthropology, Art and Aesthetics,* ed. Jeremy Coote and Anthony Shelton, 40–63. Oxford: Clarendon Press.

———. 1998. *Art and Agency: An Anthropological Theory.* Oxford: Clarendon Press.

Goody, Esther, ed. 1995. *Social Intelligence and Interaction: Expressions and Implications of the Social Bias in Human Intelligence.* Cambridge: Cambridge University Press.

Harper, Richard. 1998. *Inside the IMF: An Ethnography of Documents, Technology, and Organizational Action.* London: Academic Press.

Hoskin, Keith. 1995. The Viewing Self and the World We View: Beyond Perspectival Illusion. *Organization* 2:141–62.

———. 1996. The Awful Idea of Accountability: Inscribing People into the Measurement of Objects. In *Accountability: Power, Ethos, and the Technologies of Managing,* ed. Rolland Munro and Jan Mouritsen, 265–82. London: International Thomson Business Press.

Law, John. 1994. *Organizing Modernity.* Oxford: Blackwell.

Luhmann, Niklas. 1990. *Essays on Self-Reference.* New York: Columbia University Press.

Martin, Emily. 1992. The End of the Body? *American Ethnologist* 19:121–40.

McIntyre, Michael. 1998. Lucidity and Science, Part III: Hypercredulity, Quantum Mechanics, and Scientific Truth. *Interdisciplinary Science Reviews* 23:29–70.

———. N.d. Lucidity and Science, or the Two Sides of the Platonic. Unpublished

Ms., Department of Applied Mathematics and Theoretical Physics, Cambridge University.

Munro, Rolland. 1999. The Cultural Performance of Control. *Organization Studies* 20:619–40.

Mynott, Jeremy. 1999. Publishing: The View from Cambridge University Press. *History of the Human Sciences* 12:127–31.

Nowotny, Helga, ed. 1990. Actor-Networks versus Science as a Self-Organizing System: A Comparative View of Two Constructivist Approaches. In *Self-Organization: Portrait of a Scientific Revolution*, ed. Wolfgang Krohn, Gunter Kuppers, and Helga Nowotny, 223–39. Dordrecht: Kluwer Academic Publishers.

O'Hanlon, Michael. 1995. Modernity and the "Graphicalization" of Meaning: New Guinea Highland Shield Design in Historical Perspective. *Journal of the Royal Anthropological Institute* 1:1–22.

Power, Michael. 1994. *The Audit Explosion*. London: Demos.

———. 1997. *The Audit Society: Rituals of Verification*. Oxford: Oxford University Press.

Riles, Annelise. 1998. Infinity within the Brackets. *American Ethnologist* 25(3): 378–98.

———. 2000. *The Network Inside Out*. Ann Arbor: University of Michigan Press.

Rose, Nikolas. 1992. Governing the Enterprising Self. In *The Values of the Enterprise Culture: The Moral Debate*, ed. Paul Heelas and Paul Morris, 141–64. London: Routledge.

———. 1993. Government, Authority, and Expertise in Advanced Liberalism. *Economy and Society* 22(3): 283–99.

———. 1999. *Powers of Freedom: Reframing Political Thought*. Cambridge: Cambridge University Press.

Shore, Cris, and Stephen Roberts. 1995. Higher Education and the Panopticon Paradigm: Quality Assurance as "Disciplinary Technology." *Higher Education Quarterly* 27(3): 8–17.

Shore, Cris, and Susan Wright. 1999. Audit Culture and Anthropology: Neo-Liberalism in British Higher Education. *Journal of the Royal Anthropological Institute* 5(4): 557–75.

Strathern, Marilyn. 1997. "Improving Ratings": Audit in the British University System. *European Review* 5(3): 305–21.

———, ed. 2000. *Audit Cultures: Anthropological Studies in Accountability, Ethics, and the Academy*. London: Routledge.

Velody, Irving, ed. 1999. Knowledge for What? The Intellectual Consequences of the Research Assessment Exercise. Special issue, *History of the Human Sciences* 12(4): 111–46.

Weir, Lorna. 1996. Recent Developments in the Government of Pregnancy. *Economy and Society* 25:372–92.

Wright, Susan, ed. 1994. *Anthropology of Organizations*. London: Routledge.

7 | Documenting the Present

Hirokazu Miyazaki

HOW DO WE APPREHEND a present moment? The problem of how to access a present moment has long been recognized as an important problem in philosophy and social theory. For example, Jean-Paul Sartre notes:

> the Present is for itself. . . . There is a peculiar paradox in the Present: On the one hand, we willingly define it as *being;* what is present is present *is*—in contrast to the future which is not yet and to the past which is no longer. But on the other hand, a rigorous analysis which would attempt to rid the present of all which is not *it*—i.e., of the past and of the immediate future—would find that nothing remained but an infinitesimal instance. As Husserl remarks in his *Essays on the Inner Consciousness of Time*, the ideal limit of a division pushed to infinity is a nothingness. Thus each time that we approach the study of human reality from a new point of view we rediscover that indissoluble dyad, Being and Nothingness. (Sartre 1992 [1943], 176)

Underlying this problem is a common assumption that the present is instantaneous and therefore analytically elusive (see, e.g., Hanks 1996, 295–96). A common solution to this problem has been to refuse to apprehend the present as an instant but as a space in-between or a gap between what has come and what is to come (see Gell 1992, 223; Husserl 1964; Munn 1992; Schutz 1970). For William James, for example, the present stretches to the past and the future: "the practically cognized present is no knife-edge, but a saddle-back, with a certain breadth of its own on which we sit perched, and from which we look in two directions into time" (James 1981 [1890], 574). For Sartre, in contrast, this space is defined by an act of negation (Sartre 1992 [1943], 178): "the Present *is not*. . . . It is impossible to grasp the Present in the form of an instant, for the instant would be the moment when the present *is*. But the present is not; it makes itself present in the form of flight" (ibid., 179).

The elusiveness of the present has prompted generations of philosophers and social theorists to use the problem of the present as an analogue for more general problems surrounding the nature of self-knowledge. For example, James, Sartre and others have situated the problem of the present at the heart of their inquiries into the possibility of self-knowledge (see James 1981 [1890]; Mead 1959; Sartre 1992 [1943]). Likewise, the Marxist thinker Ernst Bloch has observed that the problem of the present and the problem of self-knowledge share a single problem, that is, the problem of how to apprehend what is too close and too immediate. As Bloch puts it, "Without distance, right within, you cannot even experience something, less represent it or present it in a right way. . . . all nearness makes matters difficult, and if it is too close, then one is blinded, at least made mute" (Bloch 1998, 120). As a solution to this shared problem, Bloch draws attention to the eschatological potential of the *now* (*jetzt*) that serves as a point of entry into a future messianic moment (Bloch 1998; see also Benjamin 1992 [1968]; Moltman 1996).

With these philosophers' analogy of the problem of the present to the problem of self-knowledge in mind, in this chapter, I turn to a particular kind of present moment that indigenous Fijian ritual participants repeatedly experience in the course of a gift-giving event. My question concerns how to recapture an elusive ritual present in an ethnographic account. I seek to identify indigenous Fijian ritual participants' own method for apprehending the present of their ritual action.

Indigenous Fijians give and receive gifts on various occasions. They describe the act of giving and receiving gifts as an act of "facing" or "attending on" (*veiqaravi*) each other. Mortuary exchange is the single most important occasion of *veiqaravi* for indigenous Fijian clans (*mataqali*). News of a death in a clan calls for a response from other clans in the form of a presentation of death gifts (*reguregu*). An act of attendance therefore constitutes a response and an act of recognition (cf. Keane 1997) or, in indigenous Fijians' own terms, confirmation (*vakadeitaka*) of the relationship (*veiwekani*) between the gift-giving and gift-receiving sides. In indigenous Fijian gift-giving, two sides, the gift-giving and gift-receiving sides, spatially face each other and exchange valuables and words (see Miyazaki 2004b; Toren 1990; Turner 1987). Regardless of the purpose of gift-

giving, an exchange event entails a movement of gifts, words and participant roles that plays on this spatial arrangement (see Miyazaki 2000; Toren
1990). During the course of a single mortuary rite, different clans (and
churches and other social groups) send their representatives to the host of
the mortuary exchange. The same form of attendance is repeated during
the course of a single mortuary exchange with the arrival of each successive
delegation.

As I have argued extensively elsewhere, indigenous Fijian gift-giving
always entails a moment of waiting for a response that I have termed a
moment of hope (see Miyazaki 2000, 2004b, 2005). In his speech presenting gifts, the spokesman for gift-givers always apologizes for the inappropriate nature of their gifts and seeks gift-receivers' forgiveness. After the
speech, the spokesman and gift-givers wait quietly for gift-receivers' judgment, hoping that the gifts will be accepted.

The analytical challenge that this moment of hopeful anticipation poses
to an anthropological observer consists in its temporary nature: the
moment of waiting ends as gift-receivers accept gifts. To the extent that
gifts are almost always accepted, it can be said that this momentary halt and
its accompanying sense of risk and hope are rhetorically manufactured so
that ritual participants may experience the efficacy of their ritual action
(see Herzfeld 1997; Keane 1997). However, this kind of interpretation
focuses on the effects of the rhetorical move and traces backward how the
rhetorical strategy contributes to the production of sense of efficacy as an
outcome. How can the "real-time" anticipatory content of the moment of
waiting be recaptured retrospectively?

My attention to ritual participants' temporal experience of gift-giving
echoes Nancy Munn's phenomenological approach to the Gawan "spatio-
temporal" experience of exchange (Munn 1986). However, my goal is to
bring to light and *borrow* indigenous Fijian ritual participants' method for
apprehending a ritual present in my own account of that present. In search
of this method, I turn to two accounts of an indigenous Fijian gift exchange
event produced by its hosting clan (*mataqali*). These are records of valuables, food, and monetary contributions received by the hosting clan in the
context of a single mortuary exchange event. Records of gifts are commonly used in Fiji (see, e.g., Turner 1987, 211) and elsewhere.[1] Anthropologists usually treat these records as sources of data about the practices
of gift-giving and the debts incurred in exchange. I instead focus on the
two documents' respective temporal location in the exchange event and
treat them as records of the present of ritual action. My goal is therefore

not to evaluate the intended purposes of these records as records of debts but to seek cues from these records for my own effort to apprehend the present of ritual action retrospectively. I suggest that the relationship between the documents and the trajectory of the mortuary exchange recorded in them, on the one hand, and between the two documents, on the other, point to a shared solution to the problem of how to apprehend an ever elusive present moment, theirs as well as ours, that I call *replication*.

My attention to replication draws from a long-standing concern in Melanesian ethnography with replication as an important operation of social reproduction. Marilyn Strathern describes replication as one of two contrasting forms Melanesian relations take (Strathern 1988). In his ethnography of gift exchange in Tanga Island, Robert Foster identifies replication as a particular mode of social reproduction mediated by what he terms "identical exchange" and contrasts it with the operation of "multiplication" that underlies *moka* and other Highland New Guinea exchange practices (Foster 1995, 16–17). In her ethnography of the Baining, Jane Fajans also uses the concept of replication to capture the role of what she terms "schemas" across different spheres of social life (Fajans 1997, 267). The ultimate goal of my discussion is to extend this concern beyond the problem of social reproduction in order to demonstrate the potential of replication as a meta-level operation or method not only for indigenous Fijian ritual participants but also for anthropologists (see also Miyazaki 2004b). At the conclusion of this chapter, I will attempt to examine the broader theoretical implication of the indigenous Fijian commitment to replication with reference to Terence Turner's work on the operation of replication in myth and ritual.

....

A Check List

The focus of my analysis is on two records prepared by the hosting clan of a six-day long mortuary exchange event that I observed in Suvavou, a peri-urban village near Suva, Fiji's capital, in September 1995. The first record that I examine is a record of death gifts the hosting clan kept during the mortuary exchange (hereafter, Document A). The second record is a descriptive account of the mortuary exchange prepared after the mortuary exchange (hereafter, Document B). In what follows, I discuss the two documents in the temporal order of their making and examine the different temporal locations they occupied in relation to the sequence of the exchange event.

Document A is a tabular record of death gifts the hosting clan received from gift-givers—clans, church congregations, or groups of individuals with a close connection to the deceased—from both within and outside the village during the course of the six-day event. For example, the first group of visiting mourners to arrive, listed in the first row of the first table, was a church group to which the deceased had belonged. The church group's gifts consisted of one *tabua* (whale's tooth), one *davodavo* (a large mat used for sleeping), and F$64 (equivalent of approximately US$45 at the time of my fieldwork) in cash. In the second row is listed two names of village women who brought one *coco* (a large mat used to cover a floor), and so on. Such tables were commonly used at the sites of all indigenous Fijian mortuary exchanges I observed in Suvavou and elsewhere in Fiji. The only difference between Document A and other specimens I observed is that while other clans drew such tables by hand on a school notebook, Document A was produced in part with the use of a word processor.

The purpose of Document A was to record the names of gift-givers and the amount of their gifts in order to determine appropriate return gifts. Document A is three-pages long and each page consists of a table of six columns and eighteen rows (the first page of the table is reproduced in fig. 7.1). The empty grid was prepared sometime after the clanswoman's death, but before delegations of gift-givers began to arrive. The first column of Document A is labeled "mortuary delegations" (*mata reguregu*) and the second to sixth columns are labeled "whales teeth" (*tabua*), "mats for the deceased" (*tevu davodavo*), "food" (*magiti*), "money" (*lavo*), and "gifts for tea" (*ti:* bread, biscuits, butter, milk, and sugar to be fed to the visitors), respectively.

The drafting of rows and columns must have demanded some anticipatory thinking about how many delegations of gift-givers would arrive and what kinds of gifts they would bring. The preparation of Document A, in other words, entailed a certain sense of expectation and anticipation.

This sense of anticipation embodied by the empty grid echoed a sense of anticipation shared by ritual participants upon the arrival of a delegation of gift-givers in a house where the hosting clan of the mortuary exchange accepted death gifts. The initial attention of both the hosting clan, that is, the gift-receivers, who waited at the "upper" end of a house, and the arriving gift-givers, who entered from "below," focused on the careful spatial arrangement of people and gifts. The gift-receivers invited the gift-givers to "move up" (*toso icake*) closer to the center of the house and the gift-givers moved up a bit and then sat cross-legged facing the gift-givers. As gift-

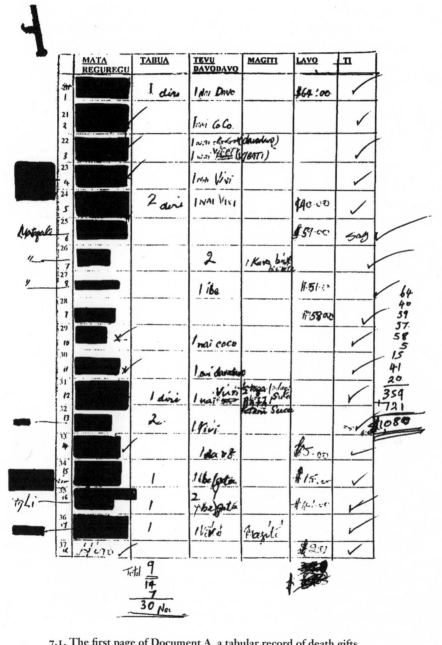

	MATA REGUREGU	TABUA	TEVU DAVODAVO	MAGITI	LAVO	TI
20 1	■	1 dina	1 Nai Davo		$64:00	✓
21 2	■		1 nai 6o Co.			✓
22 3	■		1 nai chodon (davodavo) 1 nai VEET (i/BATI)			✓
23 4	■		1 nai Vivi			✓
24 5	■	2 dana	1 NAI Vivi		$40.00	✓
25 6	■				$59.00	Sag
26 7	■		2	1 Kava biti bi hibi		✓
27 8	■		1 iba		$51.00	
28 7	■				$58.00	✓
29 10	■	x	1 nai coco			✓
30 11	■	x	1 ani davodavo			✓
31 12	■	1 dina	1 nai Vivi Baya	Stoya / Suya Sula Votani Suca		✓
32 13	■	2	1 Vivi			
33 14	■		1 da v5		$5.00	
34 15	■	1	1 iba /gata		$15.00	✓
35 16	■	1	2 ibe gata		$4.00	✓
36 17	■	1	1 Vivo	Yagili		✓
37 18	Heno				$9.00	✓

64
40
39
57.
58
5
15
41
20.
359
+721
1080

Total 9
——
14
1
——
30 Nov

7.1. The first page of Document A, a tabular record of death gifts

givers and gift-receivers faced each other, gift-givers placed a roll of mats, food, and cans of kerosene at the center of the house. At this stage of the spatial arrangement of gifts and people two kinds of gifts, whales' teeth (*tabua*) and money, were hidden from view. It is important to note that this form of ritual interaction is not specific to a particular event I discuss in this chapter but that it is an essential property of all episodes of indigenous Fijian gift-giving I have observed in Fiji. The past tense deployed in my account is simply intended to serve as a reminder of my retrospective descriptive standpoint.

A spatio-temporal movement of *tabua* and words followed this initial stillness expressed in the spatial arrangement of other gifts and people. The spokesman for the gift-givers moved forward and knelt beside the mats to make a speech. At that moment, the spokesman held *tabua* in his outstretched arms in front of him and placed an envelope containing money on the floor in front of him. The speech stressed the inappropriate nature of the presentation and asked for forgiveness:

> We thought we would come earlier but the travel was difficult. We crossed the sea so that we might join you on this important occasion today. Valuables displayed here are only small *reguregu* [lit. "kissing with the nose," meaning death gifts] from [our chief]. We thought we would bring something good. Here is a small mat, tea, food, and an envelope [referring to money] . . . but it is not useful, please forgive us.

In this speech, the spokesman raised such concerns with the size of the gifts repeatedly. Every time the gift-givers' spokesman mentioned that the gifts were "very small" (*lailai sara*), the gift-receivers immediately responded in unison, "Big!" (*Levu*). The gift-givers' humble reference to the small amount of gifts prompted the gift-receivers to confirm the appropriateness of the size of the gifts. When his speech ended, the spokesman remained still with the *tabua* extended from his hands until the spokesman for the gift-receivers got up, walked over, and silently took the *tabua* from his hands and handed it to the gift-receivers' chief. The gift-givers' spokesman then slid the envelope toward the gift-receivers and retreated before the gift-receivers' chief began to speak. The chief of the gift-receiving side pronounced that it was a good *tabua*, and then the spokesman for the gift-receivers gave a speech recognizing the effort of the gift-givers and accepting the gifts as large.

What is interesting here is that the spokesman for the gift-receivers concluded his speech by praying for God's blessing uttering a formulaic phrase: "Your valuables have been offered to Heaven so that we all may be given Heavenly blessing." This prayer brought to light the fact that the ultimate consequences of their collective ritual action were still radically indeterminate, in that God's blessing was not yet in hand. As soon as the first moment of waiting ended, in other words, yet another moment of waiting, albeit of an inevitably more open-ended fashion, was made visible.

After each episode of gift-giving, death gifts were counted and entries were made in Document A. No one started counting gifts presented by the gift-giving side until the gift-givers had left the scene of exchange. During the course of each gift-giving episode, in other words, the necessity of counting and recording gifts was backgrounded. At the conclusion of each presentation of gifts from visiting delegations, a young member of the hosting clan seated at the lower end of the gift-receiving side filled out a further row in the table with the name of the delegation and the amount and kinds of its gifts. The act of filling out a row in Document A therefore was *after the fact* and was in stark contrast to the initial prospective orientation of the document.

As soon as the completion of a presentation of gifts was inscribed in the table in the form of numbers, however, the table once again became the marker of the anticipatory quality of the ritual present. That is, when a row was filled in after each gift-giving episode, the remaining empty rows served as a reminder of the hosting clan's sense of anticipation for the arrival of other delegations. Like the moment of hopeful anticipation in each gift-giving episode, these empty rows pointed to a double sense of uncertainty and certainty regarding other expected guests' arrival. Document A thus recovered its anticipatory content.

It is important to note at this point that in gift exchange, the future-oriented nature of the ritual present was repeatedly foregrounded in the successive acts of gift-giving over the six-day event. *Veiqaravi* engaged ritual participants in a moment of hopeful anticipation repeatedly. Recall that in the gift-giving episode described above, the gift-receiving side accepted the gift; but this sense of fulfillment was once again quickly replaced with yet another kind of hopeful anticipation when the spokesman for the gift-receivers asked for God's blessing at the end of his speech.

The sense of anticipation at the end of each gift-giving episode echoed yet another kind of anticipation. After all mortuary visitors presented their gifts, the gift-receivers were expected to prepare a feast and present food. Many of the speeches made on behalf of visitors referred to this part of the mortuary rite called *i burua* as the hosting clan's obligation or "work" (*cakacaka*, meaning the preparation for the feast). The sense of hopeful anticipation achieved in each episode of gift-giving was homologous to the sense of anticipation entailed in the overall sequence of the mortuary exchange event, from successive acts of gift-giving to the final feast (*iburua*) (see also Miyazaki 2004b, 107).

Document A recorded this homological relationship between each episode of gift-giving and the overall sequence of the mortuary exchange. In the place of words that created the rhythm of alternating moments of hopeful anticipation and its fulfillment in the exchange, the alternation between the horizontal move of filling out each row with the name of a delegation and numbers of gifts, and the vertical move of listing names of delegations and their gifts across the page, repeatedly made visible this homology. Document A recorded the completion of each presentation of gifts and converted it into a marker of further hopeful anticipation that all expected delegations would arrive by the end of the period of the mortuary exchange and all the rows would be filled out.

An effect of this homological relationship between each episode of gift-giving and the overall sequence of the mortuary exchange is that it gave the present of ritual action prospective momentum and stretched the moment over time. In this sense, Document A recorded the ritual present as a temporally stretched moment. On the document, a moment of hopeful anticipation was made visible repeatedly in the grid and stretched over the entire period of the mortuary exchange event.

In the sixth column, there are ticks. The sixth column's label (*ti*, meaning "gifts for tea") indicates that the column was originally intended for another purpose. However, it so happened that because gifts for tea were recorded together with "food," column six was left almost empty at the conclusion of the successive presentations. As the identical character of the ticks suggests, unlike the successive filling out of the rows, these ticks were made at one single instance. The ticks were made as the gift-receivers prepared to present return gifts of food to visiting mourners at the conclusion of the mortuary rite to indicate that a return gift had been set aside for that delegation. From the gift-receivers' point of view, in other words, once all the rows were filled in (before the final ticks), what the document made visible was a further sense of hopeful anticipation: their hope to stage the *i burua* successfully so that the mortuary exchange might end in a "clean" (*savasava*) fashion without leaving any debts unreciprocated.

What I have sought to demonstrate is that there is an overall homology between the temporal trajectory of Document A and the temporal trajectory of the exchange it documented. Both Document A and the exchange consisted of a series of cycles of moments of hopeful anticipation and its fulfillment in which at every moment of fulfillment another sense of anticipation emerged. As each episode of gift-giving ended and left both a concrete sense of fulfillment (the fact that gifts were accepted) and an abstract sense of further hopeful anticipation (the fact that God's blessing was still not yet in hand), the act of filling in a row in Document A repeated this temporal oscillation and left the document future-oriented in the form of empty rows. When all presentations of gifts were made, and Document A had finished serving its original purpose of recording names of delegations and their gifts, the document again made evident its incomplete status (in the emergence of the need for ticks in the sixth column) and embodied the hopeful anticipation of all ritual participants for the successful closure of the mortuary exchange.

It is important to note that Document A did not record the present of ritual action real time. Recall that at the precise moment of gift-giving and speech making, the existence of the table was forgotten. It was only remembered and filled in after the exchange of speeches and valuables was completed. The document was created in a time-lagged manner, not simultaneously with the presentations. If there was a homology between the exchange and the document, the homology was time-lagged in character.

Moreover, Document A did not record all the details of the exchange event. For example, although Document A documented the temporal order of the gift-givers' arrival, it did not take notice of the passing of time. The exchange event lasted for six days but the table did not record when each delegation arrived in the village (except in terms of its place in the sequence of presentations). Document A did not record ceremonial speeches either.

In reducing ritual action to a two dimensional grid, Document A also flattened the gifts' quality as spatio-temporal markers into a series of categories—valuables lost their temporal dimension and became quantities of *tabua*, mats, and so on. As the calculations (of amounts of money received) at the margin of the table indicate, the numbers in the chart could be totaled at the conclusion of the exchange to provide a record of the scale of the exchange as a whole.[2]

What I wish to point out about the act of record keeping I have described here is that it documented the present of ritual action by *replicating* it on another terrain, that is, on its grid. The act of filling out the table tracked the process by which the spatio-temporal arrangement of persons, words and *tabua* objectified the present of ritual action stretched over the six-day mortuary exchange event. The table translated a sequence of moments of hopeful anticipation, its fulfillment into the horizontally and vertically oriented acts of filling in the columns across the page. Document A documented the trajectory of the ritual present by repeatedly converting a moment of fulfillment (filling spatial gaps) into a moment of further hopeful anticipation (making new spatial gaps appear) through the oscillation of vertically and horizontally oriented acts of form filling. At the final stage, the continuous vertical movement of the ticks encompassed all of the rows at once just as the feast encompassed all of the individual presentations. Document A documented the stretched present in ritual action as in the form of spatial gap. In both the exchange and Document A, the present was set in motion, as it were, repeatedly given renewed prospective momentum.

However, Document A only momentarily documented the ritual present by converting it into its grid. When the entire course of the mortuary exchange ended with the performance of *i burua*, Document A lost its clear temporal orientation and stopped replicating the replicative content of the ritual sequence. As a completed document (that is, after the ticks were entered in the sixth column), in other words, Document A ceased to be a record of the ritual present.

After the completion of *i burua*, the hosting clan's concern shifted to its indebtedness to its own members in Australia who had made monetary contributions to the mortuary exchange but who could not attend the exchange event. This raised the need for another document for the hosting clan, that is, the second document (hereafter, Document B), a report on the mortuary exchange that the clan prepared several days after the completion of the mortuary exchange.

....

A Thank You Letter

Document B's principal aim was to thank those overseas clansmen and women. Document A would not serve that purpose. If Document A recorded the ritual present as a gap in its grid until it completed its function as a check list, Document B was a retrospective account of the successful execution of the ritual with a particular readership in mind. Document B presents a brief account of the deceased's life. The account includes the names of the deceased's parents, the deceased's date and place of birth, the name of her husband, of her twelve children, the number of her grandchildren, the time of death, her church affiliation and her occupation. The document also includes a list of visitors and valuables received by the clan during the mortuary exchange and a balance sheet outlining the expenditure of the mortuary exchange.

Two young brothers of the hosting clan, a medical technician working at a public hospital in Suva, who often acted as the "secretary" of the clan, and a computer engineer working at the telecommunications company in Suva, prepared Document B. In late September 1995, on his way to a workshop held in Australia, the medical technician took mats as gifts of thanks along with a copy of this report to fellow clansmen and clanswomen living in Sydney. Attached to the report was a letter of thanks from six elders of the clan.

The report was the first of its kind for the hosting clan and I do not know of any other clans elsewhere in Fiji that have produced such documents. Although indigenous Fijians generally show enormous interest in documents and documentation, the hosting clan's interest in documents was particularly great. Suvavou is a village where the descendants of the original landowners of Suva have resided since they were removed by the government from the Suva Peninsula in 1882. For generations, Suvavou people have sought to reclaim the Suva Peninsula land and archival records about village history have enjoyed a privileged status among villagers (see Miyazaki 2004a, 2004b). The hosting clan of the mortuary exchange initiated an extensive "documentation project" in the early 1990s as part of the clan's long-term struggle to reclaim the clan's land in the city of Suva. The clan not only has kept all of its correspondence with the government but also has produced a number of reports on the clan's archival research, which a member of the clan conducted at the National Archives of Fiji, as well as on stories told by senior clan members. The young medical technician and his brother have used a laptop computer to prepare all of these documents. The production of Document B was motivated in part by this wider interest in documentation. The clan's transnational character may also have demanded a form of accountability as manifested in the balance sheet attached to the report. The production of Document B may also reflect some contemporary indigenous Fijians' fascination with technical and bureaucratic knowledge (see Miyazaki 2004a, 2004b; Riles 2000).

After a cover letter and a description of the deceased clanswoman, Document B provided a list of all of the delegations that presented gifts. In this list, the sequential order of the delegations' names that appeared in Document A is replaced with an implicit set of categories.[3] At the top of the list is the name of the chief of the deceased's natal clan (*weka ni mate*)—the very last delegation to arrive at a mortuary exchange.[4] It is followed by the names of the Suvavou clans and then other clans, groups, and individuals. At the very end of the list of delegations is a short list of numbers that represent the total amount of money and *tabua* received. These figures were produced by adding up the numbers in Document A. The retrospective documentation of the success of ritual action, in other words, demanded temporal flattening. This temporal flattening was facilitated by the tabular character of Document A that, in its completed form, erased the oscillation of temporal orientations it recorded in its making in favor of a spatial arrangement of numbers. In other words, the completion and associated de-temporalization of Document A enabled Document A to be read as a source of data for Document B.

On the surface, Document B did not reproduce the prospective orientation of Document A in the making and the ritual event itself. Instead, Document B's emphasis on the scale of the exchange conceptualized the exchange as a retrospective whole that belonged to the past as independent from the present moment of Document B's production. In a letter that formed the core of the report, clan elders expressed their thanks for overseas clan members' monetary contributions and commented on the excellent manner in which the mortuary rite was held:

> Our gathering has been completed. [Our mother] has been laid down peacefully and we have left news about a funeral gathering whose excellence was exceptional. They saw us working together, being respectful with one another and being united as a mataqali in the way we held this important gathering.
> This was a gathering that brought together closely once again old relatives since our ancestors' time. It was such a blessing that we the living could meet and renew the path of relations for our growing children.

Document B retrospectively described the *outcome*, not the process, of the successful execution of the mortuary exchange. The retrospective turn of Document B marked a radical departure from the prospective orientation of Document A at the moment of its making. Document B rendered its moment of production as a point of achievement and a consequence of a past success.

However, the horizon of the present moment of Document B stretched to its own future moment. In contrast to Document A, which was not imagined to have a readership or consequence after its completion, Document B was produced with specific readers in mind, and with the specific purpose of declaring the success of the exchange. In this respect, it is important to note that the temporal orientation of Document B was not simply retrospective. It was part of the hosting clan's own "attendance" on its fellow clansmen and women in Australia. One of the preparers of the document, the medical technician, as a representative of the hosting clan, took the document along with valuables to Sydney. The cover letter for Document B ends with the following passage:

> We hope that you will accept our thanks with small gifts for your large contribution to our gathering just completed. With our hope and prayers that you are doing well and that your life there is moving forward. With our love to you all, to each one of elders and children [of the clan] in Australia.

The humility and *hope* expressed here recalls the tone of the speech delivered on behalf of gift-givers discussed earlier. This part of the letter recovers the anticipatory content of the ritual present that ritual participants experienced in the exchange and that Document A dutifully converted into its grid. The present in Document B, in other words, was also stretched over a period of time between the moment of its production and the moment at which gifts of thanks were accepted by clansmen and women in Sydney.

Both Document A and Document B *replicated* the moment of hopeful anticipation ritual participants repeatedly achieved in the mortuary exchange on another terrain. As a document in the making, Document A replicated the ritual present in its spatial gaps. Document A served as a reminder of the anticipatory content of the ritual present stretched over the six-day mortuary exchange until its completion. But it fails to serve as a record of that temporal trajectory because its completion erased the ritual present it had documented as an oscillation between vertical and horizontal movements. In contrast, Document B summarizes the event, and the information and narrative it contains is temporally compressed. Yet Document B replicated the ritual present in another act of gift-giving of which the document was part. In sum, as records of a single mortuary exchange event, Document A as a completed document simply would serve as a record of the temporal order of the gift-givers' arrival and of the quantity of gifts received, whereas Document B would serve as a record of the kind of the ritual present made visible in indigenous Fijian gift-giving. Document B, in other words, should be interpreted not as a record of the way the exchange actually took place but as a *replication* of the ritual present that ritual participants repeatedly experienced during the course of the mortuary exchange.

The focus of my interest has been the implication of these two documents for the problem of how to access the ritual present. The two documents had different temporal locations in the mortuary exchange they documented. Document A was a document in the making, an act of record keeping whose temporal trajectory followed that of the exchange it recorded. In contrast, Document B was a retrospective report produced *after the fact* to summarize the event. The two documents entail different kinds of temporality. Document A as a checklist in the making was resolutely future-oriented but it lost its future direction upon its completion. Document B was a retrospective account with a particular readership in mind. The cover letter for Document B, however, turns Document B to the future (cf. Tucker 1993).

The relationship between the two documents itself is a replication of the replicative content of each gift-giving episode. The trajectory of Document A is like that of the speech made on behalf of gift-givers. If the anticipatory content of the moment of waiting evaporated when gift-receivers accepted gifts, the future orientation of Document A was lost when the ticks were entered. If the second moment of waiting in a gift-giving episode recovered the anticipatory content of the ritual present, likewise, Document B recovers the anticipatory content of Document A by replicating it in yet another gesture of hopeful anticipation in the letter of thanks.

I wish to suggest that the relationship between the documents and the event they recorded, on the one hand, and between the documents, on the other, points to replication as a possible solution to the problem of how to access the present of the ritual as well as of anthropological knowledge. What Documents A and B replicated was precisely the replicative content of the ritual present. Recall that in each episode of gift-giving, the first moment of hopeful anticipation was followed by a moment of its fulfillment, which in turn was replaced by yet another moment of hopeful anticipation. Likewise, Document A's initial future orientation was recovered repeatedly upon the completion of the retrospective act of filling in a row. Document B as a retrospective account of the success of the ritual event also replicated that moment of hopeful anticipation.

As I suggested in my initial discussion of James, Sartre, Bloch, and others' inquiries into the nature of the present, philosophers have long situated the problem of the present at the heart of the problem of self-knowledge. In these philosophical inquiries, the problem of the present and the problem of self-knowledge emerge as analogical problems albeit through divergent tropes such as temporal stretching, in the case of James, and negation, in the case of Sartre. In light of the above discussion of the indigenous Fijian operation of replication, I want to suggest that like indigenous Fijian ritual participants, these philosophers have also sought to apprehend the present by replicating its replicative content on another terrain, that is, the terrain of self-knowledge. In other words, an effort to apprehend a present moment is an effort to identify and replicate its replicative content on another terrain.

··

Replication as a Method

In his analysis of a video of a Kayapó ritual made by a Kayapó man, Tamok, Terence Turner draws attention to the replicative relationship between the video and the structure of the ritual it recorded. According to Turner, the naming ritual recorded in the video "has the form of successive performances of the same suite of dance steps, each with its own song. The video shows the three successive performances that constitute the framework of the sequential order of the ceremony" (Turner 2002, 82). In Turner's view, the operation of replication is integral to the Kayapó notion of beauty and perfection:

> In Kayapo thought, replication of originally "natural" forms (such as ceremonial songs and dances themselves, thought to be originally taught to shamans by birds, animals, or fish) though concerted social action is the essence of the production of human society. It is what specifically human behavior ("culture") consists of. The perfection of such socialized forms through repeated performance embodies the supreme Kayapó value, at once social, moral, and aesthetic, of "beauty." "Beauty," in this sense, comprises a principle of sequential organization: successive repetitions of the same pattern, with each performance increasing in social value as it integrates additional elements and achieves more stylistic finesse, thus approaching more closely the ideal of completeness-and-perfection that defines "beauty." (Turner 2002, 83)

Turner argues that Tamok's video replicates this aesthetic commitment to replication itself:

This is what Tamok's video of the ceremony also does. He faithfully
shows every repetition of every performance, each with its successive
increments of regalia and participants. His video replicates, in its own
structure, the replicative structure of the ceremony itself, and thus itself
creates "beauty" in the Kayapó sense. The master categories of social
production and cultural value, replication and beauty, thus become the
master schemas guiding Tamok's editing: his construction of his representation of the ceremony. (Turner 2002, 83)

Turner discusses the operation of replication as a more general principle of social reproduction in his earlier discussion of a Kayapó myth concerning the introduction of fire to human society (Turner 1985). In particular, Turner identifies the Kayapó concern with "control" over the process
of replication:

The principle is: that control over the power of transformation develops as a corollary of the process of transformation itself. Becoming
socialized, in other words, implies acquiring the power to replicate the
process one has undergone, which is to socialize others. This point is
the complement of the principle embodied in the form of each of the
two sequences of moves considered separately, namely that society is a
process of reflexive self-replication of the process of (re)producing a
socialized individual and the social group within which this occurs.
(Turner 1985, 97)

From this standpoint, Tamok's video is not simply evidence of the culturally specific nature of the Kayapó appropriation of video technology (cf.
Turner 2002, 80). Replication in Tamok's video as well as in the myth
about the origin of fire points to a meta-level objectification of replication
as a method and goal of self-knowledge.

I have suggested that like the Kayapó video that Turner discusses, both
Documents A and B replicated the replicative content of the ritual present.
In more specific terms, I have sought to demonstrate that this replication
entailed repeated replication of a particular kind of ritual moment across
different terrains. From this standpoint, I have suggested that for the
indigenous Fijian ritual participants I knew, replication served as a method
for apprehending their ritual present. In light of the operation of replica-

tion in philosophy and Turner's attention to the meta-level objectification of replication in the Kayapó myth and ritual, this material suggests that what is needed is more explicit attention to the operation of replication as a technique across different forms of knowledge.

....

NOTES

This chapter draws upon field and archival research I completed from August 1994 to March 1996 in Fiji. Special thanks are due to the Fiji Government for research permission and to the chief and people of Suvavou for assistance of many kinds. The research was funded by the Research School of Pacific and Asian Studies, Australian National University. I thank Caroline Bledsoe, Katherine Rupp, Simon Stern, and Matt Tomlinson for their helpful comments on an earlier version of this chapter. I benefited enormously from conversations with Jane Guyer, William Hanks, and Terence Turner on a range of topics related to this chapter. Annelise Riles drew my initial attention to documents at a very early stage of my fieldwork. I cannot thank her enough for this and many other insightful suggestions. Some of the quotations of ceremonial speeches included in this chapter originally appeared in my article, "Faith and Its Fulfillment: Agency, Exchange, and the Fijian Aesthetics of Completion," published in *American Ethnologist* 27(1): 31–51 (2000).

1. See, e.g., Monaghan 1990, 760. See also the Japanese anthropologist Ito Mikiharu's extensive cross-cultural survey on such records of gifts (1995). Ito suggests that these records be approached not simply as calculative "devices" to achieve equivalence in exchange but also as reflections of the symbolic significance of gifts recorded (203).

2. Yet it is important to recognize that Document A also retained certain formal contrasts among different kinds of gifts. Although *tabua* and money were totaled, for example, the numbers of mats and amounts of food received were not. Likewise, in the case of mats, either the specific kinds of mats presented (*coco, davodavo*, and *vakabati*) or the numbers of sets of mats (*vivivi*) were recorded in the chart. As Annelise Riles has noted, *vivivi* is "not actually a specific number of mats" (1998, 383). *Vivivi* is rather a combination of certain different kinds of mats that are layered each on top of the other to constitute a "pattern" when they are spread out together (1998, 383–85). Therefore, the mats in a *vivivi* are "counted not as concrete 'objects' but as an abstract totality" (1998, 383). What is interesting is that in Document A as well as in exchange, *tabua* and money served as markers for movement (in this case, a vertical move of totaling) while mats served as markers of stillness.

3. Evidence that these categories were created by analyzing the first column of Document A appears in the left hand margin of Document A where the words *mataqali* (clans) are scribbled next to the names of delegations that are clans.

4. *Weka ni mate* (the deceased's natal clan members in the case of the death of a woman) have a special status in Fijian mortuary exchange. They arrived last and from their arrival, they sat on the gift-receivers' side, beside the coffin, facing the guests. Their claims on the deceased's affines were signified in the fact that they

were permitted to take the body and all the mats under the coffin once the ritual was complete. This may account for why they were not listed on Document A alongside other delegations.

....

REFERENCES

Benjamin, Walter. 1992 [1968]. *Illuminations.* Ed. Hannah Arendt. Trans. Harry Zohn. London: Fontana Press.

Bloch, Ernst. 1998. *Literary Essays.* Ed. Werner Hamacher and David E. Wellbery. Trans. Andrew Joron et al. Stanford: Stanford University Press.

Fajans, Jane. 1997. *They Make Themselves: Work and Play among the Baining of Papua New Guinea.* Chicago: University of Chicago Press.

Foster, Robert J. 1995. *Social Reproduction and History in Melanesia: Mortuary Ritual, Gift Exchange, and Custom in the Tanga Islands.* Cambridge: Cambridge University Press.

Gell, Alfred. 1992. *The Anthropology of Time: Cultural Constructions of Temporal Maps and Images.* Oxford: Berg.

Hanks, William. 1996. *Language and Communicative Practices.* Boulder, Colorado: Westview Press.

Herzfeld, Michael. 1997. *Cultural Intimacy: Social Poetics in the Nation-State.* New York: Routledge.

Husserl, Edmund. 1964. *The Phenomenology of Internal Time Consciousness.* Trans. James S. Churchill. Bloomington: Midland Books.

Ito Mikiharu. 1995. *Zoyo-kokan no jinruigaku* (An anthropology of gift exchange). Tokyo: Chikuma-shobo.

James, William. 1981 [1890]. *The Principles of Psychology.* Cambridge: Harvard University Press.

Keane, Webb. 1997. *Signs of Recognition: Powers and Hazards of Representation in an Indonesian Society.* Berkeley: University of California Press.

Mead, George Herbert. 1959 *The Philosophy of the Present.* Ed. Arthur E. Murphy. La Salle, Illinois: Open Court.

Miyazaki, Hirokazu. 2000. Faith and Its Fulfillment: Agency, Exchange and the Fijian Aesthetics of Completion. *American Ethnologist* 27(1): 31–51.

———. 2004a. Delegating Closure. In *Law and Empire in the Pacific: Fiji and Hawai'i,* ed. Sally Merry and Donald Brenneis, 239–59. Santa Fe: School of American Research Press.

———. 2004b. *The Method of Hope: Anthropology, Philosophy, and Fijian Knowledge.* Stanford: Stanford University Press.

———. 2005. From Sugar Cane to "Swords": Hope and the Extensibility of the Gift in Fiji. *Journal of the Royal Anthropological Institute* 11(2): 277–95.

Moltmann, Jürgen. 1996. *The Coming of God: Christian Eschatology.* Trans. Margaret Kohl. Minneapolis: Fortress Press.

Monaghan, John. 1990. Reciprocity, Redistribution, and the Transaction of Value in the Mesoamerican Fiesta. *American Ethnologist* 17(4): 758–74.

Munn, Nancy. 1986. *The Fame of Gawa: A Symbolic Study of Value Transformation in a Massim (Papua New Guinea) Society.* Cambridge: Cambridge University Press.
———. 1992. The Cultural Anthropology of Time: A Critical Essay. *Annual Review of Anthropology* 21:93–123.
Riles, Annelise. 1998. Infinity within the Brackets. *American Ethnologist* 25(3): 378–98.
———. 2000. *The Network Inside Out.* Ann Arbor: University of Michigan Press.
Sartre, Jean-Paul. 1992 [1943]. *Being and Nothingness: A Phenomenological Essay on Ontology.* Trans. Hazel E. Barnes. New York: Washington Square Press.
Schutz, Alfred. 1970. *On Phenomenology and Social Relations.* Ed. Helmut R. Wagner. Chicago: University of Chicago Press.
Strathern, Marilyn. 1988. *The Gender of the Gift: Problems with Women and Problems with Society in Melanesia.* Berkeley: University of California Press.
Toren, Christina. 1990. *Making Sense of Hierarchy: Cognition as Social Process in Fiji.* London: Athlone Press.
Tucker, Irene. 1993. Writing Home: *Evelina*, the Epistolary Novel and the Paradox of Property. *ELH* 60(2):419–39.
Turner, James W. 1987. Blessed to Give and Receive: Ceremonial Exchange in Fiji. *Ethnology* 26(3):209–19.
Turner, Terence S. 1985. Animal Symbolism, Totemism, and the Structure of Myth. In *Animal Myths and Metaphors in South America*, ed. Gary Urton, 49–106. Salt Lake City: University of Utah Press.
———. 2002. Representation, Politics, and Cultural Imagination in Indigenous Video: General Points and Kayapo Examples. In *Media Worlds: Anthropology on New Terrain*, ed. Faye D. Ginsburg, Lila Abu-Lughod, and Brian Larkin, 75–89. Berkeley: University of California Press.

Contributors

MARIO BIAGIOLI
Department of History of Science, Harvard University

DON BRENNEIS
Department of Anthropology, University of California,
Santa Cruz

CAROL A. HEIMER
Department of Sociology, Northwestern University
and American Bar Foundation

HIROKAZU MIYAZAKI
Department of Anthropology, Cornell University

ADAM REED
Department of Social Anthropology,
University of St. Andrews

ANNELISE RILES
School of Law and Department of Anthropology,
Cornell University

MARILYN STRATHERN
Department of Social Anthropology,
University of Cambridge

Index

bookkeeping, double-entry, 19
books, consumption of, 145. *See* novels
boundary objects, 101, 117
Bourdieu, Pierre, 98, 144
Bowker, Geoffrey, 14–15, 46, 101, 117
Boyle, James, 129, 145, 152n14
bracketing: of academic knowledge, by
    bureaucratic knowledge, 78; as draft-
    ing technique, 74; of gender, 71,
    72–80; as organizational process, 74;
    as solution to problems, 74
Braunwald, Eugene, 130
Brenneis, Don, 4, 7, 13, 15–16, 17, 18,
    19, 20, 21, 23, 26, 43, 44, 46, 56, 78,
    122n4, 122n11, 191, 203n23
"bridging," 168–69
Briet, Suzanne, 28–29n1
Britain, 45, 60, 65, 66, 201n5; acade-
    mia in, 181–200; Thatcherite, 60
Brown, John Seely, 6
Brunner, Jerome, 121n1
Buckland, Michael, 28–29n1
bullet points, 25, 182–91, 195,
    196–200; as analogous to mats,
    194–95; language of, 194–96; non-
    transformativity of, 194–95
bureaucracies: and academic knowl-
    edge, 7, 40–41, 74, 78, 87–89; and
    anthropological knowledge, 72; and
    biographies, 107–8; ethnography of,
    71–73; organization of , 9–10; prac-
    tice of , 7, 8, 17, 72, with respect to
    gender, 78–80
bureaucratization, of academia, 15–16
bureaucrats, 72–76; in relation with
    academics, 7, 72, 78–80. *See* bureau-
    cracies
"bureaupathology," 97
Burke, Peter, 30n9

Callon, Michel, 153n16
care providers, documents of, 101–2
Carruthers, Bruce, 98
case analysis, 10; vs. biographical
    analysis, 108–11, 117–18, 120; of
    children, 108–11, 117–21

cases: archives of, 117; constructions of
    objects as, 97; in organizations,
    109–11
categorizations, 14, 97. *See*
    classifications
Charmaz, Kathy, 123n14
charts. *See* records
Chartier, Roger, 29n4, 153n21–22
cheating, and audit, 198
checklists, 209–16. *See also* records
childcare, and gender, 112
child development, 113–15
childhood, as social product, 116
children: biographical analysis of,
    110–11; as boundary objects,
    99–100, 117–18; bureaucratic exis-
    tence of, 100–102; care by families,
    106–7; case analysis of, 108–11; cog-
    nitive construction of, as person,
    112–13, 115–17; comparisons
    between, 110, 118; evidence of exis-
    tence of, 102–3; hospitalized,
    99–100; impact of contact with, on
    biographical analysis, 111; interests
    in, by families, 100–108; interests in,
    by neonatal intensive care units,
    102–8; medical records of, 100–106;
    as objects, 99–100; as patients,
    105–6; responsibility for, in relation
    to documents, 100–102, 108; social
    views of, 116
Chomsky, Noam, 98
Chubin, Daryl, 152n12
Clarke, Lee, 11
classifications, 10–11, 46; by docu-
    ments, 158–61; in neonatal medi-
    cine, 109–11
Clifford, James, 3, 4, 12
clinical files, Garfinkel's view of,
    164–67
cognitive conceptions, of children,
    112–13
coherence, in biographical analysis,
    117; construction of, 117–21
Cohn, Bernard, 10
collaborations, 4, 42, 44

236 □ INDEX

of, 131–38, 147–48; and scientists'
names, 131–34; traditional
definitions of, 130–31. *See also* science; science studies; scientific publications; scientists
scientific publications: consumption of,
146–47; economy of, 131–34;
method in, 136–37; vs. newspaper
articles, 136–37; vs. novels, 136; as
products, 134; "truth effect" of, 135
scientists: and authors, 135; and editors, 149; names of, 21–22, 127–28,
129, 135–37, 150–51, 147–50. *See
also* science; science studies; scientific
authorship; scientific publications
Scott, Richard, 98
Seawright, Kristie, 31n14
"self-audit catastrophe," 203n28
self-descriptions, 189, 190
self-extension, form-filling as, 172
self-knowledge, 206–7; as problem of
the present, 206–7
self-organizing systems. *See* systems;
Luhman, Niklas
self-reference, 190–92. *See also* systems;
Luhman, Niklas
semantic analysis of indigenous art,
171–72; vs. aesthetics, 171. *See also*
meaning
sense. *See* meaning
Sewell, William, 98
Shapiro, Ann-Louise, 29n8
Shaw, Harry, 23
Shepard, Daniel, 90n5
Sherman, Sandra, 30n10
Sherman, Steven, 115
Shields, 186–87
Shore, Chris, 45, 47, 67, 202n12
Shurmeyer, Walter, 28n1
Shuy, Roger, 31n14
Siegel, James, 12
signification. *See* meaning
Silverstein, Michael, 23, 43, 44
simplification, and audit, 191–92
Skolnick, Arlene, 116
Slovic, Paul, 121n2

Smart, Karl, 31n14
Smith, Richard, 150
Smith, Dorothy, 9–10, 96–97, 98
social control, of families, 106; of
home, 106; of neonatal intensive
care units, 106
social reproduction, and replication,
222–23
social systems, 202n19. *See also* systems
"societal impact," 63
sociologists, 9; of culture, 98; of organizations, 9, 97–98
South Pacific Commission, 203n24
spatio-temporal view of gift-giving,
212, 215
spatial separation, 2
Sprenger, Scott, 11, 29n7
Staffen, Lisa, 99, 112, 115, 121n3
Star, Susan Leigh, 14–15, 46, 101,
117–18
statehood, 3
statements, of university. *See* mission
statements
Steedman, Carolyn, 29n3
Stein, Gertrude, 96
Stephen, Michele, 176n2
Stevens, Mitchell, 121n3, 123n16
Stewart, Walter, 130
Stinchombe, Arthur, 9–10
Stoller, Ann Laura, 10
strategic plans, of university. *See* mission statements
Strathern, Andrew, 172
Strathern, Marilyn, 2, 4, 5, 7, 15–17,
21, 23, 24–25, 27, 43, 45, 47, 66, 67,
76, 87, 122n4, 172, 202n12, 203n22,
203n31, 209
Strub, Richard, 130
subjects. *See* agency
submission, 161–63
subversion, and audit, 198
Sudnow, David, 109
Sutton, Robert, 19
Suva and Suvavou, 209–10, 217
Swidler, Ann, 98
symbolic capital, of names, 144